11-15-71

Environmental Control: Priorities, Policies, and the Law

Frank P. Grad

George W. Rathjens

Albert J. Rosenthal

A STUDY PREPARED BY THE

LEGISLATIVE DRAFTING RESEARCH FUND

OF COLUMBIA UNIVERSITY

Columbia University Press
New York and London
1971

Foreword

In October 1969, the Sloan Foundation and the Council on Law-Related Studies made grants to the Columbia
University Legislative Drafting Research Fund for an
interdisciplinary program on Federal environmental policy,
proposed by the Committee on Science and Law of the
Association of the Bar of the City of New York. The
study was to be an independent effort conducted by
Dr. George W. Rathjens of the Massachusetts Institute of Technology, and Professors Frank Grad and
Albert J. Rosenthal of Columbia University Law School,
in consultation with the Committee. This book is the
product of that effort; it consists of papers by the
three study principals which in their initial version
were presented at a Symposium on Federal Environmental
Policy, sponsored by the Association in May 1970.

iii

For the Committee on Science and Law, the environmental policy program has been part of its continuing endeavor to contribute to the resolution of new and challenging questions of public policy posed by the interaction of technology on the one side and legal and governmental institutions and procedures on the other. The model for this endeavor has been the pioneering work of Professor Alan F. Westin, <u>Privacy and Freedom</u>, Atheneum, 1967, the product of a four-year study sponsored by the Committee.

The Committee believes that the papers of Professors Grad, Rathjens and Rosenthal will commend themselves as thoughtful approaches to some central issues of Federal environmental policy -- what should be the nation's goals and priorities, how can these be accommodated within the federal-state structure, and how can we assure that the legal system, a system of rules and sanctions, will operate to achieve the goals. I say "approaches" because it should be clear that protecting and restoring the quality of the physical environment presents choices of policy, and indeed of basic values, so pervasive, so difficult and so important that it will take an effort of years to create the new institutional and legal mechanisms required to deal with them in ways which are calculated both to achieve the desired results and be broadly acceptable in a democratic society.

Nevertheless the dramatic increase in public concern about what has been happening to our air, water and land -- a phenomenon of the last two years -- has already brought about significant improvements and will shortly bring more. There is a long way to go

but the nation is making a beginning. The legal
profession too is just beginning, but hopefully it
can make its contribution; we would like to believe
that the papers which follow will come to be regarded
as part of that contribution.

                                    William F. Kennedy

February 1971

Contents

Introduction

This work is the product of a project on federal
government policy on technology and the environment
undertaken by the Legislative Drafting Research Fund
of Columbia University. Initially conceived as a
short-term "pilot project"--i.e., a study to determine
what ought to be studied--the work was begun in the
early days of 1969. The proposal for the project had
come from the Special Committee on Science and Law
of the Association of the Bar of the City of New York,
under the Chairmanship of William F. Kennedy, Esq.,
and was funded by the Sloan Foundation and the Council
on Law-Related Studies, headed by Professor David F.
Cavers. The Legislative Drafting Research Fund of
Columbia University gratefully acknowledges their
support and encouragement.

1

It is, perhaps, a measure of the rapid development
of the field that a study such as this had a measure
of novelty when it was first undertaken in late 1969,
when institutional and legal aspects of environmental
regulation had received relatively little attention.
Since then, of course, the subject has become one of
considerable interest. The rapid development of the
field is illustrated even more sharply by the experienc€
of the writers in the course of preparing their individual contributions. Each of the papers had been
substantially completed by June of 1970, subject only--
as we thought--to formal revision before going into
print. The fall of 1970, however, brought so many
new developments in federal and state law and in the
institutional arrangements for environmental controls--
including executive reorganization plans and a new
ordering of administrative review of environmental
impacts under the Environmental Policy Act of 1969--
that substantial portions of the papers had to be
rewritten. And even while the work was already in
production, passage of the 1970 air pollution control
legislation in December 1970, in the closing stages of
the 92nd Congress, again brought some new developments
that could no longer be fully reflected in these pages.
However, it is clear that the main institutions dealing with environmental regulation have now been
shaped for some time to come, and that the legal
regulation of environmental controls has also achieved
a fairly definite direction. Institutional and legal
aspects of environmental controls, though hopefully
still open to improvement, have nevertheless been

2

sufficiently well defined to make them a worthwhile
object for an analysis of more than temporary significance.

The three papers that comprise this work were conceived as parts of a whole. Within the limits of the
study, the question that had to be faced was what subjects to select for research and discussion, in order
to provide coverage of a significant nature. In consequence, Professor Rathjens, with his unique background
in the physical and political sciences, undertook to
relate the setting of goals and priorities to the known--
and unknown--risks imposed by particular classes of
environmental insults. His paper on "National Environmental Policy" points to the need for greater discrimination in the setting of priorities as between
persistent and irreversible insults to the environment
and insults that are relatively temporary and non-
persistent. As a scientist, he regards the problems
of degradable water pollutants and solid wastes, and
of non-persistent air pollutants as essentially
solved--because the nature of the problems and the
damage produced by them is known and we have the
knowledge and technical capacity to abate them.
Consequently, in his "taxonomy of environmental
insults" he would place far greater priority on
injuries to the environment that are persistent or
that may, more or less irreversibly, alter the earth's
geophysical environment. Pushing his analysis into
the area of regulatory devices, he concludes that
cost-benefit analysis, the favorite contemporary
approach to the control of pollutants--difficult to

apply in any case--is appropriate in the area of environmental control only when dealing with non-persistent
injuries to the environment, since the cost of persistent or irreversible damages is not measurable in the
normal economic sense.

The "taxonomy of environmental insults" has far-
reaching implications in the context of setting
standards for permissible limits of emission as well--
the known irreversibility of the damage, or the mere
possibility that the damage may be irreversible, makes
standard setting a far more serious business in that
situation than in regulating more transitory phenomena.

The paper on "Intergovernmental Aspects of Environmental Controls" analyzes existing institutional
arrangements for environmental management. Though
recognizing the need for sound distinctions in the
setting of priorities and policies based on the nature
and impact of environmental insults, the writer
emphasizes the necessity for dealing with environmental
problems here and now, as we find them. Although the
problem of the non-persistent pollutants may have been
"solved" from the research scientist's point of view,
in that we know what to do about them--the problem is
still unsolved in that we have failed to do it--we have
not assigned clear institutional responsibility and we
have not provided the means to deal with the problem
effectively. The Rathjens and Grad papers fully agree
on this point--Rathjens, too, articulates the pressing
need to deal effectively with the adverse, immediate and
protracted health and economic impact of non-persistent
pollutants of the waters and the atmosphere.

4

The paper on intergovernmental aspects seeks to provide an overview of the institutions and instrumentalities that deal with environmental problems. The essay is based on the implicit premise that all problems of environmental control are inherently intergovernmental--first, because the place of emission and the place of fallout are in different political jurisdictions in all but the most minor instances and, in any case, because it is almost impossible to limit the impact of environmental insults to any one jurisdiction, and secondly, because even within a single political jurisdiction, environmental regulation generally involves more than a single agency or department of government. Exploring present institutional arrangements and their recent development, the article points to institutional gaps that exist between federal, state and local agencies, between agencies charged with developmental functions and those with regulatory ones, and between the functions of rule making and standard setting, on the one hand, and enforcement and implementation, on the other. The clear implication of this analysis is that present institutional arrangements are neither fully suited to meet the immediate regulatory needs, nor the broader, more long-range needs noted in the preceding essay with regard to the formulation of long-range policies and priorities.

The theme of the need for adequate regulatory controls is further carried out in Professor Rosenthal's paper on "Federal Power to Preserve the Environment: Enforcement and Control Techniques." In reviewing available sanctions and remedies, the essay discovers

few constitutional or other restrictions on the use
of a wide range of control techniques available to
the Federal Government if it chose to apply them.
The essay also discloses that up to now the Federal
Government has limited itself in environmental regulations to a rather narrow range of enforcement
devices. The availability--through appropriate
legislation--of a broader range of sanctions and
remedies, public as well as private, running the
gamut from administrative remedies through civil,
equitable and criminal sanctions and a variety of
positive incentives, is encouraging. To be effective,
however, traditional techniques will have to be carefully tailored to meet the special needs of environmental protection. A far broader, more flexible
arsenal of control techniques is likely to be needed
in the future, not only to carry out the enforcement
functions of existing and new institutions for environmental control, but also to implement the chosen priorities and policies for the future.

In preparing their articles, the authors had much
generous assistance. In the early stages of the study
they met in Washington with a number of legislators,
their staff assistants, and members of agencies having
environmental concerns. These meetings were most
informative and stimulating. Special thanks for their
time and ideas are due to Senator Jackson and his staff
assistant, William Van Ness, to Senator Edmund Muskie
and his staff assistant, Don Nicoll, and to Congressman
John Dingell and his staff assistant, Grant Sibers.
Our appreciation is due, too, to Richard Carpenter, of

the Library of Congress, to Charles C. Johnson, Director of the Environmental Health Services Administration (now incorporated in the EPA) and to his Assistant Administrator, Jerrold M. Michael, as well as to John Middleton, Director, National Air Pollution Control Administration, and to members of his staff. Our appreciation is due, also,to Professor Joseph Sax, of the Michigan Law School, who, while working on a special project for Resources for the Future, Inc., supplied a number of valuable insights on the uses of private litigation in environmental control.

The authors' appreciation is extended, also, to the members of the Special Committee on Science and Law of the Association of the Bar of the City of New York. The Committee acted not only as the sponsor of the study, but its members also served as an advisory committee, reviewing drafts of the papers and providing helpful comments and criticisms during one of the Committee meetings. In May of 1970, the Committee hosted an open meeting of the Association of the Bar at which the authors presented preliminary versions of their papers. Special thanks are due to William F. Kennedy, Esq., Chairman of the Committee, who not only provided continuing liaison between the Committee and the authors, but also provided encouragement, counsel, and insights based on sound experience. Special thanks, too, are due to Professor David Cavers of Harvard Law School, who, having aided in funding the project through his Council on Law-Related Studies, took a continuing interest in it, and gave freely of his time and wisdom.

Closer to home, the authors, and particularly the two authors (Grad and Rosenthal) whose base is Columbia Law School, owe a great deal to the considerable efforts of the professional and student staff of the Legislative Drafting Research Fund. Valuable contributions to the work during the research stage were made by James Mendelsohn (J.D. Columbia 1970), Terence Rice (J.D. Columbia 1970), and by Daniel Freeman, Jonathan Lehr and Claude E. Salomon (all Columbia Law School Class of 1971). An especially noteworthy research contribution was made by Michael Candido (J.D. Columbia 1970). Some of the students and former students mentioned also rendered fine assistance in the final stage of checking and production of the work, as did Michael Stolzar, Jo-Ann Whitehorn Tisman and Henry Welt, all of the Columbia Law School Class of 1972. During the summer of 1970, in particular, the burden of supportive research was borne by Robert Weiner (Class of 1972) and by Mrs. Enid Sterling (J.D. Syracuse 1949), who served as temporary professional staff assistant. Thanks are due, too, to Mrs. Audrey L. Goldberg (LL.B. Columbia 1959) who, in the last two months of her term as Assistant Director of the Legislative Drafting Research Fund, helped the study get under way.

A special note of thanks should be recorded to Professor Louis Henkin of Columbia Law School, who read the manuscript of Professor Rosenthal's paper, and made a significant contribution with his comments and suggestions.

Last, but by no means least, all of the authors wish to record their appreciation to Mrs. Laurie R. Rockett

(J.D. Columbia 1970), who made a notable contribution
to the study first as a student research assistant,
and later as Assistant Director of the Legislative
Drafting Research Fund. Mrs. Rockett took charge of
the production of the work, and assisted with great
effectiveness--and tact--in the final revision of
the work, helping to put the pieces together into a
book.

Having recorded my gratitude and appreciation, and
that of my co-authors, let me add that in spite of the
many hands and heads that contributed, the responsibility for the views expressed, and for the contents of
the pages that follow, remains entirely that of the
individual authors.

New York, January 11, 1971   Frank P. Grad
                                    Director, Legislative
                                    Drafting Research Fund

George W. Rathjens

National Environmental Policy: Goals and Priorities

When one asks the broadest questions, "How serious is the threat to the environment, and what should we do about it" one cannot but be struck by the differences in the degree of concern exhibited by different groups. At the one extreme one finds those who view the recent development of great interest in ecology as a diversion and an indulgence of the affluent who, having grown discouraged with the problems of the ghetto and the poor, now see in environmental concerns something that may be more tractable and less controversial. To the poor and the black, the problems of sulfur dioxide in the air they breathe, possible extinction of the peregrine falcon, and oil on the beaches of Santa Barbara are at most secondary or tertiary concerns. This is also true for much of the business community who recognize

that in order to maintain both a suitable environment
and image their practices may have to change, but who
hardly see the need or the likelihood of drastic
alterations in the whole structure of our society.

At the other extreme there are those who see time
running out--people who are concerned that we are
about to unleash, or may already have unleashed,
forces that will result in irreversible changes
probably resulting in the early elimination of many
living species and possibly of man himself.

One also finds corresponding variability in opinions about the viability of ecological issues as a
matter of major political concern. There are those
who see the interest of the last few years as a pass-
ing fad. Others see it having a longer life, not
because environmental alteration is a real threat,
but rather because it is, unlike the problems of the
ghetto, politically "safe" and of interest to middle
class America. And finally there are those who see
the environment as an issue of continuing and increasing concern from which we cannot escape because we
will be confronted with more and more serious ecological crises.

With such variations in concern about the seriousness of the threat to the environment and about its
viability as an issue, it is quite natural that different groups are looking for entirely different ways
of coping with the threat. We have new legislation
at both the state and the federal level, but there
are advocates of more far reaching measures--some
calling for a new federal department; some for a new

concept of the role of the federal government; and at
the extreme, others calling for a total restructuring
of society including renunciation of our Judeo-Christian
value system and acceptance of a no-growth economy.

It seems clear that without some clarification of
the seriousness of the threat it will be impossible to
approach the development of federal policy in any very
rational way. We might muddle through as we have in
the past to a large extent. However, there are reasons
for being very doubtful about such an approach. Our
concern has its basis in the fact that man has at his
disposal the possibility of modifying the ecology
globally and irreversibly--something that is largely
a phenomenon of the last half of this century. We can
deal with some of the insults to the environment as
we have in the past. Others may require very different
approaches.

A Taxonomy of Environmental Insults

In considering the problems of insults to the
environment some classification scheme may be useful.
A division into four classes is used here:
(1)   degradable water pollutants and solid wastes;
(2)   non-persistent air pollutants;
(3)   persistent toxic pollutants (in air, water or
      soils.); and
(4)   factors which may alter the earth's geophysical
      environment.

The problems which have been of concern for the
longest time--pollution of fresh water and the disposal

13

of solid wastes--we can largely brush aside in a paper
such as this at least insofar as our concerns are
technical. This is not to say that such problems are
not serious. Reversing what has happened to Lake Erie
and preventing the same from happening to Lake Michigan
and many other bodies of water is important and will,
require large expenditures and stringent regulations.
But to a very large extent we know what must be done.
We know how to measure water quality--for most purposes biochemical oxygen demand (BOD) is useful. (It
is a measure of the oxygen that would be needed by
bacteria to decompose organic wastes.) We have had
great experience in removing organic wastes that have
been traditionally troublesome in water supplies,
including bacteria that are hazards to health. We
have also begun to appreciate the seriousness of
eutrophication, and attention is now being given to
the development of tertiary treatment techniques for
removal of phosphate and nitrogen nutrients.

While the demand for pure fresh water can be expected
to rise greatly in the years ahead, the development and
implementation of public policy to meet the requirements seems straightforward--at least it seems like a
simple problem compared to some of the others with
which we will be confronted. Not only do we know what
we should do and how to do it, we can also predict the
consequences of failure to act. In addition, we can
draw some small comfort from the fact that the effects
of failure will generally be somewhat localized and
not totally irreversible. If pollution of some of our
rivers gets worse, it will not mean the end of the human

species; and in many cases it will be possible at a later date, with sufficient effort, to bring them back. The problems of solid waste disposal seem equally straightforward.

In the case of the non-persistent air pollutants-- sulfur dioxide, oxides of nitrogen, carbon monoxide, ozone, aerosols, etc.--we can also draw comfort in the fact that the effects will be more or less localized and from the point of view of the species, if not from that of individuals, generally reversible. Otherwise, however, the problems seem more difficult than in the case of solid waste and most water pollutants. Part of the difficulty is in the fact that an airshed is less well-defined than a watershed, but probably the main difficulties are others.

First, we have much less choice about the air we breathe than we do about the water we drink or otherwise use. Assuming water is available, the community or in extremis the individual householder can, albeit at some cost, treat water, almost regardless of its quality, to make it potable. No such option is realistically available with respect to air. We simply have less flexibility, the only present real hope for maintaining air quality, with the limited exception of that in buildings and vehicles, being through control of emissions of pollutants.

Second, trade-off problems may be more common and difficult to deal with in the case of air pollution. Nitrogen oxide emissions from automobiles can in principal be reduced by changes in engine design, but at the price of increasing other undesirable emissions.

15

Finally, the gaps in our knowledge of the chemistry of air are both greater and more serious than in the case of the non-persistent water pollutants. The complex reactions of various hydrocarbons, sulfur oxides, ozone, and oxides of nitrogen--many of them photochemical reactions--are not yet well understood so we do not know how best to allocate our resources when confronted with mixtures of air pollutants: whether to try to reduce them all or to look for means of reducing one or two in the hope thereby of stopping the chemical reactions that produce some of the more troublesome compounds.

When one thinks about it one will see that noise insults to our environment, although in some respects simpler, have many similarities to the non-persistent atmospheric pollutants. Accordingly, similar approaches to coping with noise may be indicated.

One might consider the persistent contaminants to constitute a third class of pollutants requiring perhaps rather different treatment than those discussed so far. Some, for example, lead and mercury, have been recognized as poisons for hundreds of years, but have assumed new importance because of vastly increased dispersion as a result of modern industrial processes. Others are new: DDT and radioactive isotopes, for example. Becaus all of these substances are removed from the biosphere only slowly by natural processes--DDT has a half life variously estimated to be months or years compared with three hours for sulfur dioxide--they may be dispersed very widely--worldwide in some cases. Because they are concentrated in successive steps in the food

16

chain, persistent pollutants can be a serious threat
to particular species even when the amounts released
and the concentrations in the air or water are low.
Particularly in the case of some of the new persistent
pollutants, there is a lack of adequate knowledge about
the effects of exposure over long periods, and a lack
of understanding of the effects of the destruction of
one species by these substances on other species.

Finally, in our taxonomy, we identify a fourth
class of environmental insults--the things which we are
doing which, while not introducing new substances into
the biosphere, nevertheless over a period of years may
produce major environmental changes. Increasing the
carbon dioxide content of the atmosphere as a result of
the burning of fossil fuels is perhaps the most discussed example. There are several others: the increase
in finely divided particulate matter in the atmosphere;
the introduction of water vapor into the stratosphere
by rockets and supersonic aircraft; changing of the
earth's albedo as a result of changing land use patterns;
the possible covering of the oceans with thin films of
oil; and the production of large amounts of heat through
combustion of fossil fuels and the use of nuclear
reactors.

It is not likely that man-produced changes of these
kinds have yet resulted in very significant perturbations
in the world's climate, but our capacity for producing
change is growing so rapidly that the possibilities
must be seriously considered. With respect to each of
these possibilities we have now reached the point, or
can see it fast approaching, when the man-produced

effects may be significant compared to our natural heritage. One could perhaps argue that the neglect of such problems was hardly serious when the amounts of substances such as carbon dioxide being added per decade to the environment as a result of man's activities were but a percent or so of natural abundance, or were small compared with geographical and other natural variations. But we may be approaching the end of that period. The carbon dioxide content of the atmosphere has increased by about 5% since 1940 and will probably increase even more by the end of the century. In the unlikely event that present trends in increasing power consumption continue, within the next two hundred years we will be producing heat at a rate equal to that which the earth receives heat from the sun. While we are not yet able to predict the effects of such changes with any confidence, there is clearly a possibility of very dramatic changes in the environment. Some of these insults might be partially offset by others: increased aerosol concentration may produce an effect opposite to that produced by increased carbon dioxide concentration. However, our knowledge is so limited that we do not know this.

Time periods of concern seem long compared to those we usually think of in discussing other pollution problems--the sulfur dioxide problem, for example--but they are very short indeed on an evolutionary time scale. While wheat rusts can develop fungicide resistant strains on the same time scale that we change fungicides, the time scale for human evolution and that of many other species will be long compared to the time

18

required for us to change our environment dramatically.

In considering this last class of environmental changes we are confronted with five very difficult problems.

First, there is lack of understanding of the seriousness of the threat. In this respect we are far worse off than in considering other environmental insults. We need both more data and better models of geophysical processes to make very useful estimates.

Second, we are confronted with the prospect of our possibly triggering environmental changes that would be catastrophic on a worldwide scale before we know what we are about, and with the possibility that we will be impotent to reverse what we may have started.

Third, in dealing with these problems it will be necessary to take serious account of what may happen in the rather distant future, something that is almost totally alien to governmental processes. In the United States it is difficult to get the President or other elected or appointed officials to give very serious attention to problems which are not likely to be troublesome during their term of office. The situation is little different in other developed countries. For example, the socialist states have five year plans, not fifty year plans. In societies that think in terms of discount rates of, say, 6 to 20 percent it is hard to generate interest in expending money and effort on programs to cope with a threat that may not materialize for several decades, if then. Only with rare exceptions have societies been willing to undertake programs with

time scales of many decades. The building of cathe-
drals and other religious endeavors are about the
only exceptions. Perhaps there is hope for the
environment in the fact that some societies, and some
people in our society, regard its preservation with
almost a religious kind of commitment. Certainly in
coping with our fourth class of environmental insults
it will clearly be necessary to do so with the perspective measured at least in decades. We should not leave
this point without perhaps noting how much poorer the
prospects will be for dealing with the third and fourth
kinds of environmental problems when the poorer nations
of the world may be responsible for much of the difficulty. For those in a subsistence economy, as is
also true of the poor in the developed countries,
concern about the future is a luxury that cannot be
afforded. Fortunately, the power and the wealth required to cause many of the more dramatic environmental changes (for example such as those that might
result from uncontrolled increases in fossil fuel consumption) are to a substantial degree concentrated in
the developed world, and within the developed world,
among those people who are sufficiently affluent that
they can afford to look beyond tomorrow. However
there are some frightening exceptions. Countries such
as China and India clearly have the capability of producing severe environmental degradation, for example by
the very widespread and wholesale use of persistent
pesticides or as a result of poor agricultural practices
which may lead to severe problems of erosion with large
amounts of atmospheric dust resulting.

20

Fourth, the effects of these fourth kinds of insults
will be worldwide (and in this respect the problem of
the persistent pesticides, radioactive pollutants, etc.,
referred to earlier will be similar). The difficulties
in achieving international control will be far more
difficult than in the case of problems that can be
dealt with on a national basis.

Fifth, there is the prospect, with some of the
insults of this class, of having to make much more
drastic social adjustments than are likely to be required to control other pollutants. At some time we
will have to cut back on the rate at which we increase
the burning of fossil fuels either because we will
exhaust them, or because of the consequences of the
addition of carbon dioxide to the atmosphere. Adjust-
ment would be difficult in that case, but mitigated
greatly by the possibility of using nuclear fuels.
The problem of thermal pollution on a global scale,
although probably more distant, will require more
radical adjustments. At some time we will have to cut
back on the rate at which we increase our use of energy
simply because if we do not the earth will become un-
bearably hot. Such prospects raise a host of questions.
When must we begin consciously to impose restrictions
on the use of energy? Does that prospect imply a zero-
growth economy or something approaching it? Would it
be possible, even if the developed world froze its
rate of resource use at present levels, for the under-
developed world ever to consume the earth's resources
and contribute to environmental alteration at the same
per capita rate we do?

21

Clearly, the seriousness of the problems raised by this last group of environmental perturbations will depend on population growth. In the view of many, that is the most serious threat of all to the environment. Limiting arguments can be made, as in the case of energy use. If population growth were to continue at present rates there would literally be no room left on earth on which people could stand four or five hundred years from now. Sooner or later then we must accept zero population growth. When? Sooner, rather than later, we will have to make choices about either reducing population growth rates or the rate of increase in per capita consumption of resources.

When one considers the fourth class of environmental insults, including uncontrolled population growth, it is clear that we have only two choices: muddling through with the result probably being far greater human misery and earlier extinction of the species than if we adopt the alternative--an effort to plan and regulate the use of resources and population growth so that our physical environment will be reasonably stable--so that it will not be catastrophically altered on a time scale that is short compared to that required for accommodation to it.

Setting Standards

In general, in attempting to develop policy with respect to pollution, one would expect to try to answer two questions. What level of a given pollutant is permissible; and what are the preferred mechanisms for insuring that that level is not exceeded?

In a few cases the first question can be easily answered by a total prohibition on the introduction of the substance in question into the environment. This is likely to be particularly true of some of the components of our third class, the persistent pollutants. The use of DDT is now prohibited absolutely in some places and lead tetraethyl may be soon. It can perhaps be reasonably argued that alternatives that are available for pest control and for improving gasoline engine performance are sufficiently low in cost to justify foregoing completely the use of these two substances.

More generally, however, the concern will be in setting a non-zero level of contamination that is judged acceptable.

We know that sulfur dioxide in the atmosphere is harmful and unpleasant; and we know that by restricting the use of fuel oil and coal to those having low sulfur content or by using various processes to remove sulfur dioxide during combustion or from exhaust gases, we can reduce sulfur dioxide concentration below levels that would otherwise result. We also have a vague idea that the costs of such practices, which ultimately must be passed on to consumers, are small, or, considering the benefits, at least acceptable. But there is something arbitrary about deciding that oil containing less than, say, one percent sulfur is acceptable while that containing more is not, or for that matter that atmospheric concentrations of 50 parts per billion are acceptable while higher concentrations are not. Why not set the limits at half these values? Fuel costs would be higher, but perhaps the savings in increased longevity, reduced

illness, reduction in corrosion, etc. would justify the
higher costs. Where is the crossover point?

A few attempts have been made to estimate the benefits of reducing certain pollutants, for example by
trying to establish correlations between property values
and air quality. However, these are hardly adequate.
Standards seem to be set, based on a combination of
expert (but generally grossly inadequate) opinion about
the adverse effects of pollutants and a judgment about
what the public will pay to maintain certain standards.
Can we do better?

The economist would probably argue that cost-benefit
analyses can be pushed further. Consider further the
case of sulfur dioxide. The economists would look for
clever ways of estimating the costs of increased incidence of emphysema and other hazards to health and property which they could in one way or another correlate
with sulfur dioxide content in the atmosphere. In
theory one would hope to establish a point where there
would be a balance between the costs of reducing sulfur
dioxide concentrations further and the benefits to be
derived from improved health, etc. Both the utility
and the limitations can be illustrated with a little
more discussion of the sulfur dioxide problem.

Reference has been made to indirect attempts to
establish the value of benefits of reducing air pollution by considering correlations between levels of
pollution and property values. In principle, the
method could be extended by using a number of cases
and multivariate analyses to estimate benefits of
reducing or eliminating individual pollutants--in the

case under consideration here, sulfur dioxide--or combinations of particular pollutants. Implementation of such an approach is, however, likely to be far more difficult than the theory. But even assuming this could be done, it is likely to result in the imputation of values to the elimination of sulfur dioxide or reductions in concentration that would be capricious in the sense that the value would have been based on misinformation or on lack of information about the adverse effects of sulfur dioxide. If information were available regarding the true extent of the adverse health effect and if this were to be made available broadly enough so that property values were to reflect it, then one could perhaps feel comfortable about using the technique. At present little information is available and what there is is not widely known. This suggests the utility of research to determine the adverse effects, and educational activities so that informed decisions are possible. (The experience of the last few years with cigarettes suggests that this is not a hopeless approach.)

If the necessary research were done on the correlation between adverse effects and sulfur dioxide concentration, one might attack the problem of estimating the benefits of reducing sulfur dioxide more directly. However, when one tries this one runs into a set of problems common to nearly all efforts to apply cost-benefit techniques to public health issues. It is relatively easy to place a value on the cost of treatment of disease and on earnings lost due to illness, but far harder to place values on discomfort and anxiety that go with illness, and, if one tries to

consider more than loss of earnings, on loss of
life.

In both of the approaches suggested, there is
the remaining fact that efforts to estimate benefits of reducing sulfur dioxide concentrations, or
if one prefers, the cost of tolerating it in the
atmosphere--the same thing--one is likely to miss
important factors. If, because of imperfect knowledge, we ascribe to sulfur dioxide increases in
the frequency of house painting, and increases in
several diseases, say emphysema, the common cold,
and lung cancer, but fail to include the potentiat-
ing or synergistic effects that sulfur dioxide may
have in initiating or exacerbating the effects of
diseases for which the primary causative agent is
some other atmospheric ingredient, then we under-
estimate the benefits of sulfur dioxide removal or
reduction. In some cases this may make the analysis
useless, but in others it still may be of value. It
will be apparent that cost-benefit analysis can be at
least useful in making a fortiori types of analyses.
If one can identify one or more adverse effects of
pollution and can impute to them costs in excess of
those involved in eliminating or reducing the pollutant, one has a sound basis for prohibition or for
lowering the permissible levels of pollution. Were
it possible to include other unknown or unquantifiable
benefits, the case would be made stronger and even
further reductions in permissible levels could be
justified. (Such a fortiori reasoning presupposes
that one can in fact measure the costs of elimination

26

or reduction of a pollutant without much ambiguity. In many cases this will be possible, but in some the price of reducing or eliminating a given pollutant may involve the introduction of other hazards or pollutants. One way to reduce sulfur dioxide concentration is to use more nuclear power in which case thermal pollution at least, and possibly other problems as well, will be greater.)

Despite the limitations of cost benefit analysis for setting standards, there is certainly room for much work along such lines. However, such approaches are likely to be useful almost exclusively in the case of the pollutants with which we have lived for some time, and which do not produce long-term effects on the physical environment, that is, for substances which comprise our first two classes.

When one turns from the short-lived air and water pollutants to the more persistent ones--those in our third and fourth categories--conventional cost-benefit techniques will be of even less utility in establishing standards. There may be cases where one can identify one or several adverse consequences, the costs of which will be sufficiently great, so that a _fortiori_ arguments of the kind mentioned above will have applicability. Such examples would, however, seem rather exceptional at least considering our present state of knowledge. For many years most of the resources and intellectual effort in trying to cope with insults of our third and fourth categories ought to be focused on simply identifying the physical and biological consequences of pollution rather than on estimating economic costs of those consequences. We make this statement simply because we know so little about the environmental effects of such insults. The literature abounds with examples of the unexpected, and in some cases catastrophic, consequence of the introduction of new pesticides and other insults to the environment. To mention only a few there are the many cases of the adverse effects of DDT on the reproductive cycle of various species of birds, the cases of concentration of radioactive isotopes in the food chain, and the reduction in the sardine catch in the eastern Mediterranean and the increase in the incidence of bilharziasis in the Nile Delta resulting from the construction of the Aswan Dam.

This suggests that in setting standards for permissi ble levels of some of these pollutants and for deciding on the approval of projects that can have long-term ecological effects, experimental work, including a care ful monitoring of the effects of new insults to the environment, and a considerable degree of modeling of complex physical and biological systems will have great utility.

Perhaps a greater use of adversary type inquiry woul also be useful: that is, the use of procedures involvin technical experts who have no stake in the introduction of the given substance into the environment, and who, indeed, preferably should be people who are likely to oppose it. What is required is that such people be given access to relevant information, in some cases resources for research, and finally the opportunity to present findings and to confront proponents of pro- grams that might result in environmental alteration.

28

But despite our efforts, and regardless of the resources available, it is inevitable that our activities
will on occasion produce effects on the environment
which are unwanted and which we have been unable to
foresee. This suggests that perhaps the single most
important aspect in setting standards and in arriving
at decisions regarding major projects with possible
environmental impact must simply be caution.

Mechanisms for Environmental Control

Although economic considerations seem destined to
have at most a limited role in helping to set standards
for environmental quality, they ought to be at the heart
of the development of techniques for insuring that the
standards will be met efficiently and equitably.

Indeed, to a very large extent the problem of
maintaining a decent environment is the example par
excellence of what the economists refer to as the
problem of the "common," that is, the problem of maintaining the quality and avoiding the exhaustion of
resources which many individuals are permitted to use,
but for which none take particular responsibility. One
must be concerned in the case of air, water, and indeed
of the earth as an ecological system with how the costs
should be apportioned so that standards of quality can
be met and maintained.

A variety of techniques for discouraging pollution
and for defraying the costs of correction are used and
have their advocates: outright prohibition on despolia-
tion with varying penalties for violation; public

subsidization of practices which will presumably improve environmental quality, or at least reduce the rate of degradation below what would otherwise obtain; and the imposition of charges or disposal costs on polluters. There are both advantages and serious problems with each of the approaches.

The case of the absolute prohibition is the simplest, but even with it there are the problems of identifying violations and of arriving at what are reasonable penalties. Obviously if the penalties are small, pollution may occur on a regular basis with those responsible simply accepting the penalties as a cost of doing business. If this becomes predictable and routine, the fines then become the equivalent of effluent charges.

The use of the latter has been much criticized as implying a license to pollute. There is something in the contention, but much of the criticism would seem to be misguided for the use of such charges can also be a mechanism for achieving efficiency in preservation of the environment. Effluent charges can lead to the efficiencies that go with specialization and economies of scale. In the interest of efficiency it may be much preferable to have a single large treatment plant downstream from several pollutant sources rather than having each source operate its own treatment plant. However, the reverse may also be true, at least in part. If several sources produce effluents requiring radically different treatment, it may be more efficient to accomplish treatment before they are mixed, or before dilution in the large volume of water in a main stream.

Obviously, the economically efficient answer is to set effluent charges high enough to cover the treatment of effluents by a publicly operated facility, leaving it to the producer of the effluents to determine whether he wishes to pay the charges, to avoid them by treating his wastes himself, or some combination of the two. Presumably he will choose the least costly solution. There are, of course, problems with such approaches to waste disposal. The distance between sources and a publicly operated treatment facility may be large in which case the utility of a significant length of stream may be impaired by pollution. Monitoring of effluents will be required to assess charges--hardly a very severe problem in the case of the liquid wastes from a large industrial concern, but something that would likely be far less practical in the case of the individual household than imposition of flat charges for sewage disposal or incorporation of the charge in property taxes. Third, and most limiting, is the fact that the setting of effluent charges based on the cost of treatment by publicly operated facilities has little role other than in water pollution and in the disposal of solid wastes. Air pollutants, and for that matter other insults to the environment, heat and noise, are not easily recapturable once released. This will also be a problem with those water pollutants not easily removed by conventional sewage treatment.

This is not to say that effluent charges can never have any role in air pollution. The output from industrial stacks could be monitored for effluents, but it would be harder to make a case for any particular

31

schedule of charges. They could not be based on the
cost of "downstream" removal since such removal would
be practically impossible. And, without more knowledge
than we now have, it would be difficult to use the
social costs of the emissions as a basis for effluent
charges. However, acceptable levels of, say, sulfur
dioxide having been established, charges could be set
sufficiently high so that it would be more economical
for power plants to burn low sulfur fuel or remove the
sulfur dioxide from stack gases. As noted earlier,
fines for exceeding certain levels may have the same
effect as effluent charges, and in this instance the
two would be indistinguishable.

In the establishment of procedures and legislation
for environmental control it will generally be desirable
in the interest of efficiency to allow those who would
pollute as much flexibility as is possible in dealing
with their wastes. Giving them the option of paying
effluent charges for liquid wastes or, alternatively,
self treatment before release is an example, but the
principle should also be applied in other cases where
feasible. Assume, for example, it is desirable to main
tain sulfur dioxide concentration in some area below
some specified level (a level which need not necessarily
be constant but which could be varied depending on
meteorological conditions). One might achieve this by
regulating either sulfur content of fuels or sulfur
dioxide emissions from stacks. In principle, the latter
would be much to be preferred since it would give those
who burn fuel not only the option of achieving the objective by burning low sulfur fuel, but also the option

of removal during burning or from stack gases, and it would provide incentives for the development of processes for doing so--including those for recapturing the sulfur in forms that could be marketed to offset all or part of the costs of removal. Such an approach would be applicable only to power plants and others whose production of sulfur dioxide was large enough to justify monitoring exhaust gases and for whom sulfur removal during the burning process was a realistic possibility. For the individual householders these will not be reasonable possibilities, and their contribution of sulfur dioxide (or particulates, etc.) can probably only be limited by controlling fuel composition.

While the foregoing has focused on mechanisms for having the polluter bear the brunt of the costs of coping with his insults to the environment, it is probably inevitable that subsidies play a prominent role in treating environmental problems as they do in other problems of the "common". This is particularly so when one sees the "common" as being the nation as a whole, or, in the case of the fourth, and to some extent the third class of insults we are considering, the world.

If the whole of a river basin or an air shed or a nation is to have its environmental quality improved, one faces the problem of either imposing standards that effect all of those who are potential polluters in the basin, air shed or nation, or alternatively of imposing general taxes in order to cope with the effects of pollution, and to provide subsidies to limit pollution. The latter course, that is, the use of subsidies, is an insidious one from the point of view of public policy

for when the polluter is relieved of the costs of pollution by subsidization, or as a result of a public
authority's having taken responsibility for removal of
his pollutants, there will be removed many of the incen
tives for process improvement to avoid pollution. If
the federal government provides most of the costs of a
municipal sewage plant, there will be diminished incentives for the municipality to impose rigid standards on
pollution and a consequent diminution in incentives for
industries in the area to treat their own wastes or
develop processes that do not produce them. There may
even be a positive incentive for pollution-prone industries to locate in the area rather than in others where
they might have to bear the full burden of treating
their own wastes.

The last point reminds us of the necessity of approaching pollution problems on the scale of the
economy as a whole, that is, within any trading area,
be it a city, a region, the nation, or the world.
Equity and efficiency will generally demand that standards of permitted pollution not be very rigorous in one
area while very relaxed in another. It hardly seems
reasonable to limit severely the emission of air pollutants in one part of an air shed while imposing no
limitations in another city within the same air shed.
Industries in the latter will benefit because of the
resulting greater tax base, while all within the air
shed (if it is properly defined) will suffer from the
results of air pollution. Does this imply the necessit
of completely uniform standards? If so, over what geographic areas?

34

1627151

For some sources of environmental degradation the standards should perhaps be uniform even on a world scale. This may be particularly true for some of the insults of our fourth class. If increasing carbon dioxide input into the atmosphere appears to be a problem, it may be hard to justify permitting a greater per capita input in, say, the United States than in some other countries. But even in this case the arguments will not be completely clearcut. One might argue that those in colder climates should be allowed to burn more fossil fuel than those in the tropics on the grounds of necessity--an argument implying to some degree that automobiles and air conditioning are luxuries, at least in a relative sense. Or perhaps it would be argued that those nations that are prepared to maintain large forested areas for the removal of carbon dioxide should be allowed to burn more fossil fuel.

For those pollutants of a more immediate concern, it will generally be even easier to make a case for variations in standards. Certainly in the case of short-lived air pollutants such as sulfur dioxide, carbon monoxide, and the oxides of nitrogen there would seem to be little basis for applying the same standards in areas prone to atmospheric inversion such as Los Angeles as to areas such as Denver where inversions are infrequent. It might be argued that the imposition of less stringent standards would put the latter city at an advantage economically. That is true, but it should be regarded as no more unfair and no more unnatural than the fact that Los Angeles has an economic advantage over Denver in terms of access to the ocean. The case then

35

for differences in air pollution standards in different
air sheds seems straight forward. But let us consider
a somewhat more difficult problem. Should there be differences in water quality standards in, say, the cases
of the Ohio and the Hudson Rivers? If there are lower
standards on one, say the former, certain industries
will preferentially locate there and the region will
benefit perhaps at the expense of New York. But the
people of New York will benefit by virtue of having a
cleaner river. Perhaps a fair exchange, and certainly
seemingly so if the two choices reflect adequately the
views of the inhabitants of the two areas. But suppose
one regards the rivers as national assets. Why should
the Ohio be despoiled for the benefit of the local
economy? In a more extreme case, certainly the public
as a whole would be outraged if our national parks were
destroyed for the benefit of local interests (just as
local interests are often outraged, as many Alaskans
now are in connection with the deferral of the pipeline construction, when national decisions regarding
the environment inhibit local exploitation).

   Not surprisingly, no clear rules emerge regarding
the question of local option with respect to environment
control. It is a bit like education: to a substantial
degree the nation feels a responsibility as a whole for
the education of its young (and for that matter to a
lesser degree for the world). Yet, if a given region
wishes to spend less on education and more on something
else, within limits, it should probably be permitted
to do so.

   Are there any generalizations about mechanisms for

36

insuring and improving environmental quality? In addition to those regarding the setting of environmental standards, discussed earlier, there are probably at least two or three.

First, to the maximum extent feasible, the costs of removing any pollutants introduced into the environment should be borne directly by those responsible. This implies that subsidies should be avoided. To some extent this is a matter of equity, but to an even greater extent, one of efficiency. All in a given region may suffer equally from the noxious output of a given plant that serves the region, and by taxing all the product can perhaps be removed. That may be equitable if the benefits resulting from the plant's existence are distributed in approximately the same way as the tax base, but it is not efficient in that the pressures for process improvement will be far less effective than if the burden for removal falls directly on the polluter, and what is even more important, the range of options that can be considered for removal will, except where economies of scale dictate otherwise, such as in the case of the individual householders, be greater if the burden of removal is at the source. Unfortunately, it is generally likely to be politically easier for the federal government to use the carrot than the stick. Thus political realism probably requires the use of federal subsidies even though they may be less equitable and less efficient mechanisms for improving environmental quality than the imposition and enforcement of tough national standards.

Second, in general standards should be set so that

37

those who would pollute have a maximum range of choice
with respect to methods of avoidance. This implies
that regulations should be imposed at the last
feasible point in industrial processes. Unless
there is no other feasible alternative, control of
inputs should be avoided. And controls on design of
plants and on equipment installed in them should be
foregone in favor of control of output because if control is limited to the former there will be little
incentive to operate and maintain waste removal equipment efficiently.

Third, the revenues obtained from effluent charges,
taxes designed to discourage pollution, and fines for
violation of pollution standards should generally be
used exclusively to deal with the pollutants in question. If they are used for general revenue or other
purposes, there is the risk of standards being relaxed
to increase revenue, in which case other purposes,
however desirable, will be subsidized by toleration of
higher levels of pollution than would otherwise obtain.

Comments on Federal Environmental Programs

There are some areas with respect to the environment where the role of the federal government must
really be paramount.

With the exception of instrumentation and process
equipment development, nearly all of the burden for
research and development as well as for monitoring
the environment must be borne by the federal government.
This is simply because most of what is done will have

national (and indeed international) payoff, and because much of what needs to be done will not be supported by sources other than the federal government. A much expanded program of measurement, research, and development is required, particularly with respect to the third and the fourth class of environmental insults. A good bit that is relevant, particularly to the fourth class, is being done, supported by the Environmental Sciences Services Administration, and, on an international scale, in the Global Atmospheric Research Program and because of the World Weather Watch Program. But those efforts are supported largely in the interest of improvement of weather prediction rather than because of concern about possible longer term changes in climate and other environmental conditions. Much more, particularly oriented to the latter problems, needs doing. Although the problems are international in scale, most of the burden for research must fall on the developed countries, particularly the United States. We consume the world's resources and are responsible for environmental alteration to a degree far out of proportion to our numbers, and we have the capabilities for doing the research. Moreover, as pointed out earlier, it is only the affluent, if they, who are temperamentally conditioned to looking more than a few years ahead.

Although we do not know how soon problems of the fourth class may really be serious, we know that sometime they will be, and there is at least serious cause for concern that that time may be measured in decades or even years rather than centuries. Accordingly, the problems of the fourth class, and also those of the third class merit high priority. They are not likely to get much attention in the government agencies concerned with more immediate problems. Some of the required expanded effort should be managed directly by the government. We have in mind particularly environmental monitoring for which there is a need on a larger scale than would be appropriate to universities or privately endowed research centers. Much of the other work with respect to longer term problems should probably be done in universities with government support.

Not only should this include investigation and modelling of physical and biological processes, but also a considerable effort in economics and the social sciences. It is none too soon to begin much more intensive studies than are now under way of the effects of crowding on human behavior, and on the problems of economies where growth rate is much reduced, including in the limiting case, studies of the nature of zero-growth societies.

The federal government should probably also take a much more active role than it has so far in setting national standards with respect to our first three classes of pollutants. This is important for two reasons.

In some respects we must regard our environmental heritage as a national one. Within limits, local option has its place, but unrestrained strip mining, pollution of the Great Lakes and major rivers, and the destruction of biological species by persistent pesticides--to give a few examples--must be considered national, if not international problems, rather than local ones.

Second, we have national markets, and in the interests of efficiency, and to the extent feasible, manufacturers should have to comply with only a minimum number of different sets of standards. This applies notably in the case of automobiles, but might also apply in other areas, for example, more than it does with respect to power plants.

The federal government should perhaps play less of a role than it does in subsidizing pollutant abatement activities. Each such project represents to some extent a violation of the fundamental concept that the charges for removal and treatment of pollutants should be borne as directly as possible by those responsible for their production.

There has been much criticism of the Administration's environmental efforts on the grounds that they were announced as a diversion from other serious problems, and that the levels of expenditure are too low-- in short, that the whole effort is cosmetic. There is probably some truth in the charge that the effort is diversionary, cosmetic, and an attempt to capture the initiative from Congressional "environmentalists". However, the charge of inadequate financial support seems less sound. A really vigorous federal commitment need not involve large direct expenditures except for research, development and measurement, but it would involve very tough legislation, including: much more stringent standards on some effluents; more caution in proceeding with programs, both federal and private, that might have adverse but presently not well understood environmental effects; provision for more rapid

41

enforcement, by the federal government if necessary; and much heavier penalties for violations of pollution standards. Such a program would result in very large economic costs, costs that would be reflected in significant reductions in the rate of increase of the gross national product. Whether the Administration is prepared to move in such a direction remains to be seen. Programs such as the supersonic transport and moves to eliminate the tax-exempt status of organizations devoted to conserving and improving environmental quality are examples that suggest it may not be.

On the other hand, there is basis for some optimism in the passage of the Environmental Policy Act of 1969, particularly in its provisions for the establishment of the Council on Environmental Quality and in the requirement that recommendations for legislation or major federal actions that might significantly affect environmental quality be accompanied by a detailed statement regarding expected effects. If this last provision is taken very seriously, particularly by the Congress as it passes legislation, the Act could prove to be a milestone.

Bibliography

1. CONTROLLING POLLUTION, THE ECONOMICS OF A CLEANER AMERICA (M.I. Goldman ed. 1967).

2. R. RIENOW AND L. TRAIN, MOMENT IN THE SUN (1967).

3. COUNCIL ON ENVIRONMENTAL QUALITY, FIRST ANNUAL REPORT ON ENVIRONMENTAL QUALITY (August, 1970).

4. U.S. DEP'T OF HEW, PUB. HEALTH SERVICE, ENVIRON-MENTAL HEALTH SERVICE, NATIONAL AIR POLLUTION CONTROL ADMINISTRATION, AIR QUALITY CRITERIA FOR SULFUR OXIDES (March, 1970).

5. Id., AIR QUALITY CRITERIA FOR PHOTOCHEMICAL OXIDANTS (March, 1970).

6. Id., AIR QUALITY CRITERIA FOR PARTICULATE MATTER (January, 1969).

7. Id., CONTROL TECHNIQUES FOR PARTICULATE AIR POLLUTANTS (January, 1969).

8. Id., CONTROL TECHNIQUES FOR SULFUR OXIDE AIR POLLUTANTS (January, 1969).

9. Id., CONTROL TECHNIQUES FOR CARBON MONOXIDE, NITROGEN OXIDE, AND HYDROCARBON EMISSIONS FROM MOBILE SOURCES (March, 1970).

10. Id., CONTROL TECHNIQUES FOR HYDROCARBON AND ORGANIC SOLVENT EMISSIONS FROM STATIONARY SOURCES (March, 1970).

11. R.L. DUPREY, U.S. DEP'T OF HEW, PUB. HEALTH SERVICE, CONSUMER PROTECTION AND ENVIRONMENTAL HEALTH SERVICE, POLLUTION CONTROL AD., COMPILATION OF AIR POLLUTANT EMISSION FACTORS (N.C. Pub. Health Service Publication No. 999-AP-42 January, 1968).

12. ENVIRONMENTAL STUDY GROUP TO THE ENVIRONMENTAL STUDIES BOARD OF THE NATIONAL ACADEMY OF SCIENCES AND

THE NATIONAL ACADEMY OF ENGINEERING, REPORT ON
INSTITUTIONS FOR EFFECTIVE MANAGEMENT OF THE ENVIRON-
MENT Part I (January, 1970).

13. A.V. KNEESE, RESOURCES FOR THE FUTURE, INC.,
ECONOMICS AND THE QUALITY OF THE ENVIRONMENT - SOME
EMPIRICAL EXPERIENCES (1968).

14. A.V. KNEESE, RESOURCES FOR THE FUTURE, INC.,
APPROACHES TO REGIONAL WATER QUALITY MANAGEMENT (1967).

15. U.S. COMMITTEE FOR THE GLOBAL ATMOSPHERIC
RESEARCH PROGRAM, DIVISION OF PHYSICAL SCIENCES,
NATIONAL RESEARCH COUNCIL, PLAN FOR U.S. PARTICIPATION
IN THE GLOBAL ATMOSPHERIC RESEARCH PROGRAM (Nat'l
Academy of Science, 1969).

16. C.D. Keeling, Is Carbon Dioxide from Fossil
Fuel Changing Man's Environment?, 114 PROCEEDINGS OF
THE AMERICAN PHILOSOPHICAL SOCIETY, No. 1 (1969).

17. G.J.F. MacDonald, The Modification of Planet
Earth by Man, 72 TECHNOLOGY REV., No. 1, October/
November 1969.

18. N.H. Brooks, Man, Water and Waste, 70 TECHNOLOGY
REV., No. 7, May, 1968.

19. R.E. McKinney, The Environmental Challenge of
Solid Wastes, id.

20. T.F. Malone, Tinkering with our Atmospheric
Environment, id.

21. J.L. Fisher, Limits on the Exploitation of
Natural Resources, id.

22. DEPARTMENT OF HEALTH, EDUCATION AND WELFARE,
PUBLIC HEALTH SERVICE, OFFICE OF PROGRAM DEVELOPMENT,
CONSUMER PROTECTION AND ENVIRONMENTAL HEALTH SERVICE,
DIVISION OF PROGRAM EVALUATION AND ANALYSIS, ISSUE
STUDY ON AIR POLLUTION (August, 1969).

23. E.D. Goldberg, Chemical Invasion of the Ocean
by Man, in YEARBOOK OF SCIENCE AND TECHNOLOGY (1970).

24. R.A. Carpenter, Information for Decisions in Environmental Policy, 168 SCIENCE, June 12, 1970.

25. W. Seiler and C. Junge, Carbon Monoxide in the Atmosphere, 75 J. GEOPHYSICAL RESEARCH, No. 21, Apr. 20, 1970.

26. O.J. Fletcher, Controlling the Planet's Climate, XIX IMPACT OF SCIENCE ON SOCIETY, No. 2 (1969).

27. I. Lyon, Nuclear Power and the Public Interest, III THE BENNINGTON REVIEW, No. 3, Fall 1969.

28. J. SNOW, RADIOACTIVE WASTE FROM REACTORS, SCIENTISTS' INSTITUTE FOR PUBLIC INFORMATION (May, 1967).

29. J.M. Pierrard, Environmental Appraisal-Particulate Matter, Oxides of Sulfur, and Sulfuric Acid, 19 JOURNAL OF THE AIR POLLUTION CONTROL ASSOCIATION, No. 9, Sept., 1969.

30. G.M. Woodwell, Effects of Pollution on the Structure and Physiology of Ecosystems, 168 SCIENCE, Apr. 24, 1970.

31. G.D. ROBINSON, LONG-TERM EFFECTS OF AIR POLLUTION - A SURVEY (The Center for the Environment and Man, Inc., CEM 4029-400, June 1970).

32. D.E. ABRAHAMSON, ENVIRONMENTAL COST OF ELECTRIC POWER (Scientists' Institute for Public Information, 1970).

33. T.K. Sherwood, Must We Breathe Sulfur Oxides?, 72 TECHNOLOGY REVIEW, No. 3, January 1970.

34. S. Miner, Air Pollution Aspects of Radioactive Substances (Litton Systems, Inc., Sept., 1969).

35. M. Ways, How To Think About the Environment, LXXXI Fortune, No. 2, Feb. 1970.

36. G. Bylinsky, The Limited War on Water Pollution, id

37. S. Rose, The Economics of Environmental Quality, id

38. T. Alexander, Some Burning Questions About Combustion, id.

39. L. WHITE, MACHINA EX DEO (1968).

40. AIR POLLUTION (A.C. Stern ed. 1968).

41. R.G. RIDKER, ECONOMIC COSTS OF AIR POLLUTION (1967).

Frank P. Grad

Intergovernmental Aspects of Environmental Controls

The scope of "environmental law" has seen such rapid
expansion in the recent past that any attempt to analyze
the part played in it by the federal, state and local
governments must first face the problem of selection of
an area in which intergovernmental considerations have
made a significant difference. Although aspects of
conservation and resource development are touched at a
number of points, the emphasis of this paper is on the
control of environmental pollution--including air and
water pollution, solid waste, noise and radiation pollution. There are several reasons for this emphasis.
Problems of pollution are the most widespread, and
many of their aspects are most acute. Moreover, there
is a well-developed technology for the control of many
pollutants, and all that is required for their successful management is the proper regulatory machinery,

properly staffed and financed. Perhaps more important,
environmental pollution is a significant metropolitan
and urban problem, and in consequence affects more
people than other aspects of environmental management.
Because it is largely an urban, metropolitan problem,
environmental pollution commonly requires the efforts
of more than any one single government for its control.
Indeed, environmental pollution has become an intergovernmental problem because its dimensions can no
longer be contained within the narrow boundaries of
municipal or local jurisdiction.

The most striking aspect of environmental controls
is the absence of any broadly inclusive federal policy.
To be sure, the passage of the National Environmental
Policy Act of 1969[1] indicates an awareness of the need
for such a policy and provides broad national policy
guidelines for the future. But the Environmental Policy
Act was superimposed on an existing scheme--to call it
a pattern would be to overstate the case--of federal,
state and local involvement in the setting of environmental policies and enforcement efforts that is both
inconsistent and bewildering. The National Environmental Policy Act expresses a general policy in favor
of the preservation and restoration of the environment
without, however, reaching in to adjust existing intergovernmental relations and without seeking to order the
variety of regulatory efforts at different levels of
government in any systematic way.

The creation in 1970 of the Environmental Protection
Agency[2] represents the first step in sorting out present
legal and administrative relationships. Although these
actions may be viewed as a promising start in the

development of national environmental policies worthy of that name, the effective formulation of such policy will require a further restructuring of relationships to make them more coherent, more logical and more effective. An examination of the laws that determine the level of government at which policies and standards are set in the control of air pollution, water pollution, solid waste disposal, noise pollution, radiation pollution and other environmental controls will serve as a useful beginning.

The Role of the Federal Government in the Formulation of Environmental Policies and Standards

The historical development of federal involvement in environmental controls has followed a somewhat parallel pattern in almost every aspect of pollution control except in the case of radiation pollution, which the federal government has viewed as a matter of national concern from the very beginning of the development of nuclear energy.[3] In all other areas of environmental controls, however, the federal government has moved from a position of self denial of powers to an ever stronger assertion of federal interest. This is understandable because the control of the environment --in the traditional sense--for the health, safety and welfare of the people--be it in the area of water pollution, air pollution or noise--had long been regarded as a proper area for the exercise of the police power by the several states.[4] The federal government, as a government of limited and delegated powers, had never

49

regarded itself as a repository of a general police
power, even though "the federal police power" has sometimes been mentioned in a somewhat metaphoric sense.[5]
The federal government has involved itself in environmental controls rather gradually. Reliance on the
commerce power in the direct control of pollution is
the most recent phenomenon of federal regulation;
initially it operated indirectly through the federal
government's power to tax and spend for the general
welfare. Thus, in most fields of pollution control the
federal involvement begins not with an assertion of
federal regulatory power but through sponsorship of
grant-in-aid programs, with federal standards gradually
being imposed as a condition of the receipt of federal
funds for purposes of environmental control. This
traditional Congressional approach to the pollution
control problem is exemplified in the policy declaration of the Federal Water Pollution Act of 1948.

It is hereby declared to be a policy of
Congress to recognize, preserve, and protect
the primary responsibilities and rights of the
States in controlling water pollution.[6]

This limitation on the federal jurisdiction was almost
entirely self-imposed.[7] Its justification lay in part
in a continued respect for the concept of federalism,
and in part in a judgment, probably accurate in 1948,
that some form of local control was a more effective
means of combating water pollution than federal controls. Consequently, under early water pollution and
air pollution control acts the federal function was
to operate in full cooperation with state and interstate agencies and with local and municipal

governments.[8] When pollution problems worsened rapidly, the wisdom of this secondary federal role was questioned.[9] The result, a new direction of the federal effort, is reflected in the declaration of policy of the Water Quality Control Act of 1965:

> The purpose of this act is to enhance the quality and value of our water resources and to establish a national policy for the prevention, control and abatement of water pollution.[10]

Though the concept of a partnership with the states still remains,[11] the unmistakable trend of federal programs has been to locate the responsibility for final decisions on water quality objectives, standards and priorities in Washington.[12]

AIR POLLUTION CONTROL

A similar development may be noted in the area of air pollution control. In 1955 the Congress enacted the first federal air pollution legislation. The law was entitled "Air Pollution Control--Research and Technical Assistance."[13] It provided grants-in-aid for state and local air pollution control agencies for research, training and demonstration projects, and gave authority for technical advice and assistance from the federal government. It also authorized the Surgeon General to collect and publish air pollution information. The limited view of the federal role in the 1955 Act is reflected in the Senate Report on the legislation:

> The committee recognized that it is primarily the responsibility of state and local governments to prevent air pollution. The bill does not propose any exercise of police power by the federal govern-

ment and no provision in it invades the sovereignty of states, counties or cities. There is
no attempt to impose standards of purity.[14]

Some eight years later, in the Clean Air Act of 1963,
the legislative finding still paid ritual obeisance to
the doctrine of primary state responsibility for air
pollution control.[15] The Act itself, however, indicated that a major change had taken place in the federal
role and in the pattern of federal-state-local relations. It gave the U.S. Public Health Service a far
broader role in handling air pollution problems and
recognized the need for regional cooperation. While
under the 1955 Act grants-in-aid had gone directly from
the federal government to the cities, under the 1963
Act the state became the focal point. In addition to
grants-in-aid and provisions for research and technical assistance, the Secretary of HEW was authorized to
publish non-mandatory air criteria and to encourage
and report on efforts to prevent motor vehicle exhaust
pollution. Grants-in-aid were also provided for air
pollution control programs and, perhaps more significant from the point of view of direct federal regulatory
involvement, the law authorized the Secretary of HEW
to intervene when air pollution was alleged to endanger
"health or welfare," when any state was unable to cope
with the problem by itself.[16] The precise nature of
these regulatory controls, which have been continued
under present federal legislation, will be discussed
at greater length in another context.[17] As will presently appear, the 1963 Act, in providing for grants-
in-aid to the states for air pollution control, exerted
an enormous influence in the development and enactment

of the states' own air pollution control legislation.[18]
Moreover, the 1963 Act, departing considerably from the
notion of strictly local control of air pollution, gave
recognition to the need for regional planning and provided tangible incentives for regional cooperation in
its grants-in-aid program--a larger proportion of the
costs of establishing, developing and improving air
pollution programs was to be reimbursed by the federal
government if the grantee agency was an intermunicipal
or interstate agency than if it served only a single
city or other governmental unit.[19]

The 1965 amendments to the Clean Air Act moved even
more toward direct federal involvement. They authorized
the Secretary of HEW to promulgate and enforce federal
emission standards for new motor vehicles, without providing for the participation in the standard setting
process by the states or localities.[20] This was one of
the early instances of clear reliance on the commerce
clause as a basis for federal air pollution control.
Based on similar constitutional authority, the 1965
amendments enabled the Secretary to act on pollution
complaints brought by international agencies or by the
Secretary of State. Such action included the ultimate
right to bring suit against the polluter.[21]

The Air Quality Act of 1967 brought the federal
government squarely into the field of air pollution
control. While continuing the provisions of the earlier
Clean Air Act for grants-in-aid for research and for
other program activities by air pollution control
agencies, for the first time the Secretary of HEW was
not only authorized but charged with the duty of

issuing air quality criteria.[22] The Act specifically
required him to designate broad atmospheric areas,
and to specify air quality control regions. He was
also required to issue information about air pollution
control techniques, and to promulgate air quality
criteria. Once criteria and control techniques had
been issued, the states were then required to set
standards and make plans for their implementation;
these standards were to be designed to meet the air
quality standards for the specific air quality regions
or parts of regions within the state's boundaries. If
a state failed to adopt standards of its own, the
Secretary was authorized to promulgate standards for
the state, following a conference with the appropriate
state officials. If requested by the state, a hearing
was required before such standards could be promulgated.
Moreover, if the state failed to enforce its own
standards or failed to enforce the standards set for
it by the Secretary, he was authorized to request the
Attorney General to commence lawsuits for their
enforcement whenever interstate air pollution was
involved.[23]

A further change in the direction of greater federal
involvement in environmental controls was evidenced by
a new power granted by the 1967 Act. The Secretary of
HEW was authorized to request the Attorney General to
bring an abatement action in any air pollution situation
which presented an imminent and substantial danger to
health, without the necessity of a prior conference or
hearing.[24] Moreover, the Secretary was granted exclusive authority to establish and improve emission

standards for new motor vehicles, except in those
instances in which a state had adopted a higher
standard for new motor vehicles prior to March 30,
1966.[25] In fact, the exception applied only to the
State of California, which had adopted such standards.[26] The Secretary was authorized, too, to
study the feasibility of national emission standards,
and was granted the power to require the registration
of fuel additives.[27] In 1970 the function of the
Secretary under the 1963, 1965 and 1967 Acts were
transferred to the Administrator of the newly formed
Environmental Protection Agency.[28] At present, in
1970, legislation is pending in Congress to authorize national emission standards.[29]

It is perhaps noteworthy that the 1967 Air Quality
Standards Act not only placed greater emphasis on
federal regulatory controls but also deemphasized
local controls to a considerable extent. The initial
burden for setting standards and for adopting plans
for their implementation to meet regional air quality
standards is placed on the states, after an appropriate
public hearing. There is, moreover, no requirement
that the local governments participate in such
hearings.[30] The shift from a local to a broader
regional, if not national, emphasis was reflected,
too, in a number of federal incentives to regional
cooperation. To be sure, the encouragement of regional
cooperation--and especially the encouragement of interstate compacts--is not exactly unambiguous. While
encouraging interstate compacts for air pollution control, the Act expressed the Congressional intention to

disapprove any interstate compact which included states not within a federally determined air quality region.[31] This limitation, as will presently appear, aborted three air pollution control compacts on the verge of adoption.[32] However, though the federal attitude towards interstate and regional cooperation is not as liberal as appears on the surface, the Air Quality Standards Act does provide for more substantial financing of air pollution control programs in interstate regions than in intrastate regions, and seeks to stimulate the establishment of air quality standards in interstate air quality regions by paying up to 100 percent of the costs of planning such interstate programs for the first two years and, thereafter, authorizing the payment of up to three-quarters of the expenses of such a program.[33] There is authority also for the Secretary to establish a federal air planning commission for consultation with the respective governors if the states fail to establish interstate air quality planning regions.[34]

The federal role in air pollution control with respect to policy making and standard setting is thus one of limited but increasingly direct involvement. For the present, the federal government merely designates air quality regions and issues air quality criteria which, in a sense, are performance standards. It is up to the states to work out emission standards and plans for their enforcement so as to meet the federal air quality criteria, the performance standard nationally established for designated air quality regions. Though the federal involvement in setting emission standards for automotive pollution is somewhat more direct, this direct involvement in the policing of standards is thus far limited to new cars, the specific area where the federal government has the means of regulation at the source. The imposition of federal standards for emissions generally is as yet in the future. Though the federal government prescribes standards for air quality generally, it is left to the states--and to the localities--to establish the emission standards which industry and others must observe and which the air pollution control personnel must enforce.

WATER POLLUTION CONTROL

The parallel developments in the history of federal regulation of water and air pollution have already been noted. Although modern developments have been very similar--indeed, much of the federal air pollution control legislation is an almost verbatim adaptation of the water pollution legislation--it is nonetheless true that the federal government asserted an interest in certain aspects of water pollution control as early as the late nineteenth century. The first such federal statute was enacted in 1886 and prohibited the dumping of refuse in New York Harbor.[35] The Rivers and Harbors Act of 1899 also prohibited the discharge of "waste materials" into any navigable waterway excepting waste which flowed in a liquid state from streets or sewers.[36] While the Rivers and Harbors Act has seen recent and fairly frequent application as an anti-pollution measure,[37] the obvious intent of early rivers and harbors legislation was

57

simply to protect navigation against floating obstructions.

Subsequent federal legislation dealt mainly with water pollution as a vector in the spread of communicable disease. The Public Health Services Act of 1912[38] authorized the investigation of the effect of pollution in navigable lakes and streams on public heal Subsequent cooperation between the Public Health Servic and state agencies resulted in the voluntary adoption of nationwide standards for the treatment of drinking water. The adoption of these standards has almost entirely eliminated waterborne diseases.[39]

When oil pollution became a problem in the 1920's the Oil Pollution Control Act of 1924[40] was enacted to combat oil discharges that were causing damage to aquatic life, mainly shellfish, and to recreational facilities and docks and harbors.[41] The Act applied onl to coastal waters and was therefore of limited use.

Between 1924 and 1948 several efforts were made to enlist the assistance of the federal government in wate pollution control.[42] Water pollution had increased drastically as a result of the wartime growth of industry and, in 1947, a number of water pollution control bills were introduced in Congress.[43] The first federal Water Pollution Control Act, which grew out of these legislative endeavors, was signed into law by President Truman on June 30, 1948.[44] The policy of this act—as stated in its legislative purpose section—was one of cooperation with state and local authorities already engaged in water pollution control.[45] Acknowledging the states' primary responsibility for water pollution control, Congress hoped that, with federal support, local programs would be able to handle pollution problems effectively.[46] The federal role in enforcement under the 1948 act was very narrow indeed. Under section 2(d) of the Act the Federal Security Administrator was authorized to ask the Attorney General to bring suit on behalf of the United States against a person polluting interstate waters, but only after affording the State in which the pollution originated a reasonable time to take action against the polluter and then only with its permission.[47] The Act was to expire in five years; in 1952 it was extended through 1956.[48]

Comprehensive and permanent federal water pollution legislation was not enacted until 1956.[49] The 1956 law, however, reaffirmed the Congressional policy to acknowledge and protect the state's primary responsibility in the area.[50] On the federal level, the Act broadened and intensified the research and training aspects of the program by authorizing research grants to public and private agencies and to qualified individuals. It also authorized grants to the states and to interstate agencies for water pollution control activities. Moreover, a substantial annual appropriation was authorized for construction grants to states, cities and other government agencies for the building of waste treatment works.[51] Other aspects of the 1956 law were to provide for simpler procedures for federal abatement actions against interstate polluters[52] and a strengthening of the Pollution Control Advisory Board that had been created under the 1948 Act.[53] The Act also established a program to control

59

pollution emanating from federal installations.[54]

There was no further federal legislation during the next twelve years, until President Kennedy threw the weight of his office behind a more active federal water pollution control effort.[55] In 1961 the federal Water Pollution Control Act was amended to strengthen certain administrative aspects of the law as well as the grants in-aid and technical assistance features of the earlier program.[56] The 1961 amendment also extended the reach of federal abatement authority. Previously the federal government had asserted authority to abate pollution in "interstate waters"; this authority was extended to include all "navigable waters" whether interstate or not.[57]

In spite of these efforts the quality of the nation's water continued to deteriorate, and in April, 1963 the Senate Committee on Public Works appointed a special Subcommittee on Air and Water Pollution.[58] This sub-committee, under the chairmanship of Senator Muskie, became the leading force in water pollution control efforts. After three sessions of debate, Congress finally passed the Water Quality Act of 1965.[59] For the first time in any federal pollution statute, the declared purpose of the Act was to establish "a national policy" for the regulation of water pollution, language subsequently adopted in the 1967 Air Quality Standards Act.[60] Thus the 1965 Water Quality Act marked the earliest assertion of federal leadership in the nation's anti-pollution efforts.

The 1965 Act assigned responsibility for the federal program to a newly created Federal Water Pollution

Control Administration (FWPCA) in HEW. It also expanded the appropriations for construction grants for sewage treatment plants and provided more substantial funds for research into pollution problems. But most important was the enactment of a timetable for the establishment by the states of water quality standards for interstate waters; these standards were to be used by the federal agency in enforcing pollution abatement.[61]

Shortly after the effective date of the new law, the President submitted a reorganization plan that proposed a transfer of the federal Water Pollution Control Administration from HEW to the Department of the Interior.[62] The purpose of this transfer was to consolidate administrative responsibility for all phases of the federal government's water resources program in a single department.[63] In 1970 the Administration was again transferred from Interior to the Environmental Protection Agency in a further consolidation of federal environmental programs.[64]

Throughout 1966 there was considerable activity both in Congress and in the executive department with hearings and reports on water pollution following in rapid succession.[65] The result was the Clean Water Restoration Act of 1966.[66] This Act further increased construction grant authorizations and authorizations for several existing and newly added research and training programs. It also provided added incentives to the states to adopt water quality standards and to contribute to the support of the construction of water treatment facilities.[67] In addition, the law extended federal jurisdiction over enforcement to international boundary waters and transferred responsibility for administration of the Oil Pollution Act to the Secretary of the Interior; the coverage of that act was also extended to include inland waters.[68]

The contribution of the Water Quality Act of 1965, as amended by the Clean Water Restoration Act of 1966, was to provide for the establishment of nationally required standards of rising quality for interstate waters.[69] The law did not provide, however, for the establishment of a single set of national standards. Instead, Congress provided for an elaborate procedure to ensure that the establishment of standards would be primarily a state responsibility, subject to federal approval.[70] Under the 1967 Act, each state was given until June 30, 1967 to adopt water quality standards applicable to interstate waters within its borders. If a state failed to meet this deadline, or if the standards submitted to the Department of the Interior were rejected, the department itself was authorized to establish water quality standards for interstate waters within that state.[71] All states, however, met the deadline.[72]

The several states set standards after the required public hearings at which testimony was heard relating to present and future demands on the waters of the particular river.[73] The present and prospective uses and the appropriate water quality having been determined, descriptive and numerical values were then established for different uses and different quality classifications. These water quality criteria were then submitted to the Department of the Interior accompanied by a plan for achieving and maintaining the standards. The plan included such components as construction schedules for treatment works, enforcement procedures and proposed steps to prevent pollution, as well as recommendations for monitoring water quality.[74] At present nearly all of the states' proposed standards have been approved and are in effect.[75] Thus, while there does not exist a general national standard, each stretch of interstate water is regulated by quality standards formulated for the particular river in recognition of the fact that each body of water has its special characteristics and uses.

The federal role has, however, gone somewhat beyond the approval of state-developed standards. Although the 1965 Act itself provided relatively little guidance to the states,[76] the Federal Water Pollution Control Agency issued guidelines to indicate the regulatory aspects of greatest concern to the federal agency.[77] The first of these provided that state standards allowing for less than existing water quality would be unacceptable. Criticized by industry,[78] this "lock in" effect was nonetheless consistent with the statutory policy of "enhancing the quality of water"and has been reaffirmed.[79] The guidelines also reflected the federal philosophy that has been described as the "clean water" approach--no standard may allow treatable waste to be discharged without the best practicable treatment or control unless there is evidence that a lesser degree of control will still provide sufficiently high water quality.[80] The guidelines thus rejected an older regulatory philosophy based on the traditional notion

of waste management, namely, to use the rivers so as to
maximize the waste dilution and assimilative capacity
of the nation's waters.[81]

The most recent federal activity in the area of water
pollution was the passage of the Water and Environmental
Quality Improvement Act of 1970.[82] A product of Congres
sional concern with the disastrous spills of recent
years,[83] the Act concentrated on strengthening federal
law on oil pollution. Federal jurisdiction was generall
extended--the ambiguous term "coastal waters" was re-
placed by "contiguous zone" and offshore facilities
as well as vessels became subject to federal regulation.
The basic provisions authorize the President to prepare
a national contingency plan for oil removal.[85] Others
include regulation of other "hazardous" substances[86] and
federal grants for training and demonstration projects.[8]
Title II of the Act creates an Office of Environmental
Quality in the Executive Office of the President to
provide administrative support for the Council on
Environmental Quality.[88] The Act, however, does not
effect the basic structure of federal-state relations
in the general control of water pollution; its provisions supplement rather than amend the 1967 Act, which
remains the basic source of federal power for standard-
setting and regulatory activities in the water pollution area.

In a sense, the federal regulatory efforts under the
recent water pollution control legislation may be
analogized to the federal effort in the air pollution
area. In both instances, there is reliance on nationall
protected quality standards to be achieved by more

specific state regulations to control emissions and effluents. In both instances there is an attempt to utilize federal regulatory power, relying on state origination of standards in the first instance. The federal attitude of regulatory reticence, however, is likely to be more effective, and indeed has been more effective, in the field of water pollution control than in the field of air pollution control. Since water quality standards for any one interstate river must be approved by the federal Water Pollution Control Agency for every state along the entire river's length, there is likely to be greater regulatory continuity than in the less well-defined context of air quality regions. Nonetheless, just as in the case in the field of air pollution control, the federally approved water quality standards are by their nature performance standards, and it is up to the individual states to deal directly with industrial and other polluters through the enforcement of standards of emission. Just as in the case of air pollution control, pending federal legislation in the water pollution area seeks to extend federal regulatory jurisdiction beyond the area of water quality standards to deal directly with emission and effluents.[89]

SOLID WASTE DISPOSAL

Air pollution and water pollution are by their very nature problems of regional if not national dimension. The ambient air clearly is no respecter of jurisdictional boundaries, and water pollution follows the pattern of river basins which, in turn, follows the

geographic scheme of the great watershed systems which
do not happen to fall within the boundaries of any one
state or locality. A slightly different problem, one
which still is viewed as primarily local in scope. is
that presented by accumulations of solid waste. Traditionally, refuse and garbage removal has been a task of
local government. Wastes collected locally are generally disposed of by incineration--usually in municipal
incinerators or by burial in sanitary landfills,
again locally regulated, generally by local health or
sanitary codes. Until recent years the solid waste
disposal problem has been viewed as a purely local
problem. Although there was a good deal of justification for this view,[90] there is evidence that it may
soon be unrealistic.[91] The impact of available disposa
systems on a region as a whole has made the disposal of
solid waste more than a local problem. If it is incinerated, an air pollution problem almost invariably
arises. If it is buried in sanitary landfills, the
leaching of chemical components into the underground
water table and the resulting pollution of the waterways will eventually affect more than the immediate
locality. Moreover, larger metropolitan communities
are running out of space for sanitary landfills and,
with growing inability to absorb the products of incineration in the atmosphere, the problem of what to
do with solid waste has assumed national proportions.
The national interest, moreover, is involved not only
because of the impact of available methods of disposing of solid waste, but also because the source of
the solid waste problem is national and not local in

66

its nature. The enormous recent increase in the amount of solid waste per person in the nation is attributable to the enormous increase in the technology of packaging and in the manufacture of goods that eventually end up as solid waste. Thus it is nationwide industrial activities, both in the general production of goods and especially in the production and use of a variety of packaging materials and of non-returnable--and non-degradable--containers that have added immeasurably to the problem.

The fact that the origin of the solid waste problem has become national in scope and that the problem itself is rapidly becoming too great for the municipalities to handle themselves, has resulted in fairly consistent involvement by the states, and some five years ago, by the federal government with the passage of the Solid Waste Disposal Act of 1965, enacted as part of the Clean Air Act.[92] If past patterns hold true, the involvement by the federal government by way of research and demonstration grants under the Act is only the beginning of deeper and more substantial continuing federal involvement.

The stated purpose of the act is

..to initiate and accelerate a national research and development program for new and improved methods of proper and economic solid-waste disposal, including studies directed toward the conservation of natural resources by reducing the amount of waste and un-salvageable materials by recovery and utilization of potential resources in solid wastes..[93]

Indeed, President Johnson himself had urged the Congress to act on the problem of solid waste disposal and had recommended legislation to assist the states in devel-

oping comprehensive programs for some forms of solid
waste disposal and to provide for research and
demonstration projects leading to more effective
methods for disposing of or salvaging solid wastes.[94]
The 1965 Act contained no regulatory provisions.
Reminiscent of early water and air pollution laws, it
authorized the Secretary of HEW (now the Administrator
of the EPA) to render financial and technical assistance
to appropriate public agencies to develop and apply
improved methods of solid waste disposal. The Secretary was also authorized to cooperate with public and
private agencies in conducting research, to make grants-
in-aid to support such research and to make available
the results of such research.[95] Grants-in-aid were also
provided to support the construction of solid waste
disposal facilities, but no grant-in-aid was to pay for
more than two-thirds of the construction costs of any
facility. Similar, too, to early air pollution and
water pollution legislation, the Secretary was in-
structed to encourage cooperative activities by state
and local governments and the enactment of uniform
state and local laws governing solid waste disposal.
The Secretary was also authorized to make grants to
state and interstate agencies for studies, and to
establish eligibility requirements for such grants.
The stated object of the research program was to find
ways of disposal that created no health hazards, and to
find ways to recycle scrap materials into production
processes. Again, interstate and regional cooperation
was encouraged--the grant program provided for payment
of up to two-thirds of the cost of local demonstration

projects and up to three-quarters in the case of regional intergovernmental projects.

A variety of disposal methods have been explored in the demonstration projects for which grants are authorized by the Act.[96] Most recently, in 1969, the Administration asked Congress for a simple extension of the Act with somewhat greater appropriations but with no basic change in policy.[97] A number of bills were introduced, however, moving in the direction of stronger federal involvement in the solid waste disposal area. These bills would provide for more federal spending on the construction of local waste disposal facilities, and would fund studies both of economical means of recovering useful material from solid wastes, and of incentives and penalties to help solve the solid waste disposal problem. Proposed legislation would also seek practical changes in current production and packaging practices, so as to reduce the amount of solid waste.[98] While neither the existing Solid Waste Disposal Act nor the newly proposed solid waste legislation sets any federal standards, it is clear that such standards are likely to be authorized in the foreseeable future if the history of earlier water and air pollution legislation is any guide.

NOISE POLLUTION CONTROL

Noise is another area of environmental pollution in which the federal regulatory interest has thus far been quite limited. "Noise pollution" is a more narrowly local problem than either air or water pollution, or even solid waste. Until fairly recently the effect of

a noise source was limited to the distance the noise
would carry. Urban noises generally, and particularly
industrial noises, have therefore traditionally been
treated as appropriate subjects for regulation by the
localities and the states. Industrial noise has commonly been dealt with through labor and safety codes
on the state level, while ordinarily city or street
noises, such as the common sounding of horns, excessive noises from radio and record shops and other
incidental noise sources have been treated by local
legislation.[99] One common source of city noise, namely
excessive noise from automobiles, has generally been
regulated by state legislation requiring the installation of effective mufflers.[100]

The only new aspect of noise pollution, one in
which the federal government has recently become
involved, is noise created near airports by powerful
jet engines and, looking towards the future, the
effects of the sonic boom which may result from the
development of a supersonic transport. In contrast to
the lack of federal law in the area of noise control
generally, regulation of airport noise, as will be discovered at a later point, has been pre-empted by the
federal government.

It has been said that federal interest in this aspect
of noise control became greater when members of a politically informed and capable group, namely upper middle
class persons with substantial homes in suburban areas
near airports, began making their power felt. From
1965 to early 1970, a total of 50 separate bills concerning noise control were introduced in Congress.

Most of these sought to bring about abatement of air-craft noise through the development and federal certi-fication of quieter airplanes, the introduction of less noisy methods of aviation, and the development of zoning restrictions to limit the use of land surround-ing airports. Some of the bills would have authorized funds for research and development in the problem of aircraft noise, and a few dealt specifically with the problem of sonic boom.[101] Only three of the 50 expressly dealt with noise as an aspect of environ-mental pollution generally.[102] Most died in committee and it was not until 1967 that a bill sponsored by the FAA, and a number of others of a similar nature reached the committee hearing stage. These all authorized and required the FAA to set noise limits in the certifi-cation of new aircraft. The FAA bill, H.R. 3400 was passed by Congress and was signed into law by the President in 1968.[103] In 1969 two regulations to control noise in the vicinity of airports were pro-posed by the FAA under that law. The first of these required that the noise nuisance factor would have to be taken into consideration in preparatory aero-nautical studies of proposed airport projects. The second set specific noise level limits in FAA certi-fication of new aircraft. After comments had been solicited and received by interested parties, the first proposed regulation was withdrawn for further study, and the second was promulgated essentially as pro-posed.[104] In addition to laws and regulations deal-ing specifically with noise, noise pollution by aircraft may be affected by § 12(f) of the Airport

and Airway Development Act of 1970 which requires the
Secretary of Transportation to consult with government
agencies concerned with environmental problems in
formulation of a national airport system plan.[105]

Aside from regulation of aircraft noise, the most
significant federal action in the area was the adoption by the Department of Labor in 1969 of a regulation based on the so-called "Walsh-Healey Amendment,"[106]
which set decibel limits for industrial noise to protect
the health and safety of employees in all industrial
concerns with government contracts in excess of $10,000.
The impact of this regulation on industry performance
is likely to be major. If the past is any guide to
the future, federal decibel limits for industrial noise
will in due course be adopted by state labor departments
that had not had such limits previously. Moreover, in
view of the relatively low amount of government contracts necessary to bring a company within the regulatory scope of the federal regulation, many companies
whose work is not primarily government contract will
probably be covered by the law. The desirability of
such regulation is beyond question since excessive
industrial noise has led to substantial hearing difficulties and deafness.[107]

Aside from some incipient regulatory efforts with
respect to airplane noise and excessive industrial noise
the federal government has exerted considerable influenc
in the development of noise pollution control standards
through federally sponsored research rather than legislation. Most of the studies completed since 1965, concerned aircraft noise and sonic boom and were authorized

72

or sponsored either by NASA or by the FAA.[108] A most
influential study on industrial noise and environmental
control[109] was sponsored by the Public Health Service
in 1967 and, in 1968, HUD published a report on field
studies involving the effects of noise in the urban and
suburban environments.[110]

RADIATION CONTROL

In the area of radiation control, the history of
federal regulation is considerably different from that
of other areas of environmental controls. While in
other areas the federal government has entered the
field gradually, leaving primary regulatory powers in
the states and localities, in many instances emphasizing
local controls when local controls were no longer
wholly appropriate, the history of radiation control
regulation moves in the opposite direction. Here,
because of the manner in which atomic energy had been
developed during the war years, preemptive federal
regulatory controls were asserted in 1946 when the
Atomic Energy Act was first passed.[111] It was not
until 1959 that the federal government released its
full preemptive sweep of power and permitted states
and localities to share part of the rule making and
standard setting powers, as well as some of the powers
of enforcement.[112]

It should be stressed that we are not concerned
with the question of reactor placement or the question
of reactor safety generally, but simply with the far
more limited issue of radiation pollution caused by
a properly functioning nuclear installation and by

the disposition of radioactive wastes. Under the
Atomic Energy Act of 1946, as well as under its subsequent amendments, the Atomic Energy Commission was
made nationally responsible for the setting of
radiation protection standards relating to nuclear
installations. To the extent that these responsibilities consisted of establishing "generally applicable
environmental standards for the protection of the
general environment from radioactive material" they
have now been transferred to the EPA.[113] Under the
1946 Act the Atomic Energy Commission was given vast
and far-reaching powers; one of its major functions
was that of advancing the development of nuclear power
for peaceful purposes. It has been criticized from
time to time--just as have other agencies that combine
developmental functions with protective functions--for
sometimes advancing its developmental interests at the
expense of the protection of the environment.[114]
   Despite the vast range of the Commission's rule-
making powers, the power to make rules for radiation
protection was not expressly stated in the Atomic
Energy Act. However, the power to enact standards of
radiation protection was held to be one of the dis-
cretionary--though not obligatory--functions of the
Commission.[115] In fact, in setting radiation protection
standards the AEC relied over the years on the advice
and guidance of the National Council on Radiation Protection and Measurement, a highly regarded scientific
organization founded in 1921[116] to represent the professional interests and knowledge of radiation
physicists and physicians in radiologic medicine.

Although it does not have any official standing as a government agency, its publications and handbooks are relied on as if it were. In addition to the National Council on Radiation Protection and Measurement, the Atomic Energy Commission was assisted by the Federal Radiation Council which was established on August 14, 1959 by Executive Order[117] and is now part of the EPA. The Federal Radiation Council is composed of the Secretaries of Defense, Commerce and HEW and the Chairman of the Atomic Energy Commissson and the Administrator of the EPA. The Special Assistant to the President for Science and Technology is authorized to participate in its deliberations, and each executive agency represented on the council, as well as every other federal agency, is to give the council whatever technical and other assistance it may need. The purpose of the council is to advise the President with respect to

...radiation matters directly or indirectly affecting health, including matters pertinent to the general guidance of executive agencies by the President with respect to the development of such agencies of criteria for the protection of humans against ionizing radiation applicable to the affairs of the respective agencies. The Council shall take steps designed to further the interagency coordination of measures for protecting humans against ionizing radiation.[118]

The federal standards for radiation protection and for the management of radioactive wastes have retained their unquestioned authority in spite of the passage in 1959 of a far-reaching amendment to the Atomic Energy Act which provided for cooperation with the states.[119] What was of particular interest in the 1959 amendment is not the fact that the states were given an opportunity

75

to share in the development of atomic energy, but that, despite the provision for federal-state cooperation, the entire effort was to be on terms laid down by the federal government. Moving from a position of absolute preemption, the amendment authorized the Atomic Energy Commission to enter into agreements with the governor of any state to arrange for the discontinuance of the regulatory authority of the commission under certain subchapters of the Atomic Energy Act. Aside from the fact that no general delegation of authority to deal with atomic energy was granted to the states, but rather a limited authority to act within a narrow sphere, defined in each instance by separate agreement, the law is clear that certain areas that involve secrecy or major risks may not be delegated to the states under any circumstances. Among the subjects which may not be delegated is the disposal into the oceans of specified nuclear waste materials.

An agreement delegating to a state certain regulatory functions with respect to nuclear energy may be entered into only if the government of the state certifies that it has "a program for the control of radiation hazards adequate to protect the public health and safety with respect to materials within the state covered by the proposed agreement. . ."[120] Moreover, to enter into such an agreement the commission must find that "the state program is compatible with the commission's program for the regulation of such material, and that the state program is adequate to protect the public health and safety with respect to the materials covered by the proposed agreement."[121] The effect of this limited

76

delegation has been to make the federal radiation protection standards the dominant ones in the field.

Until the recent past when two separate attacks
were leveled against them, there had never been any
substantial criticism of the adequacy of federal
radiation standards. The first attack, by Dr. John
W. Gofman and Dr. Arthur Tamplin of the Biomedical
Division at the Lawrence Radiation Laboratory in
California, charged that the emission standards were
entirely too low, and that, given the current population of 200 million, if there were a more than 20
percent contribution to U.S. power needs from nuclear
power plants yielding the maximum emissions permitted by the Atomic Energy Commission, 16,000
radiation deaths a year would result.[122] It is
expected that by the year 1980, 20 percent of the
power needs of this country will be met by nuclear
reactors.[123] This attack has been rejected by the
Atomic Energy Commission[124] and by the Chairman of
the National Council of Radiation Protection and
Measurement.[125] Basically, the difference of opinion revolves around the issue of whether radiation
in any amount is damaging, or whether there is a
threshhold tolerance for radiation for the population at large. The other attack on the federal
standards has come from the State of Minnesota
which has sought to impose higher radiation emission
standards to permit the siting of a new nuclear
installation, in spite of the fact that an Atomic
Energy Commission license had already been obtained
for the particular site. This matter is presently
pending.[126]

FEDERAL ENVIRONMENTAL REGULATION--IN GENERAL

It is evident from the brief survey of the role of the federal government in setting standards and in making regulations for environmental control that most areas have developed along similar lines. Since most aspects of environmental pollution initially appear as subjects appropriate for regulation under the states' police power, the federal interest initially has been to bolster the exercise of the states' and the localities' power through grants-in-aid, grants for research and development, and grants for inter-governmental cooperation in dealing with environmental pollution. As it has become apparent in area after area that environmental problems are not easily suscep-tible to state or local resolution, but are indeed of regional or national scope, the federal interest has been enlarged and the federal government has taken on more and more of the burden of standard setting and regulation. As will presently appear, standard setting and regulation have not necessarily brought about a more direct federal involvement in enforce-ment activities for, on the whole, the federal govern-ment has traditionally sought to work through state and local instrumentalities in the control of the environment. It is also clear that federal standards --whether direct regulatory standards as in the case of radiation pollution or automotive emission standards, or indirect regulation through the use of the grant-in-aid device--have had an enormously stimulating effect on the states' and localities' own standard setting and rule-making endeavors. Since the passage of the

78

Air Quality Control Act of 1967, when the federal
government first set motor vehicle emission standards, for instance, some 28 states have enacted
legislation to deal with vehicle pollution.[127]
It is evident, too, that many of the state regulations for water pollution control were passed in
response to federal grants conditioned on the states'
enforcing appropriate standards, as provided in the
1965 Water Pollution Control Act.[128]

Another aspect of federal involvement in environmental controls needs to be mentioned. Until very
recently, with the passage of the Environmental
Policy Act of 1969,[129] the federal concern for the
regulation of environmental pollution has proceeded
on a totally piecemeal basis, with each environmental
problem being taken up in turn, often without regard
to its impact on other aspects of environmental quality.
Aside from regulatory controls in the area of air
pollution, water pollution, noise pollution, etc., the
federal government's own involvement in programs that
have significant environmental impact, such as highway,
airport and research development activities, has proceeded separate from, and without regard to, the policies implicit in some of the regulatory efforts. The
lack of coordination between regulatory programs on the
one hand and the broad developmental programs on the
other raises a significant question relating to the
consistency of federal environmental policy. Unless
federal programs with broad environmental implications
can be reconciled with federal regulatory efforts in
the control of the environment, no sustained coherent

federal environmental policy will emerge.

If the Environmental Policy Act of 1969 is to have any purpose whatever, it will be to fulfill that need. But the Environmental Quality Council, created under that Act, has no regulatory power, although it has broad scope to investigate and coordinate the efforts of other agencies.[130] Although the creation of the Council is a promising development, it is of course too soon to evaluate the potential of this new organization. If the Council is to serve any function, it will have to address itself particularly to the question of a general federal environmental policy that harmonizes the federal government's own developmental activities with the regulatory purposes of federal legislation that deals with water pollution, air pollution, and other injuries to the environment.

The Role of the States and Municipalities in Standard-Setting

The states and localities have dealt with environmental problems under the states' police power practically from the beginning of time. Much of what is presently referred to as environmental legislation finds its origin in rather primitive early regulations promulgated in the state or local sanitary code as part of the regulation of the public health. So, for instanc the origins of air pollution control can be traced back to early colonial legislation and to even earlier English regulations that dealt with smoking chimneys and the nuisance created by smoke, fly ash and cinders.[131] The origins of water pollution controls may

also be found in the early local regulations which
prohibited a man from placing his cesspool too close
to his own or his neighbor's well.[132] Frequently, such
regulations preceded even the scientific knowledge
which would have justified them, for the placement of
a well near a cesspool was regarded as dangerous even
prior to the knowledge that insufficient filtration
could cause contamination of the well from the cesspool.
So, too, local regulation of noise nuisances antedates
by many years the clear evidence that excessive noise
results in hearing loss. Thus, there has never been
any real question that the states or the municipalities,
by delegation from the states, had the power to enact
laws or regulations that protect the health, safety and
welfare of the people against adverse effects of environmental pollution.

AIR POLLUTION CONTROL
    It is of course a long way from a local smoke
ordinance to a sophisticated state or municipal air
pollution control code. Generally the states and
localities developed such codes in response to federal
grant-in-aid programs that made it desirable for them
to do so. So, for instance, following the initial
federal air pollution legislation in 1955 which provided funds for research and development, the Council
of State Governments first called the states' attention to the need for air pollution regulations and
proposed some general standards through appropriate
recommendations of one of its governors' conferences.[133]
Today, almost all states have enacted state air pollution

control legislation, some of the most recent enact-
ments having occurred in response to the 1967 Federal
Air Quality Act.[134] Typically the state laws designate a state agency or establish a new commission to
promulgate standards and codes.[135] In most states the
enforcing agency is the state health department,[136]
although in some states separate air pollution control
agencies have been created.[137] Most of the state laws
allow local governments to enact air pollution codes
or regulations of their own, but do not generally
require it. A number require the state agency, board
or commission to encourage local units of government
to handle air pollution programs and to provide them
with technical advice and assistance.[138] Under most
state laws local units of government are empowered to
enact laws or ordinances regulating air pollution, but
the standards set by such local units must be consistent with, or more stringent than, the state regulations. A few states have even more detailed provisions
to insure a coordinated state-local effort. In Florida, for instance, the state agency must review local
standards before they become effective;[139] in Colorado
the law requires a mutual review--local units must
review state regulations and the state agency must review the local regulations before either becomes effective.[140] In some states, county and other governmental
units are given the authority to study and investigate
pesticide problems and to report them to the central
air pollution control agency for review and action.[141]
A few states, too, require municipalities and other loca
governments to participate in area-wide regulation, or

else to become subject to direct state regulation.[142] Regional cooperation is authorized and provided for in many states' air pollution control laws, though none of them expressly require it.[143]

A recent draft of model state air pollution control legislation proposed by the Council of State Governments[144] requires local regulatory action by state law in a direct and effective fashion. Section 14 of the proposed law requires municipalities to establish and administer air pollution control programs. Local standards must be stricter than, or at least consistent with, those of the state and must provide for administrative and judicial sanctions. Moreover, the state agency is required to approve the program. If the local unit of government does not act, or if it does not carry out its responsibilities adequately, the state may, after a hearing, administer the program directly, and may charge the local unit for the expense. Interlocal cooperation is provided for, and the state agency may require area-wide air pollution control programs where considered necessary. If the local units of government do not cooperate in the establishment or administration of such a regional program, the state is authorized to administer the program directly. Finally, if the state agency determines that a particular class of air pollutants is more amenable to state regulation than local regulation, the state may assume exclusive jurisdiction.

The proposed model state air pollution control act is significant in that it deals with a number of problems that have arisen in state air pollution control

programs and that existing legislation has failed to
address. Generally, state and local air pollution
control programs are structurally independent of one
another. While the state theoretically exercises
supervisory control over local programs, in fact there
is considerable disjunctiveness both on the standard
setting and on the enforcement level. The state
generally exercises little or no supervision over the
standards promulgated by local air pollution control
agencies and the question of inconsistency between
state and local standards is not likely to be raised
at all unless a person charged with violating the
local code raises the issue in defense to a criminal
prosecution or other enforcement action. The disjunctiveness of state and local air pollution control programs within a single state is even more sharply pro-
nounced in the area of enforcement and will be referred
to in greater detail in that context.[145]

Originally, one of the most troublesome aspects of
state and local air pollution control programs was the
composition of the air pollution control agency empowered to set standards and make regulations. Normally
state and local air pollution control agencies operate
on well-established administrative law principles.
The agency is established by law and is given power to
promulgate an air pollution control code consisting
of emission standards and such other standards as the
enabling legislation may refer to in a general fashion.
The enabling legislation normally prescribes the membership of the commission or board that is empowered to
promulgate the code or other standards under the law.[146]

It has been the practice in air pollution control legislation to give substantial representation to the very industries that were the most serious polluters. For many years, membership in standard setting boards in many of the states was based on something of a tripartite formula, with industry having approximately one-third of the seats and with the public, labor groups, and professionals with specific knowledge or interest in air pollution technology holding the other two-thirds.[147] Most of the professionals who were likely to be knowledgeable in air pollution control matters, however, were either employed by industry or were closely identified with industry's point of view. Consequently, many states' air pollution control agencies were for a long time industry-protection oriented, and would not recommend air pollution control measures that were costly or otherwise objectionable to industrial polluters. Moreover, state air pollution control legislation often contained safeguards from the very beginning that were protective of industry.[148] Provisions that require the agency to set air pollution control standards, taking into account "economic feasibility," were especially likely to result in standards that permitted economic factors to outweigh the claims of public health.[149]

State and local air pollution codes differ widely with respect to coverage and technical sophistication. On the most primitive level, all of them deal with visible emissions and set limits (usually in terms of the Ringelman chart) in terms of the density of emissions.[150] Most codes go beyond this primitive smoke-emission standard and deal also with gaseous emissions, whether visible or not.[151] On a yet higher level stand the codes that relate the amount of emission to the amount of heat produced by the apparatus--in effect, requiring minimal standards of heating efficiency.[152] Other, more advanced regulatory approaches limit certain harmful particulate emissions, including process dust, often relating the amount of permissible emissions to the weight of the bulk involved in the manufacturing process.[153] More advanced codes, moreover, impose not merely emissions standards, but also fuel standards, reflecting an appreciation of the fact that the nature of the emission is directly related to the nature of the fuel.[154] Finally, the most advanced codes provide for a system of permits and licenses both for the construction of factories, power plants, or other pollution producing installations, and for their operation.[155] The considerable variety in the nature of air pollution control codes is significant because the more sophisticated the code, the more complex the monitoring system, and the more highly trained the personnel required for its enforcement. Particularly in smaller municipalities, the means for the enforcement of a sophisticated code are not likely to be available. In consequence, there are serious limits on the capacity of a local air pollution control agency, for instance, to enforce a highly technical and sophisticated state air pollution control code.

86

WATER POLLUTION CONTROL

The history and development of state and local controls in the area of water pollution is again not too
dissimilar from that in the area of air pollution. As
in the case of air pollution, water pollution control
by states and localities is based firmly on the police
power.[156] Initially the individual had no realistic
protection against water pollution beyond the possibility of a suit for damages and injunction against an
upstream polluter.[157] And even private litigation suffered from the absence of any generally accepted standards of water purity against which to measure the
degree of pollution.

Initial steps towards governmental control of water
pollution came in the form of measures to protect
domestic drinking water supplies[158]--as for instance,
the sanitary regulation, previously referred to, that
prohibited the placing of one's cesspool too close to
one's neighbor's well. Other measures of similar nature
took the form of statutes that made the dumping of offal
and refuse into the waters a criminal offense.[159] Municipalities were often granted extraterritorial powers
to abate pollution contaminating municipal water supplies,[160] and local boards of health were empowered to
monitor the quality of water used for domestic purposes.[161] Frequently, however, local success in keeping water supply pure was often achieved by sending wastes
downstream,thereby harming other localities.[162]

As pollution became more severe and its threat to the

public interest became more apparent, the need for comprehensive state action was realized. In this second
evolutionary step, several state agencies were typically
given pollution control authority in their respective
spheres of operation.[163] Where a single agency was
assigned primary responsibility it was usually the state
health department.[164] This assignment reflected the
public concern of the times which focused almost exclusively upon the public health aspects of water pollution
Hines summarizes the main faults of this period as being
(1) inadequate statutory authority, (2) lack of forceful
administration, (3) inappropriateness of the public
health dominion, and (4) lack of centralized authority.[165] These shortcomings became apparent whenever
concerted action was required.[166]

The present practice is to create a single state
agency and to assign to it the authority to make the
major policy decisions relating to all aspects of water
quality control.[167] In many states a number of agencies
with lesser jurisdiction antedated the creation of the
single dominant state agency. Many states, therefore,
were faced with the choice of either creating an entirely
new agency to assume jurisdiction from all existing
ones, of creating a special statutory coordinating board
or commission, or of singling out one of the existing
agencies and granting it dominant powers over all other
water pollution control agencies in the state. An
example of the first type of agency is the Texas Water
Quality Board. Directed by law to "set water quality
standards for the waters in the state. . .,"[168] it in
effect has achieved major master planning functions in

the water areas for the state as a whole. The board is composed of seven members, of whom three are appointed by the governor and confirmed by the Senate; the four others are the chief executives of the Texas Water Development Board, the health department, the Parks Department and the Railroad Commission.[169] Generally, the appointed members are community leaders.[170] An executive director, who is full-time, operates as liaison for the part-time board members and supervises the execution of policies through an appointed staff.[171] Florida, which had initially entrusted water pollution control powers to the Department of Health, ended up by creating the Florida Air and Water Pollution Control Committee, composed of the governor, the secretary of state, the commissioner of agriculture, and two additional members appointed by the governor and confirmed by the senate.[172] Provision is made for a director with qualifications in bio-environmental or sanitary engineering.[173]

The coordinating committee approach is exemplified by Oklahoma. There the department of pollution control, created in 1968, consists solely of the pollution control coordinating board and of any special task forces that might be assigned to the department.[174] The pollution control coordinating board consists of the chief administrators of the five enforcement agencies--the Oklahoma Water Resources Board, the corporation commission, the state department of health, the state department of agriculture and the state department of wildlife conservation. The board's primary function is to coordinate the efforts of the various agencies in

order to avoid duplication of effort and to promote
efficient pollution abatement. The board was granted
authority to prescribe water quality criteria, standards
of water quality and the beneficial uses of the state's
waters.[175]

The third approach of vesting control powers in
existing agencies was adopted in New York. The New
York Public Health Law gave the water resources commission the power to classify waters and to adopt
standards. The enforcement of the program, however,
was delegated to the State Department of Health. The
Water Resources Commission, though it promulgated
classifications and standards for the Department of
Health to enforce, was an independent body nominally
within the structure of the Conservation Department.[176]
In April, 1970, New York abandoned this structure,
transferring the functions of the Water Resources Commission and the Conservation Department to a newly
created Department of Environmental Conservation which
has general standard-setting and enforcement authority
in environmental matters.[177]

A number of state water pollution control efforts
have been criticized on structural grounds--it is said
that separating standard setting and rule making powers
from enforcement powers has proved unsatisfactory.
According to this view, the coordinating committee
would seem likely to be the least effective form of
agency since by definition it has coordinating powers
only and may not enforce directly. Conversely, a
centralized agency, such as that of Texas, with its
own staff and extensive enforcement authority, is

likely to be far more effective. It has been charged,
for instance, that the reason for the lack of effectiveness of the old New York law was the absence of
close coordination and cooperation between the Water
Resources Commission, the policy maker, and the
Department of Health, the enforcement agency.[178]
The implications of separating standard setting and
rule making from enforcement responsibilities ought
to be taken into account when considering the recent
trend towards the establishment of coordinating and
standard setting agencies for environmental controls
at large. There is evidence that the establishment
of coordinating agencies, or the separation of policy
making from enforcement activities is of dubious
effectiveness even within any one field of pollution
control, such as water or air pollution. Why, then,
should there be greater effectiveness expected of a
state-wide pollution control agency with responsibility
for policy-making in water pollution, air pollution,
noise pollution, solid waste disposal and all the rest,
but leaving enforcement responsibilities to specific
divisions within the overall pollution control
agency? That is not to say, however, that interagency coordination is not both desirable and necessary. It is true, for instance, that water pollution
problems cut across many lines of interest and require
many different kinds of technical knowledge.[179] Even
a unified water pollution control department may find
it difficult to administer its program if it does not
take cognizance of the expertise and interests of
other agencies.

The composition of water pollution control boards differs from state to state but, just as in the case of air pollution control boards, follows a number of set patterns. When a board's function is primarily advisory, the representation of interests on the board is likely to be very broad,[180] although some advisory boards consist wholly of officials of state agencies involved in various aspects of water pollution control, serving on the board ex officio.[181] In many instances advisory boards or boards charged with standard setting functions consist of officials of enforcement agencies and of persons representing interests most directly concerned with the regulation of pollution.[182] Ordinarily, when a water pollution control body has not only supervisory or standard setting authority but also exercises enforcement functions, it is likely to be composed primarily of agency officials.[183] The question of whether or not it is desirable to include members of the regulated industry on a standard setting or rule making body has been previously referred to in the context of air pollution regulation. It has been suggested in the context of water pollution control that the members of the regulated industry, who are likely to be the major contributors to the pollution that is sought to be regulated, should not be given an official position in the standard setting agency because their views have usually been adequately represented in the legislature in the course of legislative hearings, and by counsel in board hearings on proposed regulations. It is likely that in water pollution standard setting agencies, just as in air pollution standard setting agencies, the presence of industry board members has hindered the regulatory effort by at least as much as it has advanced it.[184]

State agencies differ considerably with respect to their jurisdictional scope, and this of course has considerable implications for the kinds of standards and the reach of the regulations that they may impose. Some state statutes limit agency jurisdiction by giving it regulatory control only over specified waters, or by exempting certain waters from regulation.[185] Other states exempt ground water pollution thereby ignoring the integral relation between the quality of ground waters and surface waters.[186] The more up-to-date and comprehensive statutes generally and expressly include all waters within the pollution control effort.[187] The presence of certain political and economic pressures is clearly visible on the face of certain of the water pollution control statutes. Thus, for example, Pennsylvania makes its act applicable only to sewage and exempts from coverage all wastes from coal mines, tannery and municipal sewage systems existing at the time the act was passed.[188] Sometimes, too, the regulatory scope of the law is limited by a very narrow definition of the wastes capable of creating a condition of pollution.[189] It is clear that inclusive coverage is not difficult to achieve statutorily through a broad grant of jurisdiction and a liberal definition of activities to be regulated.[190]

State agencies' powers differ considerably with

respect to the kind of water quality standards they may impose. Though on their face modern state water pollution control laws grant broad powers to the control agency,[191] not all of them grant full powers to the agency to set water quality standards across the board. Many states that have the power to establish water quality standards are approaching the task in gradual stages. Some states have never gotten beyond the promulgation of broad minimal standards, while other states have not set state-wide standards but have proceeded area by area.[192]

The New York law and the regulations promulgated under it offer a good example of a comprehensive program of water classification and the adoption of quality standards. The waters are classified on a "best use" basis, which means that the existing or potential use requiring the highest degree of purity is used to set the standard.[193] Public hearings are required in the standard setting process. Standards of purity are assigned to the various rivers and streams based on the following criteria:

1. Stream characteristics, including size, temperature, and drainage area;
2. Character and use of the surrounding area;
3. Existing and potential uses of the stream; and
4. The extent of present defilement or pollution.[194]

In order to avoid standards from becoming permanently fixed at too low a level of quality, the New York Water Resources Commission had the power to repeal, modify, or alter standards from time to time. The water classi-fication program in New York has been attacked as an unconstitutional delegation of legislative authority. The constitutionality of the law and the regulations were upheld, however, by the highest court of the state.[195] Similar water classification schemes have been upheld in other states against constitutional attacks based not only on improper delegation but also on due process and equal protection grounds.[196]

Where a state's water pollution regulations have been adopted, there is relatively less scope for rule making on the local level, except insofar as such local regulatory efforts may be expressly sanctioned or authorized by state law. In the main, however, the local regulatory effort is likely to support the state effort by assisting the municipality in meeting the requirements imposed on it by state law. This happens to be one of the unusual areas of the law in which local governments have been sued by state water pollution control agencies to compel compliance with state regulations. This is particularly true in instances where the locality has failed to provide adequate sewage treatment facilities to treat raw sewage before it is discharged into one of the state's waterways.[197]

In many localities local subdivision regulations require developers of entire subdivisions or developers of sizeable tracts to provide for community disposal systems and for community-operated treatment plants instead of individual septic tanks.[198] The aim is to help meet the state's water purity standards. In many jurisdictions, developers may not proceed with building operations until the local

agency has been assured--by way of submission of
plans for certification--of the developer's intention to make adequate provision for sewage treatment
in his development.[199]

In water pollution control there has been far
closer correlation between state and local agencies
than in air pollution control. The reason probably
lies in the different character of water and air pollution. In the case of water pollution the problem
is generally well defined by a river bed which
touches many municipalities within the state. Consequently, the failure to conform on the part of one
municipal agency becomes immediately apparent not
only to the state agency but to all other municipal
agencies downstream. The problem of air pollution is
far less well defined because air pollution, though
it may move with prevailing winds, does not move in
clearly defined channels, and the contribution of
any one municipality to the total amount of air
pollution in a region is not only difficult to
gauge but also difficult to prevent. Consequently,
disjunctiveness of effort in the air pollution control
field is less likely to become immediately apparent
than would be a similar disjunctiveness of effort
in water pollution control.

SOLID WASTE DISPOSAL

Other areas of environmental control, such as solid
waste disposal and noise control are by their nature
far more local in character, and in each instance the
federal concern is thus far reflected primarily in

96

grants-in-aid legislation for research and development and, to a far more limited degree, in federal regulations.[200] Solid waste disposal has been handled thus far by local regulation, generally subject to state enabling legislation.[201] The manner in which solid waste is to be collected, the manner in which the householder is to store his solid waste and get it ready for collection is generally treated in state or local sanitary, health,[202] or housing codes.[203] The subsequent disposition of wastes collected by municipal sanitation departments or by private garbage collectors is also regulated by local ordinances, subject again in most instances to state enabling legislation.[204] Thus the proper method for sanitary landfills and the required quantity of clean soil to bury waste are regulated by state or local health codes.[205] The manner in which wastes may be incinerated, either in a municipal incinerator or in a privately operated incinerator, or by burning on the lot, is generally subject to state or local air pollution control regulations.[206] What is noteworthy in this context is the fact that the relationship of solid waste management to air pollution control or to water pollution control is not articulated in any state law or regulation--in spite of the fact that some jurisdictions have had that connection brought to their attention--rather forcefully--as in New York, where an order to shut down apartment house incinerators led to a garbage removal crisis.[207]

The statutory treatment of solid waste disposal is also interesting, in that it appears to be concerned to

a far greater extent with the economic rather than the
environmental aspects of the problem. Provisions for
the issuance of bonds for incinerators and other disposal systems abound, and special districts for this
purpose are sometimes authorized.[208] In large cities,
considerably more attention is devoted to the licensure of private garbage collectors--a sometimes racket-
ridden industry--than to the sanitary aspects of waste
collection and movement.

On the whole, state laws relating to solid waste
disposal exist in their own statutory compartment just
as does water pollution and air pollution control legislation.[209] While some states are beginning to reflect
the recognition of the interrelationship of different
aspects of environmental pollution through the establishment of coordinating committees and agencies of
various kinds, no effective means appears to have been
found as yet to reflect the close interrelationship
of these matters in operative regulations.

NOISE POLLUTION CONTROL

The subject of noise regulation is in some respects
unique; though there has been some recent federal
development in the area,[210] the states and the municipalities have on the whole dealt with quite distinct
aspects of it. State regulation of noise is essentially
limited to muffler legislation intended to reduce
noise produced by motor vehicles,[211] and to regulations relating to industrial noise for the protection
of workmen.[212] Aside from these two separate areas,
the regulation of noise has been largely a local

responsibility, and the local regulation involved has been of a rather minor kind, namely the establishment of miscellaneous prohibitions collected in local codes under some such heading as "police ordinances." Usually these are composed of matters too trivial to appear in the state's general code, and they generally concern matters too neglected in modern times to be included in public health law or the like.

The fact that the states have generally not legislated against noise and that such local laws as exist are largely recompilations of old ordinances, suggests that very little attention is presently being paid to the problem, and that there is little expectation that the local laws will be actively enforced. This point is substantiated by looking at the anti-noise laws in a few American cities. In New York City, the relevant provision of the Administrative Code prohibits "the creation of any unreasonably loud, disturbing, or unnecessary noise" or of "noise of such character, intensity and duration as to be detrimental to the life or health of any individual."[213] This is followed by a list of specific acts that "among others" shall be deemed to be violations of the general prohibition. Some of these themselves are phrased in terms of "loud" or "unnecessary" or "disturbing" noises of various kinds. Included, too, are such concrete examples as horn blowing, except as a danger signal, failure to use a muffler, and construction work between 7 p.m. and 6 a.m. on weekdays except by special permit. Other provisions regulate sound trucks and other amplifying devices used in public.[214]

Philadelphia's code of ordinances prohibits unnecessary noise in the handling of trash cans, and construction work between 6 p.m. and 6 a.m. It also
contains special provisions to protect the quiet of
hospitals, churches, court houses and schools, and
prohibits the use of outdoor amplifying devices for
advertising purposes, unnecessary horn blowing and
"all other loud and unnecessary noises upon or near
to the streets or other public places in the city,"
and provides for the regulation of street peddlers.[215]
Chicago, in addition to some of the more standard
provisions, provides that "rails, chimneys, and columns
of iron, steel, and other metal which are being trans-
ported on the public ways of the city" shall be loaded
so as to avoid the creation of loud noises.[216]

What all of these city ordinances lack is a coherent scheme of noise control. Typically they are col-
lections of specific prohibitions drafted and enacted
from time to time by the local legislative body in
response to some special problem, and not subject to
revision, review and updating by an administrative
agency having the requisite expertise to deal with
noise problems in a consistent fashion. There are,
however, some notable improvements on the horizon.
Modern zoning ordinances, especially the 1960 New York
City Zoning Resolution, deal with industrial noise
and similar environmental insults, such as vibrations,
not only by the ordinary zoning technique of requiring
separation of incompatible uses, but also by imposing
specific performance standards for the more frequent

pollutants. Thus decibel standards for particular zones
are imposed to set permissible standards for noise,
just as standards for vibrations, smoke, dust and other
particulate air pollutants, odor, toxic emissions,
fire and explosive hazards and other onerous environmental hazards are dealt with in relation to the use of
particular zones for designated purposes.[217] A modern
zoning ordinance also can, and should, deal effectively
with the problem of effective airport zoning. Certain
facilities--such as schools or hospitals--should be
excluded from neighboring zones unless properly sound-
proofed. Imaginative use of the zoning power can
protect the airport without placing a complete bar on
other development in the area.

At least two building codes, in New York[218] and in
New Jersey,[219] require sound insulation in new buildings
as a condition of a building permit or a certificate of
occupancy. In addition to requiring adequate sound
insulation against noise from outside the building or
from other parts of the building, these codes also provide for adequate protection against noise sources from
within the building itself--i.e., ventilation and heating
equipment, elevators, ducts and other machinery and
facilities.

Unlike earlier municipal noise regulations which
were enacted from time to time by municipal legisla-
tures, these newer regulatory efforts are not only more
comprehensive but are also the result of technical work
done by knowledgeable and technically qualified administrative agencies with special competence in the field.

101

The Role of the Federal Government
in the Enforcement and Administration
of Environmental Regulations

While there has been a gradual move towards the consolidation of standard setting responsibilities at
higher levels of government, the major responsibility
for seeing that air pollution, water pollution and
other environmental standards are actually enforced
rests at the lower level of the governmental hierarchy.[220] In part, the fact that the responsibility
for enforcement activities is not centered at the
federal level reflects the earlier assumption that
environmental controls are primarily a local responsibility. In part, too, the primary emphasis on enforcement powers at the local or state level reflects the
realistic appreciation that there is local and state
enforcement machinery--i.e., a staff of inspectors and
a force of clerical back-up personnel--while there are
very few federal enforcement officials who are concerned
with matters of day-to-day enforcement against individual violators of the standards, rules and regulations.

The consequence of a predominantly local emphasis in
enforcement is that in air pollution and water pollution
control, as well as in any number of other areas of
environmental protection, federal enforcement against
persons who violate standards is not only infrequent
but is viewed as a rather extraordinary measure. Thus
under federal air pollution legislation there were
virtually no federal enforcement powers prior to the
Clean Air Act of 1963, which, for the first time,

provided for abatement procedures for interstate air pollution.[221] The 1967 Air Quality Standards Act retained these abatement procedures and added one or two others which clearly and on their face indicate that they, too, were remedies reserved for extraordinary or extra-hazardous situations.[222]

As presently constituted, federal law provides for federal abatement procedures in four separate situations. If solely intrastate air pollution is involved, the Administrator of the EPA may take action only if requested by the governor of the affected state. But he may not proceed if he determines that the effect of such pollution is not of such significance as to warrant the exercise of federal jurisdiction. This section is inapplicable to interstate air pollution.[223]

A second procedure, added in 1967, authorizes the Administrator to seek immediate court action to stop emission of pollutants where there is evidence of "imminent and substantial endangerment to the health of persons" and where state or local authorities have failed to act.[224] The section is intended as a remedy for emergency situations only, and the Congressional intent embodied in the House Report that accompanied the legislation was clearly to make the remedy inapplicable as a continuing control for chronic or generally recurring problems of less than calamitous nature.[225] Local authorities do not have the power to require the Administrator to act under this section. The Congressional intent regarding the section was clearly to have it used only in such extraordinary situations as, for example, the incidents in Donora,

Pennsylvania in 1948, in New York City in 1953, and
such incidents as the London killer smogs of 1952 and
1962.[226]

A third procedure is provided for if the interstate air pollution occurs in an air quality control
region with established air quality standards.[227]
Federal enforcement is authorized only if the Secretary finds that air quality has fallen below the
prescribed standards, and that the state itself has
failed to take reasonable action to implement and
enforce the applicable standards.[228] While the
Administrator may act on the basis of the complaint
from one of the states affected, he is not required
to act on the basis of such a state complaint, and
it is up to him to determine whether the state com-
plained of has or has not taken "reasonable action"
to bring about abatement. First provided in the Air
Quality Act of 1967, the procedure was never invoked
by the Secretary of HEW and has not as yet been used
by the Administrator.

Finally, the fourth procedure which may bring the
federal government into an active enforcement role
is that which was initially provided by Section 105
of the Clean Air Act of 1963. The procedure is applicable only in instances of interstate air pollution
where the source of the pollution is in one state and
the adverse effect in another. The Administrator is
required to call a conference whenever requested to do
so by the governor or by a state air pollution control
agency of one of the states affected, or with their concurrence, by a municipality, if there is evidence of

air pollution "which is alleged to endanger the health
or welfare of persons in a state other than that in
which the discharge originate(s)."[229] The Administrator
is also free to call a conference on interstate air
pollution on his own initiative after consultation with
the officials of the affected states.[230] It is noteworthy that this is the only instance under the law in
which a state or municipality can require the Administrator to act. However, an individual citizen cannot
require him to act under this or any other federal
enforcement provision.

When a conference is called by the Administrator,
the interstate, state and local agencies involved participate in it, and an appointee of the Administrator
presides. The person responsible for the discharge
may be invited by one of the member agencies, but there
is no legal requirement that he attend the conference,
and it has been held that due process does not require
his presence since the conference is neither rule-making
nor adjudicative.[231] The conference meets on thirty
days' notice accompanied by a preliminary report made
by HEW. Advance notice is also given to the public by
publication on at least three different days in a
newspaper of general circulation in the area.[232] The
conference itself is informal and does not have the
character of an administrative hearing.[233] Following
the conference, HEW prepares and distributes a summary
of the conference discussions, and the Administrator
may recommend necessary remedial action. The law
provides that the polluter must be allowed six months
to take the remedial actions recommended. If six

months later the Administrator is dissatisfied with the progress made, he may call a formal public hearing before a hearing board of five or more persons appointed by him. Each of the states affected may choose one member, and each federal department which the Administrator determines has a special interest in the matter may choose one member. One member must be a representative of an appropriate interstate air pollution control agency, and a majority of the members must be persons other than officers or employees of HEW.[234] The appointment of a formal hearing board is entirely at the discretion of the Administrator,[235] and the complaining state or municipality has no role in the initiation of this step. All interested persons must be given an opportunity to present evidence at the hearing, and the board makes recommendations for affirmative action to abate the pollution on the basis of the evidence presented. The findings and recommendations of the board are forwarded by the Administrator to the alleged violator and to the agencies involved, together with a notice specifying a reasonable time of not less than six months for compliance.[236] Neither the board nor the Administrator has been granted authority to issue a binding order following the hearing, and the Administrator is not authorized to impose any sanctions for the violator's failure to comply with the directives of the conference. It has been held that, though more formal in character, the hearing is not adjudicative and the alleged violator cannot obtain a judicial review at this stage for he has not as yet been subjected to any legally binding order.[237] If the alleged violator, however, fails to comply with the hearing board's directions within the time set for such compliance, the Administrator may then ask the Attorney General to file suit in the federal district court to secure abatement.[238] This is the first and only instance in the lengthy procedure that a sanction has been provided for failure to comply. However, the complaining state or municipality cannot require the Administrator to take this step. Whether or not the Administrator decides to ask the Attorney General to file suit is again left entirely to his own discretion. When suit is brought, the court may receive any transcript of the proceedings before the board and a copy of the board's recommendations, along with any other evidence which the court deems proper.[239] The board's findings and recommendations will not be received as evidence to prove any facts recounted in them, but will be evidence only as to what the public interest and the equities of the case may require. Both the government and the defendant have an opportunity to produce additional evidence.[240] The court considers all pertinent factual and legal issues de novo and in making its determination,

> The court, giving due consideration to the practicability of complying with such standards as may be applicable and to the physical and economic feasibility of securing abatement of any pollution proved, shall have jurisdiction to enter such judgment, and orders enforcing such judgment, as the public interest and the equities of the case may require.[241]

Although this procedure has been available since the enactment of the Clean Air Act of 1963, its effectiveness

has been minimal. It is most cumbersome and slow,
and in the past seven years it has been invoked in
only nine interstate areas.[242] In only one instance,
moreover, has the case gone beyond the conference
recommendation stage, i.e., beyond the very first
formal step. That case involved the Bishop Processing Company of Bishop, Maryland, which was charged
with emitting such vile odors from its chicken offal
processing plant as to endanger the health and welfare of persons in Selbyville, Delaware, two miles
distant. In that case, administrative proceedings
were initiated by a request from the Delaware State
Air Pollution Authority which, with the state of
Maryland, had been engaged in futile efforts since
1959 to induce Bishop to abate its pollution. A
formal hearing was subsequently held in May of 1967
after the company had failed to make satisfactory
abatement efforts. The company was directed, following the hearing, to abate the pollution by
December, 1967. On July 28, 1968, some two and a
half years after the proceedings had begun, the
district court in Maryland denied the company's
motion to dismiss the government's suit seeking
abatement. In the fall of 1968 the Bishop Company
agreed to a settlement requiring it to cease operations upon the filing of an affidavit by the Delaware
Water and Air Resources Commission, stating that the
company was causing air pollution in Delaware. The
affidavit was not filed until March of 1969. In
September an order was issued directing the company
to cease operations. The order was, however, stayed

during Bishop's appeals to the Court of Appeals
and Supreme Court and did not become final until
spring of 1970--five years after the inception of
the federal procedure and eleven years after the
state governments first became concerned with the
situation.[243]

The range of federal enforcement powers under
federal water pollution control legislation, as
amended by the Clean Water Restoration Act of 1966,
is similar to--and appears to have been copied from
--that in the air pollution area. The bases for
federal intervention, closely paralleling those in
air pollution, are: (1) pollution of interstate and
navigable waters in or adjacent to any state or
states that endangers the health or welfare of any
persons, (2) a governor's request for federal intervention when pollution in one state affects the
health or welfare of persons in another, "unless
the effect of such pollution on the legitimate
uses of the waters...is not of sufficient significance to warrant federal jurisdiction."[244] In
addition, action may also be instituted when the
Administrator of the EPA has reason to believe
that pollution in interstate or navigable waters
creates substantial economic injury resulting from
inability to market shellfish or shellfish products
in interstate commerce, and, finally, whenever the
Administrator has reason to believe that pollution
of interstate or navigable waters endangers the
health or welfare of persons in a foreign country
and the Secretary of State has requested him to abate

GRAD

such pollution.[245] The procedure consists of three
stages. First, a conference with participation by
state and interstate agencies and the alleged polluters, followed by recommendation by the Federal
Water Pollution Control Administration to the
state agency to take action within a period of not
less than six months. Second, a formal hearing
before a board appointed by the Administrator,
and, after such hearing, again a direction that
abatement measures be taken within a reasonable
time of not less than six months. Finally, a dis-
cretionary request by the Administrator to the
Attorney General to bring suit for an injunction
on behalf of the United States.[246] Sone 43 informal conferences were held through 1968; only four
continued to the hearing stage. Of these, only
a single case was taken to court.[247] Another
provision allows compliance action by the Attorney
General upon 180 days' notice to the polluter; no
court action has as yet been taken under it.[247a]

Both in air and water pollution enforcement,
the federal government relies primarily on informal
negotiations rather than on hard enforcement, for
it is clear that the established enforcement devices
do not meet the need for the swift and decisive
action that may be necessary. Hence federal enforcement under both the air and water pollution control
acts is only as effective as informal procedures
prior to court action can make it. This is well in
line with long accepted principles of public health
compliance techniques which rely primarily on

110

education and on negotiated cooperative measures.[248]
It is clear, however, that these measures are not
designed to gain compliance from a hard-core violator
who sees no immediate reason for prompt compliance
when it is costly and burdensome. Under both the federal air and water pollution control acts such a
violator knows that he has two to three years from
the time when the federal government commences its
laborious proceedings until he may actually be compelled to take abatement measures. There is virtually
no incentive for him to take earlier action, because
neither the Air Quality Standards Act nor the Clean
Water Restoration Act penalizes his delay--no fines
or other sanctions are provided for dilatory action.

Oddly enough, it is older and far less sophisticated federal legislation that provides more immediate
sanctions in the field of water pollution. Although
the Rivers and Harbors Act of 1899 was not initially
intended as a water pollution control measure, it has
been increasingly used for this purpose through re-
peated interpretation and reinterpretation,[249] and,
although penalties under it are not very substantial,
the Act does provide a far more immediate method of
getting at industries that pollute navigable rivers
and harbors and for criminal prosecution and maximum
penalties of $2,500.00.[250] Recent federal enforcement
activity, much of which has gleaned headlines considerably beyond its importance [251] has been based on
Rivers and Harbors Act prosecutions which, though not
a major deterrent to violators, provides a mechanism
for prompt, direct action.

Of special note are efforts in areas of enforcement
in which the federal government has asserted its preemptive interest. These areas are, notably, the area
of automotive pollution by new cars and airport noise
pollution.

Title II of the Air Quality Act of 1967 directed the
Secretary of HEW to set national standards for emissions from new motor vehicles. Once such emission
standards have been set, no manufacturer may produce
for sale or for rental any vehicle which does not meet
the standards. The law provides that the courts may
by injunction stop any manufacturer from distributing
motor vehicles which do not meet the federal emission
standards and provides a fine of up to $1000 per
vehicle that exceeds the standards of emission.[252]
The responsibilities of the Secretary have been transferred to the Administrator of the EPA.[253]

In spite of the law's apparent stringency, the
present regulations fail to control the field effectively. First, the coverage of emission standards is
less than complete. The Act applies to manufacturers
that import vehicles into the United States, but
vehicles imported for purposes other than sale or
resale are not covered. This leaves uncovered the
thousands of cars imported by individuals from abroad
for their own personal use. Second, the method of
seeking compliance with automotive emission standards
for new vehicles does not assure that vehicles coming
off the assembly line in fact meet national emission
standards. Under § 2 of the Air Quality Standards Act,
any automobile manufacturer may request the National

Air Pollution Control Administration to determine whether a particular new motor vehicle or new motor vehicle engine meets the applicable emission standards.[254] If the test vehicle meets the standards, the Secretary of HEW must issue a certificate of conformity for a period of not less than one year. Thereupon any new motor vehicle or engine which "is in all material respects substantially the same construction as the test vehicle or engine for which a certificate has been issued,"[255] is considered to have met the applicable emission standards. In consequence the thousand-dollar penalty per non-complying vehicle is totally meaningless, because a manufacturer whose prototype model has been certified is immune from the penalty, regardless of whether subsequent automobiles of the same model coming off the assembly line meet the emission standards in actual operation on the road. The evidence is clear that many of the automobiles that roll off the assembly line indeed do not perform as well as the certified prototype.[256] It is also evident that emission control devices become less effective the longer the car stays on the road, so that by the time a vehicle has been driven for more than 20,000 miles, its emission control devices have generally lost most of their effectiveness.[257] Thus, the inadequacy of enforcement of federal automotive emission standards appears clear. Moreover, they have exerted, through preemption, an inhibiting effect on state developments, (with the exception of California, whose standards antedate the federal ones).[258] Since the federal government does not purport to exercise any control over older vehicles, that area of enforcement has been relegated to the states to cope with as best they can under their various motor vehicle inspection laws.

Federal regulations with respect to aircraft noise appear to be preemptive in intent.[259] While both the courts and the Federal Aviation Administration have asserted that operators of airports have the ultimate right to decide which aircraft can or cannot use their facilities as long as their judgment is not discriminatory, whatever decisional law there is seems to hold that local governments may not pass airport noise regulations or ordinances more stringent than the standards adopted by the FAA--though they may promulgate such standards in their proprietary capacity as airport operator.[260] Thus, although there has been considerable dissatisfaction with the federal aircraft noise standards,[261] municipalities have been severely handicapped in defending their inhabitants against excessive noise from aircraft in interstate commerce. The suggestion is readily at hand that preemptive federal standards, both for automotive emissions and aircraft noise, are as much designed to protect the particular industries affected against more stringent controls by the states and municipalities as they are to protect the public.[262] This point may gain in force in light of recent federal participation in the development of the supersonic transport plane, for the regulation of sonic booms, it seems, is also a federal monopoly under the same legislation that authorizes FAA regulation of aircraft noise.[263] Another example--which has since been resolved--is

that of federal preemption under the Atomic Energy Act
of 1946. Under that Act the federal government exercised broad and apparently wholly preemptive jurisdiction over all nuclear plants. The federal intent was,
of course, to regulate all aspects of a nuclear installation in which there was a clear federal interest in
the development of nuclear energy and in safeguarding
a secret technology. A nuclear installation, however,
also has ordinary boilers and a cafeteria and wash-
rooms for its employees, as well as elevators in its
office buildings. In the early days of the reactor
industry, city boiler inspectors, city health inspectors, city elevator inspectors were refused access,
on the alleged grounds that the plant as a whole was
under federal regulation and that any regulatory
effort by any other government was entirely outlawed.
Clearly this had not been the federal intent, because
the federal interest extended only to matters having
a direct relationship to nuclear development. The
federal legislation had not been intentionally designed to prevent normal city and state inspections
of sanitary and safety features of nuclear installations
that had no particular direct or indirect bearing on
the nuclear installation itself.[264] In spite of this,
it was years before the issues were fully resolved
in the course of the general revision of the Atomic
Energy Act.[265] That revision, of course, went far
beyond the simple matter of permitting state and local
health and safety inspectors to carry out their duties
in parts of the installation that were not directly
connected with nuclear development. Indeed, the

1959 revision of the Atomic Energy Act provides the basis for federal-state cooperation in the field. The role each state is to play in the partnership is to be fixed under the law by a formal agreement entered into between the state and the Atomic Energy Commission, and the precise range of state regulation is subject to that agreement.[266] Although atomic energy legislation is no longer fully preemptive, the states clearly play the role of junior partners.

Difficulties created by partial federal preemption of a field are demonstrated too by the current state of the law with respect to the control of jet plane noise. The federal regulations set by FAA are preemptive in that no state or local government may set higher standards than the standards established by the federal agency. On the other hand, the federal agency has repeatedly stated that its regulations provide a minimum requirement only and that the proprietors and operators of airports throughout the nation are free to set standards of their own--i.e., each airport may decide that it will not permit its facilities to be used by planes that exceed a noise level set by that airport even though the level set by the airport itself may be higher than that set by FAA.[267] In actual fact the purported permission to airports to set standards of their own is wholly illusory because, as a practical matter, airport operators cannot enforce higher standards. In this instance the federal standard is entirely more preemptive than it purports to be. The assertion that it is not wholly preemptive serves the purpose of the federal regulatory agency, however, because whenever the federal standard comes under attack, the agency can respond that the local airport is free to require more stringent compliance if it wants to do so. Here, too, federal preemption has created a no-man's land in which there is federal abstention from standard-setting without any concomitant grant of power to the state or municipality to take up the slack.

The Roles of the States and Municipalities in the Enforcement and Administration of Environmental Regulations

AIR POLLUTION CONTROL

Regulations to control environmental pollution are generally enforced on the state or local level, if they are enforced at all. Whether particular enforcement efforts are the responsibility of a state agency or local agencies depends on the state's administrative or structural arrangements. In most states the agency primarily responsible for environmental controls is still the state health department.[268] State health departments differ from state to state with respect to the degree of centralization and the degree of their interrelation with local health agencies. In some states the department operates primarily as a standard setting or rule making agency which may have advisory and other "staff" functions for the state as a whole, but which takes little or no "line" responsibility for the activities of individual municipal or county health departments. In many instances the supervision by the state health

agency of the activities of local or municipal health
agencies is minimal indeed. The state health department does not supervise the day-to-day operations of
local or municipal agencies, and may be called in
only to take steps when some major failure on the part
of municipal or local health agencies has occurred.[269]
In other states the responsibility for enforcement of
health laws and regulations is much more centralized
in the state health department, with county and municipal health agencies directly responsible for their
routine performance, and accountable to the state
health agency for all of their programs.[270] In those
instances a true "line" relationship exists between
the local or municipal health agency and the state
health department. A variety of more or less inter-
mediate patterns exists, but in almost every instance
the primary responsibility for standard setting and
rule making is in the state health agency, and the
actual enforcement function is lodged lower down in
the hierarchy--whether or not the local agencies are
directly responsible to the state agency or operate
more or less independently from it.

The relationship of state health departments to
county and municipal health departmens is further affected by a variety of legal relationships dependent
on the state constitution and on legislation that
defines the relationship of counties and municipalities to the state generally. In many states, for
instance, incorporated municipalities, such as villages
and cities, will have health departments of their own,
and in addition there will be a county health depart-

ment which may or may not be an administrative branch
of the state health department. This county health
department will commonly have jurisdiction to operate
within the unincorporated areas of the county, but
each of the cities and villages will be free to regulate its own affairs, consistent, however, with
whatever standards the state health agency may have
prescribed for the state as a whole.[271] Moreover, the
extent to which health departments in incorporated
municipalities, such as villages and cities, may
manage their own affairs may depend to a considerable
extent on the degree of home rule granted to such
municipalities, either by state constitution or
general municipal legislation, or by their own individual charters. In terms of air pollution legislation, for instance, this means that there is likely to
be a statewide air pollution control code[272] to meet
the requirements of the 1967 Air Quality Standards Act
for the air quality regions federally determined for
that state. This statewide air pollution control act
and the state code adopted pursuant to it indubitably
set the minimum standard for the entire state. These
standards are probably the only standards applicable
to the unincorporated areas within the state. Additional requirements may have been set by a county
air pollution control agency, and these standards,
though consistent with the state code, may be higher
for the county as a whole.[273] The county standards,
depending on some of the factors previously mentioned,
may apply to the entire county or merely to its unincorporated areas--or it may apply to all of the

unincorporated areas in the county and to such of the incorporated areas, i.e., villages and cities, that have not adopted air pollution control codes of their own. Any major village or city, however, particularly if it has a substantial amount of industry, is likely to have an air pollution control code of its own which will have to be consistent with the county code, if any, and certainly with the state code. It may be more stringent than either one of them, particularly if it can be shown that the municipality has special problems of pollution caused by particular topographical or industrial features that are not shared by the rest of the county or state.[274]

The question raised by this array of overlapping, albeit supposedly consistent, codes is which agency enforces any one air pollution control code. As a rule of thumb it may be stated that each municipality or other jurisdictional entity enforces its own code, without much regard to the code of the next higher jurisdiction in the hierarchy.[275] Each municipal air pollution control agency has a staff of air pollution inspectors and some monitoring or other surveillance equipment of its own, and each of these staffs and their equipment are used for the purpose of cutting down on emissions from within the jurisdiction so as to accomplish compliance with that jurisdiction's code. None of the municipalities have extraterritorial powers, and in practice, each jurisdiction can abate only the emissions emanating from sources of pollution within its own borders.[276] Thus the air pollution inspector is stopped absolutely in his enforcement

efforts by the local boundary line. If City A has the
most advanced air pollution control code but receives
most of its pollution from industrial sources in City B
located within the same county, the air pollution control inspectors of City A cannot enter City B to serve
a violation notice on the industrial pollution source
in B. Only the air pollution control inspectors in
City B can do so.[277] If the main consequence of
emissions in B is pollution fallout in A, and if the
source in B is a major employer of B's population,
enforcement may not be overly zealous. There is also
a question in many states whether the air pollution
control inspector of the county in which both A and B
are located can go into either of the cities to serve
a violation notice because he, in turn, may be limited
by provisions of law that grant enforcement powers
within their own boundaries to incorporated municipalities. While air pollution is no respecter of
jurisdictional boundaries, air pollution control
agencies are, by reason of the law under which they
operate. The consequence of jurisdictional limits on
enforcement has frequently been to render helpless
municipalities which themselves produce few emissions
but which, by reason of topography or prevailing
winds, receive all or most of the fallout from
neighboring municipalities. There are even a number
of instances on record when inventive owners of
manufacturing establishments combined to incorporate
industrial enclaves as cities or villages, as a
defensive measure against the imposition of pollution
controls.[278] Thus a highly industrial area with a

daytime working population of several thousand persons
and a nighttime population limited to a few watchmen
may effectively eliminate the possibility of having
environmental pollution controls enforced against them.
All of the surrounding residential communities may
enact the most sophisticated air pollution control
ordinances, but since the source of emissions is in
another incorporated area, the residential community's air pollution control codes will have little
effect, because its air pollution control agency has
no jurisdiction to enter the incorporated industrial
area for purposes of enforcement. The only possibility
to secure adequate enforcement under such circumstances is to grant enforcement powers for county and state
agencies even within the incorporated areas. In the
past, however, enforcement staffs have been lodged
at the local level and in many states where the structure of health departments depended on local enforcement efforts, there was no effective enforcement staff
on the state or county level. These structural
hindrances to effective environmental controls are not
the result of willful obtuseness on the part of state
or local officials. When the business of health departments consisted primarily of epidemiologic controls
or of controls of food establishments, eating places,
barber shops, swimming pools, etc., the kind of division
of labor between state, county and local departments
involved here made good sense and was appropriate to
the problems for which it was designed. It is only the
realization that environmental problems have spread
beyond narrow jurisdictional boundaries and affect

incorporated and unincorporated areas alike that makes much of the traditional governmental machinery for public health enforcement archaic and inappropriate for the uses to which it must be put.

WATER POLLUTION CONTROL

A somewhat different pattern of enforcement is encountered in the field of water pollution control. The municipalities generally are in charge of enforcing certain aspects of the purity of the water supply--i.e., it is generally the municipality's job, either under appropriate health code regulations or under subdivision ordinances, to see to it that necessary septic tanks and private sewage disposal systems are built and that they are built in a manner that will prevent pollution of well water and other sources of water supply.[279] Normally, non-compliance is punishable as a misdemeanor,[280] and usually the construction of a private sewage disposal system requires a permit from the local health agency with the frequent requirement that the system not be covered up or buried before a sanitary inspector has had an opportunity of checking it.[281] In addition, the municipality generally is in charge of enforcement against malfunctioning private sewage disposal systems and usually has the power of summary abatement if these systems develop into nuisances.[282] The municipality may have a requirement, too, that as soon as public sewers become available, the householder is under an obligation to connect his own facilities to the public sewer, paying whatever special assessments there may be for that service.[283] In some instances,

subdivision developers may be compelled by local law
to provide community sewage treatment plants for the
development as a whole.[284]

Aside from local enforcement of the nature previously mentioned, water pollution control is generally
lodged at either the state level or the regional water
basin level in those instances when the state relies
on separate agencies for separate river systems rather
than on a central water pollution control agency.[285]
In either case, the agency may itself seek out violations of standards through inspections or through
a monitoring system, or it may respond to complaints.[286]
Most state laws require that a hearing be held whenever
a probable violation is discovered and that the alleged
violators be afforded an opportunity to appear and
answer the charges.[287] Some state laws contain provisions for emergency procedures that allow the
agency to dispense with hearing prior to issuing an
order; under those circumstances a hearing must normally be held as soon as possible after the order has
been issued.[288] Following the hearing, the usual
remedy is the issuance of a cease and desist order.[289]
In New York, for instance, the Commissioner may issue
"such final order or make such final determinations as
he deems appropriate under the circumstances."[290]
Failure to comply with such an order may generally be
penalized by both civil and criminal sanctions.
Violations are usually treated as misdemeanors.[291]

Civil penalties are recoverable separately by civil
action. The range of penalties for failure to live
up to water quality standards is rather wide from

state to state, just as is the range of penalties for
air pollution violations. In some states, the maximum
fine may range only up to one or two hundred dollars
per violation. In others it may go as high as $3,000.
In Florida, for instance, the civil penalty is $1,000
for each offense, and the criminal penalty for a misdemeanor is a thousand dollar fine and a year in jail
for each offense.[292] In New York the criminal penalty
may include fines from five to twenty-five hundred dollars and imprisonment of up to one year for each offense.[293] In a number of states, each day of non-compliance may legally constitute a separate offense.[294]
Most state statutes also provide for injunctive relief
when the violator has failed to comply with earlier
agency orders.[295] All of the state laws provide for judicial appeal and for review of agency orders.[296] Generally such a review will be based on the record of the
hearing before the agency,[297] although a minority of jurisdictions require a de novo review by the courts.[298]

Although enforcement procedures under state water
pollution control acts are fairly similar throughout
the country, enforcement in different states varies
considerably in effectiveness.[299] The major reason
for such differences appears to be the relative aggres-
siveness of the responsible agency.[300] Water pollution
control is one of the few areas of enforcement in which
a significant number of cases can be found where the
state agency has actually sued a municipality to compel
compliance by the local government with state standards relating to sewage treatment, water purity and
permissible emissions.[301]

SOLID WASTE DISPOSAL

With respect to solid waste disposal, enforcement is an entirely local matter. As has been pointed out previously, many states have extensive legislation dealing with the municipality's obligation to collect wastes and to dispose of them either by incineration or by sanitary landfill methods. Almost all municipalities have detailed regulations with respect to placement of wastes outside the home for collection and many of them go into significant detail with respect to the kind of containers that are permissible, where they may be placed and how soon they must be taken in after trash and other wastes have been picked up.[302] Violations of such laws and regulations are generally treated as minor misdemeanors, and the fines imposed are likely to be very low.[303] Sanitary landfills, however, may be subject to a system of licensure in some jurisdictions.[304] A number of municipalities have enacted some special legislation or regulations to deal with the ever-increasing problem of the thousands of old automobiles that are junked or abandoned at the roadside.[305] Generally the trend of such legislation or regulation is to provide both penalties for unlawful abandonment of old cars and a service program to make it easier to leave old cars for sanitation department pick-up instead of abandoning them to become an eyesore and a possible hazard. Again, the responsibility for enforcement is generally that of the municipality, which is handicapped in applying the criminal sanctions because the ownership of abandoned cars is

usually very difficult to trace after the license
plates have been removed.[306]

NOISE POLLUTION CONTROL

Enforcement of noise control, traditionally a matter
of local concern, generally involves police prosecution,
with minor criminal penalties.[307] The states, however,
have long exercised jurisdiction over industrial noise
through their industrial codes administered by the
state labor department. Criminal penalties for violations, as well as cease and desist orders and injunctive relief are commonly available; administrative
procedures before the state labor department usually
precede prosecutive and other judicial remedies.[308]
With the greater concern for automobile noise, state
muffler legislation has become almost universal, and
violations are commonly punishable as misdemeanors.[309]
In addition, such legislation is also enforced through
state motor vehicle inspection laws.[310]

RADIATION CONTROLS

A particularly diversified pattern of state and local
enforcement is encountered in the area of radiation
pollution. Although radiation standards are primarily
set at the federal level--and even in instances where
they may be set at the state or local level they will
commonly follow the federal pattern--the enforcement of
radiation protection standards is presently dispersed
among a variety of federal, state and local agencies.
The enforcement of standards, both within reactor
installations and outside of such installations,

127

is entirely subject to Environmental Protection
Agency supervision, as successor, under the 1970
Reorganization Act, to the Atomic Energy Commission.
The disposal and storage of atomic wastes, however,
remains an AEC responsibility.[311] As previously
indicated, however, under the 1959 amendments to the
Atomic Energy Act, the states were invited to make
agreements with the Atomic Energy Commission to
arrange for the assumption of responsibilities for
the development of nuclear power and particularly
for radiation safety within the state.[312] State
regulations and state involvement in the enforcement of radiation protection measures vary considerably in scope and detail. There are a few
states that have no legislation on the subject at
all,[313] but most have at least a provision requiring
nuclear materials to be registered.[314] A number of
states have rather elaborate registration and licensing provisions[315] and some share regulatory burdens
with municipal governments within the state.[316] One
of the most sophisticated systems is that of the
State of New York which will be used to illustrate
the various interests and agency involvements that
may be encountered in this rather complicated field.

Both the State and the City of New York have
comprehensive radiation protection codes to protect
against overexposure to ionizing radiation, whether
from isotopes or from X-ray machinery. The state
code is a part of the State Sanitary Code promulgated
by the State Public Health Council pursuant to the
State Public Health Law.[317] It applies throughout the

state except in New York City. The City's radiation
code is part of the New York City Health Code, promulgated by the City Board of Health, under the New
York City Charter.[318] Both codes contain elaborate
administrative provisions for permits for holders of
certain radioactive materials, and for the registration of the materials themselves. Both codes, moreover, prohibit the use of X-ray equipment by persons
who are not licensed in the healing arts, or persons
under their supervision. The sale or rental of X-ray
equipment to persons not authorized to use it is also
prohibited. The State Public Health Law itself, in
fact, regulates the practice of X-ray technology.[319]

Both the State Sanitary Code and the New York City
Health Code expressly limit themselves to the regulation of emissions of radiation not otherwise regulated
by the Atomic Energy Commission, or by the State
Industrial Code. The federal government retains
exclusive power over emissions from nuclear reactors,
and the disposal of radioactive wastes.[320] The
State Labor Department, under the Industrial Code,
regulates the use of radioactive substances and equipment in its industrial applications.[321] Again, a
detailed administrative permit and regulation requirements are provided for. In addition to administrative
remedies of permit revocation, hearings and cease and
desist orders, violations of each of the respective
codes are also punishable as misdemeanors.[322]

The New York City Health Code also regulates the
transportation of radioactive materials within the
City.[323] Shipments of nuclear materials are under

the jurisdiction of the Atomic Energy Commission,
but as a matter of comity the Commission provides
the City with reports of all of its major movements
of such materials within and through the City.[324]
While the State and City radiation codes do not
contain any such express provision, because reactor
uses are regulated by the Atomic Energy Commission
while industrial uses are controlled by the State
Labor Department, the enforcement and regulatory
activities of the state and city health departments
are primarily concerned with medical uses of
ionizing radiation.

Intergovernmental Cooperation — the Use of Interstate Compacts

There has been relatively little intergovernmental
cooperation in the area of environmental regulation
or enforcement. In the main the intergovernmental
cooperation has involved cooperation imposed from the
top down, rather than among governments at the same
level. In a sense one may view the arrangements under
the 1967 Air Quality Standards Act and in the 1966
Water Restoration Act as examples of intergovernmental
cooperation, because in both instances the federal
government sets requirements and requests the states
to meet them, keeping in reserve the federal power to
impose standards if the particular states involved do
not undertake to do so on their own.[325] So, too, the
various grant-in-aid arrangements for the construction
and maintenance of sewage treatment plants and water
purification installations are instances of intergovern-

mental cooperation, in that the federal government and the states or the localities cooperate in their establishment.[326] Another instance of intergovernmental cooperation can be discerned in the field of atomic energy where the states and localities have taken over some aspects of radiation safety control under contractual arrangements.[327] What is true of all these apparent instances of cooperation is that they are not freely entered into by all of the participants. In every instance the cooperation is either enforced by the federal government, or, in the case of arrangements under grants-in-aid, operates on the terms set by federal law or regulation. There are, to be sure, some instances of interlocal cooperation, particularly in the area of water management and sewage disposal. In those areas a number of states have authorized the establishment of water districts or sewage districts which exceed the territorial limitations of any one of the localities within them.[328] Such water or sewage districts are generally regarded as municipal corporations established for a special purpose; they normally assume some of the powers of the local governments included within them and may have limited taxing or other revenue powers in order to carry out their assigned tasks.[329] Normally, however, arrangements for such special purpose authorities or districts are made cooperatively after voter approval by the different localities and governments involved. The municipalities located within such a district generally cede or delegate to the district the particular municipal powers involved or at least abstain from exercising those powers after the special-purpose district becomes operative.[330]

In the conservation field, too, special authorities or park districts have been created in a number of states, again exercising powers for conservation and recreation purposes that would otherwise be exercised by the municipalities affected.[331] However, in the instance of such recreation, park or conservation facilities, the establishment of the agency is normally the result of state action and not the result of cooperative planning on the part of the municipalities or local governments involved.

Over the years a number of schemes have been proposed to provide a framework for cooperation of the numerous municipal governments that usually compose the total area of a metropolitan region.[332] These schemes, intended to provide for more effective metropolitan planning and to cut down on the inefficiencies and overlaps of governmental efforts within metropolitan regions, are not primarily designed for cooperative arrangements to regulate environmental pollution, but since a substantial part of the business of government in metropolitan areas is concerned with the environment, they would have an obvious impact on environmental controls. Particularly schemes such as annexation of unincorporated areas abutting on the central city, city-county consolidation or metropolitan combinations of government would have an obvious impact on the enforcement of air pollution, water pollution, noise and other environmental regulations, and on the rendition of services to improve the city environment. The history of these devices has been most disappointing, and few metropolitan areas in the country can point to successful forms of metropolitan government combinations. One which has been recurrently advocated is that of the formation of a metropolitan government council with representatives from all of the local governments that make up the metropolitan region represented. Such a metropolitan government council serves essentially as an organization for liaison, coordination, mutual information and advice. It has proved to be acceptable to a number of metropolitan areas simply because it is entirely advisory and makes and enforces no decisions.[333] Its uses in connection with the management of environmental pollution are difficult to document, though it is clear that such a council could serve as a ready forum, for instance, to bring to the attention of the representative of each municipality in the region that its air pollution emissions were causing a problem in another municipality within the same metropolitan area. Whether or not this will ultimately help to resolve the problem is a different question. On the whole, experience with advisory and coordinating bodies that are free to inform but have no power to decide or enforce has not been very impressive.

Perhaps the only device for intergovernmental cooperation which has had some experience behind it and has some possible uses before it, is the interstate compact. Originating during colonial times as a

device to settle boundary disputes, the interstate
compact has long been recognized as a proper method
for the exercise of state power and, more recently,
even of federal legislative power in any area in
which Congress has the authority to act.[334] The
Supreme Court has expressly recognized the validity
of the interstate compact in the exercise of the
power to "promote the general welfare through large-
scale projects for reclamation, irrigation, or other
internal improvement..."[335] The constitutional basis
is found in the compact clause of the Constitution,
which allows the states to enter into such agreement
with congressional consent.[336]

Before 1920 interstate compacts had generally been
used only for the settlement of boundary and other disputes between contending states, and did not involve
the creation of agencies authorized to carry on
governmental functions for an unlimited period of time
on behalf of the states involved.[337] In the 1920's,
the New York Port Authority, which has since become one
of the most powerful interstate compact agencies, was
established by a compact between New York and New
Jersey.[338] At the same time, the western states
joined to form the Colorado River Compact,[339] which
established a commission to allocate the waters of
the Colorado River. These two compacts opened the way
to a consideration of the utility of the compact device
to carry on a variety of governmental functions over an
extended period of time.

Since the early interstate compacts had established
compact agencies with delegated powers over river and

harbor management, it is not surprising that they soon were thought of in connection with water pollution control. The first such compact was joined in 1935 by New York, New Jersey and Connecticut. Known as the Tri-State Compact, it created a permanent agency, the Interstate Sanitation Commission.[340] The initial purposes of the compact were relatively limited--it dealt primarily with coastal, estuarial and tidal waters and was primarily concerned with the protection of fish and shellfish against contamination by sewage and other effluents. The Commission consists of 15 commissioners, five of whom are appointed by the governor of each of the three states. All decisions of the Commission require the concurrence of three of the five commissioners from each state. The Commission sets water standards and is empowered to issue abatement orders which are enforceable in the courts of each of the member states. Because it has both standard setting and enforcement functions, the Commission is considered to be relatively powerful.

The compact commission created in 1940 under the Potomac River Compact between Maryland, West Virginia, Pennsylvania, Virginia and the District of Columbia, demonstrates an entirely different pattern.[341] Though the Commission includes federal representatives for the District of Columbia, appointed by the President, it has no rule-making or enforcement powers--its functions consist purely of research and advice to the member states. A new and stronger compact for the Potomac River with effective enforcement powers is presently pending.[342]

Another variety of regulatory compact is illustrated by the New England Interstate Water Pollution Control Compact which was approved in 1947 by New York and the New England States.[343] Under that compact the Commission is authorized to adopt standards, but the enforcement of the standards is left entirely to the seven member states. The Commission itself has neither investigatory nor enforcement powers.

A compact agency with substantial powers has been established under the Ohio River Valley Water Sanitation Compact, ORSANCO.[344] This compact was approved by the states of Illinois, Indiana, Kentucky, New York, Ohio, Pennsylvania, Tennessee and West Virginia in 1940, but did not go into effect until 1948. The ORSANCO Commission has standard setting as well as enforcement powers; however, its scope and enforcement is somewhat limited by the fact that any determination of the Commission must be approved by a majority of the commissioners from a majority of the member states, as well as by a majority of the commissioners from the states affected by the determination or order.

The two commissions with substantial enforcement powers, namely, the Interstate Sanitation Commission and ORSANCO, have both issued a number of compliance orders, but only the Interstate Sanitation Commission has thus far sought enforcement of its orders in the courts. It has generally succeeded in having its orders upheld.[345]

In addition to the compacts that deal specifically with the control of water pollution, a number of other water compacts affect water pollution problems incidentally. In some of them, while pollution control is mentioned, the major purpose of the compact is a different one, be it water allocation, flood control, recreation or soil conservation. One other major and perhaps the most comprehensive interstate compact in the water regulation field is the 1961 Delaware River Basin Compact between Pennsylvania, New York, New Jersey, Delaware and the national government.[346] This compact is unique in that the federal government is a full party to the Compact and is a full member of the compact commission. The compact is also unique in that it is concerned not with isolated phases of river basin management, but with all aspects of the development of the Delaware River basin. Among its many powers are the power to regulate water allocation and use in the basin, to make provisions, and to take preventive measures, for flood control, to develop recreational uses of the river, to develop the river for hydroelectric power purposes and to set and enforce water pollution standards. A compact of somewhat similar jurisdictional reach has been proposed for the Susquehanna River basin. Passed in New York and Maryland, that compact is still pending in Pennsylvania.[347]

The development of the compact device in the field of air pollution control has been much less advanced than in water pollution control. Although interstate cooperation in the field of air pollution control has been encouraged in federal legislation ever since the first federal Air Pollution Control Act in 1955, no air pollution control compacts are presently in effect.

The only and somewhat inconsequential exception is the
New York-New Jersey-Connecticut Interstate Sanitation
Commission which, by amendment of the water pollution
compact, was given some limited authority over tri-
state air pollution as well.[348] In the air pollution
field, however, its jurisdiction is merely advisory and
has been of little effect. While federal legislation
purports to encourage the use of the interstate compact
device for air pollution control,[349] the federal legislation in other respects has served to inhibit rather
than advance such compacts. At present three major
air pollution control compacts, the Ohio-West Virginia
Control Compact,[350] the Indiana-Illinois Air Pollution
Control Compact,[351] and the Mid-Atlantic States Air
Pollution Control Compact,[352] are pending before
Congress. In addition, a fourth, rather far-reaching
compact has been proposed and is presently pending in
a number of states.[353]

It is unlikely that any one of them will obtain the
necessary federal consent. All of the three proposed
interstate compacts were pending when the 1967 Air
Quality Act became law. In the course of passage of
the Act, a House amendment was proposed to delete the
provision of the Clean Air Act encouraging states to
enter into air pollution control compacts. This provision was restored in conference between the House
and the Senate,[354] but with a most important caveat,
stating the intent of Congress that no future air pollution control compact would be approved if its jurisdiction encompassed an air quality control region
including any state not included in whole or in part

138

in the designated region.[355] Subsequent steps in
the passage of the law provide a guide to its interpretation. The Senate Judiciary Committee, which has
jurisdiction over compact approval, referred the
three compacts to the Subcommittee on Air and Water
Pollution of the Committee on Public Works because of
its special familiarity with the subject matter. In
a statement and testimony on behalf of the Department
of Health, Education, and Welfare on March 26, 1968,[356]
and in the Public Works Committee's report back to the
Judiciary Committee,[357] interstate compacts were again
endorsed as desirable ways of carrying out the policies
of the Air Quality Act. However, the Act was construed
as providing some rather specific limitations on compact activity. The Department found the three compacts
unacceptable as submitted, largely because of their
alleged incompatibility with the Air Quality Act.[358]
The Subcommittee concurred in substantially all of the
Department's objections. The Committee report recom-
mends that Congress approve the compacts on condition
that the states enact appropriate amendments.[359]

A number of the objections made were based on general considerations of effective air quality control
enforcement. For example, it was stated that the
enforcement agency under the proposed compacts should
have the full range of powers--which it did not--
including the right to obtain injunctions against
violations, and that pollution should be defined so as
to reach potential as well as presently injurious
effects. Other objections reflected the usual Congressional reluctance to commit itself to a greater

extent than necessary. The reservations preserve
national emergency powers, insure Congress' right to
alter or amend its grant of consent, and provide that
consent to any compact does not represent a determination that the compact agency necessarily qualifies
under the Air Quality Standards Act.[360]

None of these objections would pose significant
obstacles in the case of a well-designed compact.
In certain other respects, however, the Act, as interpreted by the Department and the Committee, imposes
major constraints on compact structure. These relate
chiefly to two matters. The first arises from the
statutory provision noted above, i.e., that no compact which relates to control of air pollution in an
air quality control region may provide for participation by states not included in whole or in part in
such region. The Department views this as an absolute
requirement, and also adds the converse requirement
that an interstate compact must include all the states
with territory included in the air quality region.[361]
Although the Act does not further state that the
specific territory governed by a compact must consist
solely or primarily of the designated region, both the
Department and the House Committee on Interstate and
Foreign Commerce (which added to the Act the language
containing the limitation on compact membership) have
indicated that compacts should ordinarily only cover
specific metropolitan areas or groups of closely
related communities which share a truly common air
pollution problem.[362] The total effect of this interpretation rejects an arrangement like the Mid-Atlantic

compact which was designed to cover several entire
states and to include two massive air pollution
problem areas, New York and Philadelphia. Thus
federal policy will bar virtually any air pollution
control compact which goes substantially beyond the
boundaries of a single air quality control region.
The second major effect of the Act on future
compacts arises from the Department's insistence
on separating the compact agency from any official
tie with the federal government. The Act, technically speaking, imposes the duties of adopting and
enforcing air quality standards on the states themselves. The Department of Health, Education, and
Welfare is prepared to view an interstate compact
agency as being the arm of the states for purposes
of compliance with the Act, subject to certain requirements as to the nature of the compact as follows:
a. The federal government is not to have voting
    membership in any compact. The Department deems
    this as a conflict of interest with its duty to
    pass on the adequacy, under the Air Quality Act,
    of the standards that the compact commission
    will issue. Non-voting federal representation,
    however, is considered   highly desirable.
b. The compact agency is to be an agency or instru-
    mentality solely of the states, rather than of
    the states and the federal government.
c. Despite the compact's possible status as federal
    as well as state law,[363] standards and rules under
    the compact would only have the status of enact-
    ments of the state, not of the federal government.

The principal practical effect of such a characterization is that the compact standards generally
would not be binding on the agencies and operations of the federal government.

d. Finally, since the compact machinery would be
solely the creature of the states, the federal
government would not share in financing its
operations as a party to the compact. Federal
support of the operations of the compact commission would come solely through the grant-in-aid
programs authorized under the Air Quality Act.[364]
It is perhaps worth noting that virtually all of these
issues had been present when the Delaware River Basin
Compact was before Congress, and at that time Congress
saw fit not only to consent--but to consent to full
federal participation as a contracting party.[365]

Since the appropriate Senate committees have made
their recommendations, the Ohio-West Virginia compact
has been revised and the revisions approved by the West
Virginia legislature.[366] The revision, however, is
still pending in Ohio.

The draft of the fourth proposed compact, the
Penjerdel compact for the Pennsylvania-New Jersey-
Delaware region, which includes the Philadelphia-
Camden-Wilmington area, was undertaken with the criticisms of earlier air pollution control compacts in
mind, and there is thus a possibility that once passed
by the states, it may find Congressional favor. The
supporting materials for the proposal contain a great
deal of detailed and reasoned support for air pollution
control compacts with broad regulatory powers. In

supporting the compact the agencies involved in its
preparation examined other alternatives to regional
air pollution control management and concluded that--
short of federal regional air pollution control--the
interstate compact furnished the only viable possibility for true regional air quality management.[367]
The Penjerdel compact, going even beyond the proposed
Mid-Atlantic Air Pollution Control Compact, projected
a "coordinated regional program of continuing action--
planning, monitoring, research, informing and persuading,
rule making, enforcement--not just coordinating law
making at the outset."[368] It proposed the establishment
of an interstate compact agency with extensive enforcement powers of its own, and with staff and enforcement
personnel separate and distinct from that of the parti-
cipating states. It did, however, anticipate that in
many instances enforcement would be undertaken with the
cooperation and the assistance of personnel of the
member states. It concluded that other devices, such
as uniform legislation or the use of special authorities or districts would be inadequate to cope with
the "fragmented and grossly inadequate"[369] effort to
manage and control the particular region's atmosphere,
and that an interstate compact was the only device
capable of overcoming the jurisdictional deficiencies
caused by the mosaic of state and local political
boundaries dividing a geographically related and
economically interdependent region with air pollution
problems.

    While the interstate compact device, properly
managed, has indisputable potential as a tool for

regional air quality management, interstate compacts
have been subjected to a number of criticisms. The
establishment of an interstate compact is a lengthy
procedure. It has taken an average of eight years
and nine months from the time a compact is proposed
to the time Congressional consent was obtained.[370]
The compact is thus clearly not a device to deal with
emergency situations. In addition to the ponderous
machinery necessary to enter into a compact, some of
the compact agencies have been no less ponderous in
their actual operations. Since they are not normally
responsible to any particular constituency, the main
difficulty with compact agencies is their lack of
responsiveness to public needs. They have often been
charged with delays in decision making caused by
commissioners who, frequently regarding themselves
as ambassadors from their own states, seek instruc-
tions before they will join in decision making. It
has also been said that compact procedures themselves
delay decision making. Although compact agencies
are generally designed to operate by majority vote,
they will commonly tend to rely on unanimity.
Decisions of compact agencies may, therefore, be
geared to the lowest level of agreement, i.e., that
level which the least developed member state can
agree to.[371] Moreover, there is an inevitable
tendency to logrolling between commission members
with a tendency to agree to vote for one state's
project in return for a promise to vote for the
other state's project. Interstate compacts may also
be hampered in their work because Commissioners will

often primarily be concerned with the protection of the parochial interests of their own state rather than with the interest of the region as a whole.[372] Another criticism which is perhaps less valid today than it used to be in the past is that of inadequate representation of the national interest in compact agencies. Today a representative of the federal government is likely to participate either as a member or as an observer of a compact commission. Moreover, interstate compact agencies, to the same extent as the states themselves, are dependent on the federal government for a great deal of the support of their activities. Indeed, the 1967 Air Quality Act encourages and provides financial incentives for the use of interstate mechanisms, including interstate compacts. There is, in consequence, adequate provision for federal oversight of compact activities. Finally, the compact has been criticized as non-representative in that it lacks a constituency and gives an equal voice to every member state, regardless of size and degree of interest.[373]

The interstate compact device, in spite of the criticisms that have been leveled against it, is the only workable device for regional pollution control management short of general federal controls. In view of the unwillingness both on the part of the federal government to assume, and on the part of the states to surrender, wholesale responsibility for pollution control, efforts should be directed to devising interstate compact mechanisms that will meet the criticisms and that will enable interstate compact agencies to function free from the obstacles

that the configuration of particular compacts has
frequently imposed on such agencies in the past.

Problems Presented by Present Legal and Administrative Arrangements—A Critical Recapitulation

As indicated by the previous review of environmental legislation, one of the major problems that
the present pattern of rule making and enforcement
in environmental law presents to effective environmental management is the lack of a unified policy and
the disjunctiveness of regulatory and enforcement
activities. This lack of integration and disjunctiveness is two-fold. First, there is no integrative
principle that in some way ties federal and state
development programs into the state and federal
environmental control effort. Second, present legislation too often separates the responsibility for
rule making and standard setting from the responsibility for enforcement by lodging them at different
levels of government. Although there may be adequate
reasons for the division of labor, it frequently
renders the regulatory effort less effective.

The earlier portion of this paper dealt primarily
with specific regulatory efforts in the control of
pollution. But as previously noted, when discussing
the lack of integration of policy between development
programs and the programs of pollution control, we
must consider governmental involvement more broadly.
So, for instance, the federal and state highway
program has a most significant environmental impact

146

which heretofore either has been disregarded or
dealt with in a manner wholly separate and unrelated
to programs to regulate environmental pollution. The
highway program--aside from possible damage to scenic,
historic and aesthetic values--has major ecologic
effects in that it may interfere with watershed management, and may adversely affect forests, wildlife and
other resources deserving of protection. Just as
important as any of these, it may have a major impact
on the spread of air pollution from automotive sources.
The federal government's support of extensive road-
building programs[374] constitutes federal support for
internal combustion engines, by encouraging greater
use of private automobiles and refined fuels, and in
consequence, of automotive air pollution and other
environmental affects that stem from fuel refining
operations. The production of more automobiles in and
of itself makes considerable demands on power resources
which in turn require industrial and combustion processes with broad environmental implications. Without
entering into any detailed discussion of the social and
economic implications of federal road building programs,
and even on the basis of a very cursory overview, it
is apparent that to consider federal regulatory activities that deal with air pollution, water pollution,
and other major environmental pollutants without
reference to the federal government's own activities
that have a direct or indirect impact on the environment
is to tell less than the full story. Thus, federal
controls on automotive pollution may be largely
neutralized. The present policy preference for road-
building over development of means of mass transpor-

tation is, thus, a policy which has to be considered
as part of the air pollution control picture, as well
as, of course, a matter having huge planning, land
use, and urban developmental implications.

Numerous other examples of disjunctiveness in
policy-making could be provided from present federally-
supported programs. One of them is the atomic energy
program. The Atomic Energy Commission has not only
been given regulatory powers over the use and development of atomic energy, but also has the affirmative
obligation to encourage and develop nuclear power
sources.[375] Leaving aside the question of disposal
of nuclear wastes, which has in and of itself become
a major environmental problem, there is no indication
that environmental values were considered when the
Atomic Energy Commission received as part of its
charter the task of helping to develop nuclear power
plants. Nuclear power plants share with fossil fuel
power plants the problem of thermal pollution resulting from the use of river water as a coolant. Nonetheless, even at the present, relatively advanced
state of technology there is clear evidence that nuclear power plants produce a great deal more thermal
pollution than conventional ones.[376] In addition, in
the early phases of nuclear power, not enough consideration was given to the question of the cumulative
effects of even the low permissible emissions of a
radioactive nature from nuclear power plants.[377]
Clearly the needs for power are so great that some
price must be paid for its availability in terms of
adverse environmental consequences. The purpose here

is not to say that such adverse consequences must be
avoided at all costs, but simply to point out that
there ought to be coherence in the policy-making
process between the promotion of new government-
sponsored projects and the agencies of government
that are charged with the protection of the environment against known hazards.

Numerous other examples of this kind of disjunctiveness in policy-making could be cited. Some of
them have been the subject of caricature for a long
time. So, for instance, the efforts of the Corps of
Engineers at land reclamation could be juxtaposed
with the concern of the Department of Interior for
wetlands preservation.[378] Another instance was the
effort of the Department of Agriculture to advance
the use of agricultural insecticides and fertilizers
without regard to the Department of Interior's efforts
at water pollution control; many of the fertilizers
advocated create precisely the kind of runoff which
contributes to the eutrophication of the rivers.[379]
Another instance was the schizophrenic nature of the
Department of Interior's own activities--which, by the
way, are shared by many of the states' departments of
conservation and resources. On the one hand, the
department was charged with development functions
involving the improved exploitation of resources,
particularly in mining operations. On the other hand,
many of these mining operations result in the production of tailings and the destruction of the topography in such a manner as to contribute greatly
to the pollution of the rivers which the Department

of the Interior was also charged with cleaning up.[380]
With the creation of the Environmental Quality Council
in 1969 and the transfer, in 1970, of the environmental aspects of these functions of the Departments of
Agriculture, Defense, Interior and the Atomic Energy
Commission to the Environmental Protection Agency,
first steps have been taken to eliminate disjunctiveness between development programs and environmental
protection on the federal level.

As to the second aspect of disjunctiveness in
environmental policies and programs, it is clear that
the dispersal of responsibility among federal, state
and local agencies frequently creates confusion and
results in ineffective enforcement. A review of the
situation in the field of air pollution control
provides a focus for our discussion. While clearly
air pollution is a regional problem in its impact and
the development of regulatory policies and actual
standard setting functions is moving toward the federal
government, as we have seen, all of the effective regulatory controls remain lodged on the local level.[381]
The federal government still is responsible only for
approving regional air quality standards (except in
the case of emissions from new automobiles where some
federal emission standards have been set). While all
of the states have by now enacted state air pollution
control codes that set limits on the emission of air
pollutants in order to live up to federal standards
for the ambient air, it is clear that no fixed formula
determines the relationship of emission standards to
ambient air quality standards, and the presence of

federal air quality standards does not by itself
impose upon any state the obligation to reduce emissions from particular sources. Legislative developments already point to the eventual adoption of
federal emission standards, possibly national and
most certainly regional in scope. But even with
adequate federal and state emission standards,
enforcement is likely to remain at the municipal
level. As pointed out earlier, enforcement is
limited by the geographical boundaries of the jurisdiction. Since effective air pollution control must
take place at the source of emissions, the jurisdiction
which receives the fallout and which suffers the
consequences of the emissions is frequently not the one
which can regulate the source. In view of the fact
that most municipal or other local enforcement agencies
operate independently of the state air pollution
control agency, enforcement is likely to be very
spotty indeed. Moreover, though the standards may be
relatively high, having been set at the state level,
enforcement at the local level may reflect a response
to political pressures which were not present to the
same extent at the level at which the policies were
first adopted. Thus, though the federal government
or the state may limit particular emissions stringently,
local enforcement is likely to be lagging when the
enforcement effort would result in limiting the
activities of a major employer in the locality.

Present arrangements for policy-making are thus
in need of substantial review with a view to restructuring environmental programs on a national or at

least regional level. Enforcement activities are similarly in need of review. Traditionally, much of the environmental enforcement effort has been lodged at the local level. Recently legislative developments have begun to place policy-making and standard-setting at higher levels of government, reflecting the insight that effective standards and policies for environmental control cannot be limited within narrow jurisdictional boundaries. The question arises whether what is true of policy-making and standard-setting is not also true of enforcement. Can we rely on the local jurisdiction to enforce the state, regional or national standard if the impact of stringent enforcement will fall primarily on industrial and commercial establishments within the local municipality? While a national air pollution control program would be difficult to operate with thousands of air pollution control inspectors and other enforcement personnel responsible to the National Air Pollution Control Administration in Washington, D.C., new instrumentalities and new enforcement devices should be considered to overcome the constraints that local administration puts on effective enforcement.

A major part of the difficulties in the regulation of environmental pollution is posed by the persistent attempt to deal with regional and national problems on a state or local level, in spite of the fact that problems of environmental pollution have outgrown the limits of the state or local police power. The insight that environmental pollution is increasingly a regional if not a national or even international

problem is very recent, and our traditional institutions
and modes of dealing with it reflect a cultural lag.
It is important to remember that less than ten years
ago air pollution could still be regarded as a primarily
local problem, and that it has been a mere fifteen
years since the federal government has involved itself
in the regulation of water pollution. Originally the
dimension of these problems was such that they could be
regarded as local in nature, but air pollution and
water pollution are no longer local or even state
problems; they have become national problems quite
simply because the amount of pollution and the adverse
environmental effects have become so great as to burst
beyond the boundaries of narrow local jurisdictions.
They have simply become too great for municipalities
and states to handle on their own. The process is
still going on--initially local problems still grow
into matters of national concern in environmental
pollution. The solid waste disposal problem is an
example. Still treated as a primarily local matter,
it is becoming more apparent every day that no major
municipality has enough land to bury its waste or
the facilities to incinerate it without creating
major water or air pollution problems that will spill
over municipal--and state--boundary lines. Another
example is that of noise. Though noise is relatively
limited in its range, many sources of noise, such as
jet aircraft (not to speak of the proposed supersonic
transport), cannot be regulated locally but are by
their very nature subject to national controls. And
even when noise is more locally defined--as in the

case of more insulation of residences--unequal local
requirements create competitive disadvantages for
the localities that impose the higher standards.

The persistence of the belief that problems of
environmental pollution that are regional and national
in their impact can somehow be handled on the local
or municipal level continues to have adverse consequences on the effectiveness of regulation. It has
been demonstrated that the territorial jurisdiction
of many municipalities and local governments--and
even the territorial jurisdiction of many states--
is inadequate to cope with problems of regional
air or water pollution. Within metropolitan areas,
in particular, the source of emission and the place
of fallout are likely to be under different governments. Since local governments have no extraterritorial powers and since state governments rarely
intervene in local intergovernmental disputes--
particularly where the dispute has its origins in
the activities of a private operator--there is
frequently no agency that is responsible for abatement.
What holds true of different municipalities within
one metropolitan area also holds true of interstate
regions. When the source of emissions is in one state
and the impact is in another, the only available
remedies are either federal or else, far less frequently, remedies provided under some interstate
compact. The only other remedy, an original suit
in the United States Supreme Court is even less
frequently invoked.[382] Thus far the federal government has exercised its enforcement powers with

great restraint--rarely, and only after lengthy delays, and in emergency situations.

In addition to weaknesses in enforcement caused by limited territorial jurisdiction, disabilities have also been caused by inadequate legal power. This is particularly true of powers granted to local and municipal governments. The powers of municipal government under state constitutional or state legislative provisions are often narrowly circumscribed.[383] Even in instances where a municipality has been granted home rule status, the question whether it may carry out particular functions is often unclear, especially when the state has already asserted a regulatory interest by enacting general legislation.[384] Assuming that the municipality's power to exercise a power on its own is clear, the question of consistency of the local and state code still remains, and unless the local code merely duplicates the state code, there will always be a question whether a different regulatory approach is consistent or inconsistent with the state regulations. When the state merely regulates emissions, may the municipality add fuel regulations, or would such fuel regulations be considered inconsistent with the state action? There simply is no clear answer.

Problems of consistency aside, local governments are commonly granted more limited powers of enforcement than state governments. Most of the state codes are presently enforceable by a variety of criminal, and civil (including administrative and equitable) sanctions. On the local level, however, enforcement

155

is likely to be by criminal prosecution as for a misdemeanor, and the use of civil penalties or equity
proceedings is either not authorized at all, or else
is only rarely invoked. The limits of the criminal
process for effective environmental enforcement
have been discussed elsewhere.[385] In view of the
relative ineffectiveness of the criminal process to
bring about improvements or abatement of conditions,
a municipality that can do no more than to prosecute
an environmental offender is severely handicapped in
its efforts.

In a few areas the federal government has seized
hold with full vigor and has claimed preemptive effect
for its laws and regulations. While federal preemption
may be necessary in some areas, it may also create
problems of its own, as, for example, in the area of
control of airplane noise and atomic energy. Essentially, federal preemption has tended to create a
jurisdictional no man's land where state and localities fear to tread though full regulatory jurisdiction
has not been expressly exercised. Federal preemption,
both with respect to regulation and enforcement, is
clearly called for in many areas of environmental
control--when national uniformity is essential by
the nature of the problem, or the consideration of
regulatory efficiency proves persuasive. The arguments
for federal preemption, however, need to be examined
and clearly articulated in every instance. When a
decision is made to use federal power preemptively, it
should be made wholeheartedly, to cover the field
clearly and decisively in order to avoid the peripheral
jurisdictional uncertainties.

INTERGOVERNMENTAL ASPECTS

The federal government could, constitutionally, assume control of the regulation of all environmental pollution, and it could establish broad interstate regions to carry out its regulatory activities, but it is unlikely to do so both for political reasons and for reasons of administrative economy. Short of such federal assumption of power, the only viable mechanism for regional pollution control management is the interstate compact. As has previously been indicated, although the interstate compact has not been used to full effect in the regulation of environmental pollution, it appears to be an instrument of considerable flexibility and potential. There are a number of problems with the interstate compact device which will need to be resolved, however, before its full potential may be realized. Considerable attention should be given, first, to redefining the appropriate federal role in such an interstate arrangement. With the dominant federal interest in navigable waters (and, therefore, indirectly in all waters), interstate compacts affecting waterways have invariably had federal representatives, observers, or participants on the regulatory commission.[386] With the exception of the Delaware River Basin Compact, however, interstate compacts have not enjoyed direct federal participation, and the federal government has thus far not seen fit to exercise federal power through interstate compact agencies. The possibility that the federal government might well use interstate compact agencies as executors of federal policy was contemplated and accepted in the promulgation of the Delaware Compact.[387] In order to make the interstate

157

compact device more effective and less likely to conflict with closely related federal interests, the possibility of working out similar relationships in other
water pollution compacts, as well as in air pollution
control compacts that have been proposed, ought to
be considered.

One of the major obstacles to full federal participation, and to the use of interstate compacts as
carriers of federal policy, is the concept of "equal
sovereignty" which has inhibited the use of compacts
as effective institutions. The problem is not an easy
one. Theoretically, there is ready acceptance of the
notion that in a compact like the Delaware Compact the
interests of the State of New York are considerably mor
extensive than the interests of the State of Delaware,
in terms of population served, industrial development,
use of the river basin, and capacity to contribute
financially to the development of the basin and to the
operation of the interstate compact agency. On the
other hand, there is a political and constitutional
tradition that each of the states is an entity of
equal sovereignty. In any interstate compact, therefore, all of the states ought to be regarded as
sovereign equals, just as are parties to a treaty.
The equal sovereignty concept has given far greater
influence to the smaller states, and has sometimes
put the larger state at the mercy of a combination of
the smaller states who are members of the compact,
because traditionally each state has equal representation on interstate compact commissions.[388]

The equal sovereignty problem aggravates the difficulty of federal participation in a partnership role.
If the federal government is to be treated as just
another party--i.e., as having no more impact on the
decision making process than a small state, then
federal reluctance to enter into compacts on that
basis may be easily understood. That is not to say
that in the political sense, when particular issues
are before the interstate compact commission, the
federal government's unique position would not be
readily apparent, both because of the very real federal
power to unmake most compact decisions, and because
of the major role of the federal government in financing compact projects. Nevertheless, the fact that,
structurally, interstate compacts provide for equal
sovereignty gives some of the smaller states the
power to delay and to affect decisions to a far greater
degree than their participation would otherwise warrant.
    Another interstate compact problem stems from the
fact that interstate compact agencies have no political
constituencies. Normally, the commissioners of an
interstate compact agency are appointed by the governor
of each of the party states. They are not responsible
to any electorate, nor, for that matter, are they
responsible to the governor himself, because the term
of a commissioner of a compact agency commonly exceeds
that of the governor who appoints him. This makes for
great political independence, but it may also make for
a lack of responsiveness.[389]
    The recent interstate compact proposal, for the

Penjerdel region seeks to accomplish political responsibility by requiring the election of some of the
compact commissioners. The proposal, quite novel in
its concept, raises a number of other political
problems, for example, potential conflicts between
elected and appointed commissioners from the same
jurisdiction; it is likely to be opposed by the
existing interests in the states affected. To make
interstate compacts more effective, a solution will,
however, have to be found not only for the problems
of the federal relationship with the compact agency
and equal sovereignty, but also for the problem of
political responsiveness of the interstate compact
agency. If compact agencies are to assume major
policy-making regulatory and enforcement functions
that directly affect the people in their region, the
answers to these problems will become vitally important.

Government Structure for Environmental Management: Approaches to Solutions

In the planning for effective environmental controls,
a question recurring throughout this paper has been
that of the appropriate level of government to make
policies and rules and to carry out or enforce them.
Brought down to its simplest terms, the question is
how wide must a government's territorial jurisdiction
be to operate effectively in the control of environmental pollution. To a considerable extent, the
question is one in which administrative and legal
arrangements ought to follow scientific and technological determinations relating to airsheds, watersheds,

etc. Thus, while there is considerable agreement
that local control of air pollution is no longer
appropriate because the problem by now clearly exceeds local boundaries, there still remains a question as to whether the state, the region, or the
nation as a whole is the appropriate regulatory
entity.

Under the Air Quality Act, the federal government has chosen a rather narrow regional approach,
operating largely through individual states. There
has been some criticism of this approach,[390] and
answers must be sought from science and air pollution
technology to determine whether effective controls
require broader regional management. The scientists
and technicians need to tell us, generally, what can
best be controlled and where. Thus, for instance,
it is clear that for the present, automotive pollution will largely have to be controlled at the time
and at the point of manufacture of the automobile
when appropriate pollution control devices may be
installed most effectively and at the least cost.
It is a technical determination, too, whether control
at point of manufacture necessarily means that
uniform national standards need be applied. Is it
possible, for instance, to require the installation
of a variety of air pollution control devices at the
point and time of manufacture, each of which meets
the particular state standards in the purchaser's
state? Thus far the determination has been the
other way, with only federal standards and the
California standards (which antedate the federal

161

ones) being applied to the actual installation of control devices.

For adequate pollution controls, a set of criteria ought to be developed to help determine the conditions which make uniform national or regional standards desirable or necessary. Enough experience has probably been collected in the regulation of air and water pollution to make such criteria possible. Such a set of criteria would then be properly applicable to the planning of mechanisms for the control of other pollutants as well. Thus, the problem of solid waste disposal is clearly emerging from a local and state issue into a national one. The nice question which will have to be answered before long is, when is the lack of a local solution to a problem so fraught with regional and national consequences that it properly becomes a regional or national concern? Some developments that invite comparison are taking place in noise pollution control. Because the jet plane--which has brought about the demand for noise controls--is clearly in interstate commerce, federal controls have been developed. In the case of muffler legislation for automobiles--though the automobile is involved in interstate commerce no less than the jet airplane--reliance has been placed on state legislation.[391] Muffler legislation is more effectively enforced as part of state motor vehicle inspection programs, but the need for national uniformity in the case of automobile mufflers may be no less great than the need for uniform standards affecting jet engines.

In all of these instances the problem is two-fold. The issue is not only what level of government should appropriately regulate the problem, but whether policy making and standard setting functions need to be the responsibility of the same level of government that is primarily responsible for enforcement. Thus far these issues have been resolved pragmatically. Since state and local governments were historically concerned with the environment in the traditional exercise of the police power, and since state and local governments, in consequence, were the ones that had staffs of inspectors, sanitarians and other enforcement personnel, enforcement has generally been lodged at the state and local level,[392] although policy making and standard setting has begun to move in the direction of higher levels of government. Thus, though regional air quality standards may be approved by the federal government, the emission controls--if enforced at all--are enforced by the local air pollution control officer. Whether policy and rule making, and enforcement should be divorced in this manner ought to be examined systematically. While the enlargement of federal enforcement machinery is generally looked upon with distrust, if not hostility, the question whether federal standard setting should not, in due course, lead to greater federal involvement in enforcement activities might well be explored. At the very least, devices must be found to prevent narrow local interests from determining the direction and rigor of the enforcement effort.

A recurring issue--raised again most recently in
the context of the establishment of the National
Council on Environmental Quality[393]--is the kind of
agency suitable for effective environmental management generally. Traditionally, each field of environmental control and development has been treated
separately and has had its own history of administration. Highway departments build highways and may from
time to time be brought up short on environmental
and scenic issues.[394] Generally, conservation departments and recreation departments manage the state's
recreational areas and forests quite independently
from the concerns of the highway departments, which
may build the roads which will bring people to
recreational or wilderness areas. Neither the conservation and recreation department, nor the highway department directly concerns itself with problems
of air or water pollution, which each of their
particular activities may have bearing on.

With a growing concern for environmental management as a whole, questions have been raised whether
the interrelationship between enforcement and development programs should be reflected in government
agencies that have broad across-the-board responsibilities. The federal response has been the creation
of the EPA, coordinating many environmental functions
previously dispersed among other federal departments
in a single agency. In a number of states this concern
has led to the establishment of coordinating boards or
agencies, frequently with ex officio membership drawn
from among the commissioners and other department heads

that have primary responsibility for enforcement and
development programs with environmental implications.[395]
Normally these coordinating boards or agencies have
little power except to coordinate and advise. Their
essential purpose is to make sure that commissioners
of departments with responsibilities in related areas
are aware of each other's programs, so that all of the
programs in the state may consistently follow a common
design. It is not clear whether such coordinating
boards or agencies are effective. The common experience
with ex officio agencies of that kind has not been good,
quite simply because each commissioner or department
head is responsible for his own program and is not
likely to give coordination with other programs in the
state a high priority. The legislation that established
coordinating boards or agencies usually makes provision
for department heads to send deputies to meetings,[396]
and in practice such coordinating boards or agencies
consist of middle level government executives who are
not free to make policy decisions themselves, but who
must bring each decision back to their department head
for consideration and approval. Consequently, coordinating boards and agencies have provided the outward
appearance of coordination, though there is very little
of it actually. The coordinating board or agency
normally has no "line" functions, and the various
departments have no line responsibility to it. At
best they are likely to function as staff agencies
with power to advise and cajole, but no power to direct
and implement.

It is considerations of this nature that lead to

an attitude of "wait and see" with regard to the impact
of both the National Environmental Policy Act of 1969
that created the Council on Environmental Quality,
and the subsequent establishment of the Environmental
Pollution Administration under a Federal Reorganization
Plan that became effective in mid-1970. The enactment
of the National Environmental Policy Act and the
creation of the Council were greeted with high hopes
and enthusiasm. Indeed, the Act has even been
referred to as a long-awaited "environmental bill of
rights."[397] A more balanced analysis of the new
legislation demonstrates that its future effectiveness depends to a far greater extent on agency and
interagency cooperation with the Council's recommendations and on the support of the President than
on any of the relatively limited powers the Congress
has conferred upon it. To be sure, the initial response to the new legislation is promising, and it may
be hoped that the early momentum of the Act will
extend its effectiveness into the future. On its
face, the Environmental Policy Act establishes the
Council of Environmental Quality as an advisory
body to the President.[398] It has no line responsibility in any area of environmental development or
regulation, and it has no authority to supervise, or
in any way to inject itself into, the regulatory
activities of any agency, or even to fulfill any
coordinating role between agencies. It does not
serve as a national environmental "ombudsman,"
empowered to mediate or arbitrate among agencies
and groups of competing interests with regard to the

ecology. Its three members are appointed by the
President (with the advice and consent of the Senate)
and serve at his pleasure. Though the Council is to
be "conscious of and responsive to the scientific,
economic, social, esthetic, and cultural needs and
interests of the Nation; and to formulate and recommend national policies to generate the improvement
of the quality of the environment,"[399] all of its
recommendations, legislative and otherwise, its
studies, surveys, and annual reports are to be
addressed to the President, to whom alone the Council
is responsible. The Act requires the President to
report annually to Congress on the state of the
ecology, and provides that the Council is to assist
him in preparing the report.[400] The first annual
Council Report on the "State and Condition of the
Environment" was presented to the President and was
published in August 1970.[401] It is a skillfully prepared document of great significance.

The present Council is indeed a most prestigious
body which appears to have the President's ear.
Whether, in the long run, it can exercise a real
influence on such operating agencies as the Environmental Protection Administration, the Department of
Transportation or the Atomic Energy Commission remains
to be seen. Early comments from at least one
cabinet member--the Secretary of the Interior--would
indicate that the effectiveness of the Council will
depend entirely on the continuing support of the President. That cabinet member's rather pointed comments
reflected the not uncommon attitude of agency heads

toward advisory bodies. Secretary Hickel, in an
interview, said that the Council on Environmental
Quality "is basically a watchdog" and "has great
merit in interdepartmental coordination." He added,
however, that the Council "obviously doesn't have
the responsibility and I think that anything in
government that has authority without responsibility
finally becomes a very unworkable thing. . . .I don't
know where they could stick their head in, to mean
anything. You know, they're not going to run mines
and minerals, they're not going over to HEW and run
their programs."[402] Comments from other agency heads,
however, were more favorable, stressing the Council's
capacity to act as a coordinating body that would
avoid interagency disputes regarding the preservation
of environmental values.[403] It will clearly be able
to carry out this function as long as it has Presidential support.

The initial expenditures authorized for the
Council on Environmental Quality were rather slender,
and there was some question whether the Council would
be capable of operating effectively on such a small
budget.[404] Although it is not clear whether the move
was favored by the Administration, the Council received
some added assistance with the passage in 1970 of the
new water pollution control act,[405] which, in Title II,
created an Office of Environmental Quality in the
Executive Office of the President, and authorized
additional funds for it. The Office of Environmental
Quality provides additional staff for the Council.
Originally, in competition with the bill that eventually

became the National Environmental Policy Act, the
provisions of the law creating the Office of Environmental quality were ultimately adjusted so as to
designate the Chairman of the Council on Environmental
Quality to be the director of the Office. The bill
does, however, provide for a deputy director, named
by the President and subject to Senate confirmation.
The position has not as yet been filled and thus the
question of possible conflict between the Council and
the Office has been avoided.

The National Environmental Policy Act, in one of
its key provisions, contained in Section 102, directs
that, "to the fullest extent possible" all agencies
of the federal government interpret the policies and
laws in accordance with the policies of the Act, and
that all agencies shall

(A) utilize a systematic, interdisciplinary approach
which will insure the integrated use of the natural
and social sciences and the environmental design arts
in planning and in decisionmaking which may have an
impact on man's environment;

(B) identify and develop methods and procedures, in
consultation with the Council on Environmental
Quality established by title II of this Act, which
will insure that presently unquantified environmental amenities and values may be given appropriate
consideration in decisionmaking along with economic
and technical considerations;

The legislative history of the Act shows some Congressional concern over the meaning of the words "to the
fullest extent possible."[406] In any event, the direction to the agencies contained in the subsection
quoted is a strong mandate to take environmental matters
into account, not because they carry any very clear

meaning, but because they convey a significant mood.
The more specific mandate to federal agencies is
contained in subsection (C) which requires them to

(C) include in every recommendation or report on
proposals for legislation and other major Federal
actions signficantly affecting the quality of the
human environment, a detailed statement by the
responsible official on--
(i) the environmental impact of the proposed
action,
(ii) any adverse environmental effects which
cannot be avoided should the proposal be
implemented,
(iii) alternatives to the proposed action,
(iv) the relationship between local short-term uses
of man's environment and the maintenance and
enhancement of long-term productivity, and
(v) any irreversible and irretrievable commitments
of resources which would be involved in the
proposed action should it be implemented.

Consultation with agencies, federal, state and local,
that are concerned with particular environmental impacts is provided for; the statement, accompanied by
the views of such other agencies, is to be made available to the President, the Council on Environmental
Quality, as well as to the public, pursuant to the
Freedom of Information Act.[407] The Act is silent on
what the Council is to do once it receives the statements, but it is clearly intended that the Council review
the statements and take such informed action, directly
or through advice to the President, as may be appropriate to advance the policies of the Act. Moreover, the
availability of the reports to the public will give
assurances that interested citizens and groups will be
able to review the evidence supporting particular decisions that may have substantial environmental impact.

In an Executive Order that followed the enactment
of the Act, the President directed the Council to
issue guidelines to federal agencies for the preparation of Section 102(2)(C) statements;[408] interim
guidelines were promulgated on April 30, 1970.[409]
These guidelines, in turn, required the several
agencies to establish formal procedures to identify
agency actions requiring environmental statements,
and for the preparation of the statements themselves.
Based on the Act's legislative history, the interim
guidelines freed the federal environmental protection
agencies, such as NAPCA and FWQA, from the preparation of such statements. The interim guidelines make
it clear that a serious, substantial review of environmental impact is required, rather than a mere formal
finding that the environmental impact of proposed
action will not be adverse, or cannot be avoided.

By September, 1970, a large number of Section 102
statements had been received by the Council, most as
yet in preliminary form. The statements are being
reviewed by the Council for compliance with the law
and the guidelines.[410] It is apparent that many
agencies are devoting major attention and a great deal
of time and effort to the development of these statements; this, in turn, has served to delay a number of
agency actions. Whether gains to the environment
will justify these delays is not as yet clear, for
there is as yet no evidence one way or the other
whether the required review of environmental impacts
will result in policy changes, or will merely result
in more elaborate justification of policies determined

on other grounds. Paradoxically, the careful and pains-
taking preparation of Section 102 statements may have
the result, in some instances, of protecting the
agencies from the environmentalists, rather than the
environment from the agencies. When an agency is challenged on some project by conservation or environmental
protection organizations, judicial review is more likely
to uphold agency action if it is supported by a detailed
statement on environmental impact that covers every
angle. If usual principles of administrative review
are followed, the court will not substitute its judgment for that of the agency as long as the agency can
show that it has, indeed, considered and verified all
of the relevant facts in deciding to move ahead on
some project that casts a burden on the environment.[411]
While agency activity in compliance with the requirements of the Act has been encouraging in the first
six or eight months, it is too early to gauge the
legislation's long-range effectiveness.[412]

The early impact of the National Environmental Policy
Act was encouraging in some other respects; in the first
three months after its effective date, it was relied on
in at least two judicial and three administrative decisions, and in every instance projects with adverse
scenic or environmental impact were held up for further
review--one of these decisions was the temporary injunction issued by the Federal District Court in Washington,
D.C. forbidding the Interior Department to grant a permit to a group of oil companies to build a road across
federal land in Alaska, preparatory to the construction
of a planned oil pipeline across the Alaskan tundra.[413]

Although the policy of the Act may aid environmental litigation, it carefully stops short of the express creation of a personal "right" to a clean environment. The Act declares that "The Congress recognizes that each person should enjoy a healthful environment and that each person has a responsibility to contribute to the preservation and enhancement of the environment."[414] The Senate-passed version of the bill had provided that "each person has a fundamental and inalienable right to a healthful environment," but this assertion was eliminated in conference.[415] Thus, the extent to which the Act will provide a basis for private litigation, or for litigation on behalf of the public interest by private groups remains uncertain.

The question, whether the responsibilities for enforcement ought to be lodged in specialized agencies having expertise in the management of particular aspects of environmental pollution or whether agencies charged with environmental protection generally are more appropriate, has been answered for the time being on an operationally significant level, by some recent state legislation[416] as well as by the new Federal Reorganization Plans.

The federal government has gone strongly in the direction of general protection under Reogranization Plans Nos. 3 and 4, submitted to Congress on July 9, 1970, effective sixty days later.[417] Reorganization Plan No. 4 established the National Oceanic and Atmospheric Administration whose primary purpose will be to coordinate research relating to the sea and

the atmosphere with an emphasis on securing future
food, mineral and other resources. It is not
directly concerned with the control and regulation
of the environment but is significant in that it
separates and recombines research functions of
operating agencies. Thus, for instance, the Reorganization Plan abolishes the Environmental Science
Services Administration in the Department of Commerce,
established under Reorganization Plan No. 2 of 1965
which had transferred the regulatory control of water
pollution to that department.[418]

Of far more immediate significance is Reorganization Plan No. 3 which established the Environmental
Protection Agency. Significantly, the agency is not
a separate department nor is it made part of any
department. It is headed by an administrator who does
not appear to have cabinet rank, assisted by no more
than five assistant administrators.[419] The Agency,
which will have some five or six thousand employees
transferred from existing operating agencies, will
operate with a budget of $1.4 billion as previously
allocated.[420] It is given no new powers but is the
recipient of all of the powers legislatively granted
to the component agencies transferred into it. The
agencies and functions now combined in the Environmental Protection Agency are the following:
1. The Federal Water Quality Administration, essen-
    tially with all of the functions that had
    previously been transferred to the Department of
    Interior under Reorganization Plan No. 2 of 1966,
    as well as the functions vested in the Department

of Interior with respect to studies on the effects of insecticides, herbicides, fungicides, and pesticides upon fish and wildlife resources, and with respect to some other pollution-related studies.

2. The Environmental Health Service, in the Department of HEW, including the National Air Pollution Control Administration and the Environmental Control Administration, with the Bureaus of Solid Waste Management, Water Hygiene and Radiological Health. Not transferred are the functions carried out by the Bureau of Community Environmental Management, the Bureau of Occupational Safety and Health, and the Bureau of Radiological Health insofar as its functions pertain to regulation of radiation from consumer products, radiation used in the healing arts, occupational exposure to radiation and research, technical assistance and training related to any of them.

3. The functions vested in the Secretary of HEW relating to the establishment of tolerances for pesticide chemicals under the Federal Food, Drug and Cosmetic Act.

4. The functions of the Atomic Energy Commission, as administered through its Division of Radiation Protection Standards, insofar as such functions consist of establishing generally applicable environmental standards for the protection from radioactive materials, as well as the functions of the Federal Radiation Council.

5. The functions of the Secretary and Department of Agriculture under the Federal Insecticide, Fungicide,

175

Rodenticide Act, as well as the functions relating
to that department under the Federal Food, Drug
and Cosmetic Act and those administered through
the Environmental Quality Branch of the Plant
Protection Division of the Agricultural Research
Service.[421]

Transferred also were the Water Pollution Control
Advisory Board and the Air Quality Advisory Board from
the Departments of Interior and HEW, respectively, and
"so much of the functions of the Council on Environmental Quality under. . . the National Environmental
Policy Act of 1969. . . as pertains to ecological
systems."[422] In submitting these reorganization plans
to Congress, the President expressed the hope that the
new Environmental Protection Administration would set
environmental baselines for industry to follow and that
it would work closely with the Council on Environmental
Quality. He described the new agency's general job as
that of focusing "on setting and enforcing pollution
control standards."[423]

While the creation of the Environmental Protection
Administration may be viewed as a significant first
step in a coordinated attack on environmental pollution
problems generally, it creates--as must every major
reorganization of this kind--a number of problems of
its own. First, while the new agency may successfully
coordinate the Federal Government's attack on environmental pollution, it cannot deal with environmental
problems generally because it has no jurisdiction over
federal development programs that affect the environment
nor does it have any role to play in conservation effort

176

of other agencies and departments. To be sure, this coordinating function might be played by the Council on Environmental Quality, though, as has been noted, its express powers are not exactly designed to accomplish this purpose. The new Environmental Protection Administration, in combining many agencies whose primary purpose is to fight pollution, had to relinquish some of the research functions which had previously been a part of those agencies and which are now continuing separately in the National Oceanic and Atmospheric Administration. There is, moreover, no guarantee that the different functions of the new Environmental Protection Administration will be carried on in any clearly integrated fashion. Each of the separate agencies transferred will still operate under its own basic law. The question remains whether a full and complete integration of functions will not require some basic changes in procedures and administration, thus necessitating basic changes in the underlying law.

There is a certain neatness in putting all or most environmental protection activities under a single agency. Clearly, there are important trade-offs in the field of pollution control, and the control of one aspect of pollution frequently affects another. If we have separate air pollution and water pollution control agencies, the argument goes, then whatever choices are made by one agency may improperly affect another, in the absence of a single locus of responsibility for the protection of the environment as a whole. On the other hand, it may be that the effective-

ness of regulatory controls is not necessarily enhanced by the establishment of larger departments
with a multiplicity of responsibilities. While solid
waste disposal, for instance, raises both water pollution and air pollution problems, the technology of
water pollution control and air pollution control
differ so widely, and the personnel that is employed
to manage either effort differs so widely in background and training, that the establishment of a
single agency to deal with both does not necessarily
enhance the effective regulation of either. The suggestion has been made from time to time that since
so many governmental development programs affect the
environment, agencies charged with environmental protection ought to have a full range of responsibilities
including such matters as road building, resource
development, wetlands development, open space planning
and recreation areas as well. Such experience as is
available casts doubt, however, on the wisdom of
lodging both regulatory and developmental responsibilities within a single agency. At this juncture, the
establishment of the Federal Environmental Protection
Agency, limited to the control of pollution, reflects
the better of the available choices. But conscientious
study and sound deliberation are still needed to develop
agencies charged with broad responsibilities for environmental protection generally, with operating departments
that develop expertise in particular areas of concern;
integrated policy approaches then would be the
business of the highest level of the agency. Clearly,
there are no easy answers. The need for a broad,

coordinated policy for environmental protection as a whole has been recognized and acknowledged. The need for expertise in particular agencies and the question whether such expertise may be developed within the framework of a department with broader, more general responsibilities has not been fully explored. To be sure, the two approaches are far from mutually exclusive. The assumption, however, that a contribution to environmental control is made simply by a legislative combination of existing pollution control and conservation agencies into one mammoth department is probably ill placed. Unfortunately, much of the recent legislative effort at the state level has been precisely of this nature.[424]

A consideration of intergovernmental aspects of environmental controls would not be complete without a mention of some emerging governmental issues and priorities. In the present national concern for the environment, it is generally assumed that there is a national uniformity of interests in environmental protection and that there are no large political differences among the proponents of better environmental management. In actuality, there is a variety of interests involved in environmental protection, not all of which are wholly consistent with one another. One of the larger issues which is likely to develop among the environmentalists is the cleavage between the urbanist and the conservationists. While the environment is but a single, interrelated system, differences in approach are likely to be raised in terms of priorities and claims on scarce appropriations. Stated simplistically,

179

if a choice has to be made, shall we spend our resources to save the redwoods or preserve the cities?
The preservation of the cities may well require the
further expansion of power sources and the creation of
more power plants and transmission lines that will
have at least some deleterious effects on conservation
and aesthetic values.[425] We can have both conservation
and scenery and the power, if we are willing--and able
--to pay for it.[426] But if not, then a political context for scarce resources is likely to develop and will
need to be resolved by the legislature and by appropriate administrative agencies.[427]

Without denigrating the aims of the conservationists,
it may be well to remember that, broadly defined, the
environmental problems of the cities have given rise
to grave and immediate political pressures. On the
other hand, the legislatures--including the Congress--
have often appeared to be more responsive to non-urban
constituencies. A restructuring of governmental
machinery for environmental controls will have to
take account of such imbalances and try to make provision for their resolution.

Another aspect of environmental concern with
intergovernmental implications, not referred to
previously, is that of population control. By general
consensus, no degree of environmental protection can
restore the ecological balance, unless population
growth is controlled.[428] The legal machinery for
population control is as yet undeveloped, though
more liberal abortion legislation in a few states,[429]
and government programs for the dissemination of

family planning advice and health programs to make such advice effective[430] are moves in that direction. There are a number of intergovernmental aspects in population regulation. Though population control has become a matter of national policy[431] and although there are federal programs to advance family planning, the states provide the laws relating to abortion,[432] and, until recently, they also controlled the issue of whether or not birth control and family planning information could be readily disseminated.[433] A question which needs investigation is whether existing state laws regulating dissemination of planned parenthood information and other aspects of medical care that impinge on procreation, stand in the way of effectuating the national policy.

Finally, there is the inevitable problem of balancing economic growth and environmental exploitation.[434] Emphasis on economic growth and industrial development has in the past lessened the concern for environmental protection. When industrial development and the creation of employment opportunities are emphasized, air pollution and water pollution control are likely to become secondary. In fact, numerous instances may be cited where conscientious choices were made to sacrifice environmental, recreational, and scenic values for the sake of economic development of a particular river or region.[435] Any approach to intergovernmental aspects of pollution control has to include consideration of the fact that industrial and economic development is not uniformly advanced in all of the states and regions of the United States.

Hence, environmental controls are likely to fall most
heavily upon those parts of the country that would
now have the same freedom to exploit--and abuse--the
environment for purposes of economic advancement as
did other parts of the country some fifty or one
hundred years ago that now find themselves in advanced
stages of development. A national policy of environmental protection must find ways of ensuring that
newly developing areas of the country are not kept
in an industrially and economically backward state
at the price of environmental protection for the rest.
In most instances, economic growth is possible without
undue burdens on the environment; it may simply be
more costly. To the extent that economic development
with adequate protection of the environment may be
more costly than it was during the days when the
environment was being despoiled, a way must be found
to see that the environment policies of the present
provide means to equalize the competitive advantage
enjoyed by earlier exploitation.

Notes

1. Pub. L. No. 91-190, 83 Stat. 852 (1970).

2. Reorganization Plan No. 3 of 1970, H.R. DOC. NO. 91-364, 91st Cong., 2d Sess. (1970) [hereinafter cited as Reorganization Plan No. 3].

3. For a discussion of the direction of the national interest in the development of nuclear energy--and in radioactive protection--see p. 73, infra.

4. Jacobson v. Massachusetts, 197 U.S. 11, 25 (1904); Town of Shelby v. Cleveland Mill and Power Co., 155 N.C. 196, 200, 71 S.E. 218, 220 (1911); Berman v. Parker, 348 U.S. 26 (1954).

5. U.S. v. Carolene Products Co., 304 U.S. 144 (1938); Speert v. Morgenthau, 116 F.2d 301 (D.C. Cir. 1940); U.S. v. Patterson, 155 F. Supp. 669 (N.D. Ill. 1957).

6. Ch. 758, 62 Stat. 1155 (1948).

7. Hines, Nor Any Drop to Drink: Public Regulation of Water Quality, Part III: The Federal Effort, 52 IOWA L. REV. 799, 800 (1967).

8. Id. at 800.

9. Id.

10. The Water Quality Control Act of 1965, Pub. L. No. 89-234, § 1(a), 79 Stat. 903 (1965), 33 U.S.C.A. § 1153 et seq. (1970).

11. Id., § 1154.

12. Hines, supra note 7, at 802.

13. Ch. 360, §§ 1-7, 69 Stat. 322 (1955).

14. S. REP. NO. 389, 84th Cong., 1st Sess. 3 (1955).

15. Pub. L. No. 88-206, § 1, 77 Stat. 392 (1963).

16. Id. §§ 3(c)(3), 4-6 (now 42 U.S.C. §§ 1857b-d and subch. II (Supp. V, 1965-69)).

17. P. 103, infra.

18. See NATIONAL CENTER FOR AIR POLLUTION CONTROL, U.S. PUBLIC HEALTH SERVICE, A DIGEST OF STATE AIR POLLUTION LAWS (1967).

19. Pub. L. No. 88-206, § 4, 77 Stat. 392 (1963) (now 42 U.S.C. § 1857c (Supp. V, 1965-69)).

20. Motor Vehicle Air Pollution Control Act, Pub. L. No. 89-272, § 102 et seq., 79 Stat. 992 (1965) (now 42 U.S.C. subch. II (Supp. V, 1965-69)).

21. Id. § 204(s) (now 42 U.S.C. § 1857f-3(b) (Supp. V, 1965-69)).

22. Pub. L. No. 90-148, § 2, 81 Stat. 490 (1967), 42 U.S.C. § 1857c-2 (Supp. V, 1965-69).

23. Id. 42 U.S.C. §§ 1857c-2 and 1857d.

24. Id. § 1857d(k).

25. Id. §§ 1857f-1 and 1857f-6a.

26. Ch. 200, § 1 [1959] Cal. Stats. at 2091 as amended; Ch. 36, § 1 [1960] Cal. Stats. at 380 (repealed 1970); Ch. 2031, § 1 [1965] Cal. Stats. at 4606 (repealed 1970). Emissions standards are now authorized by CAL. HEALTH AND SAFETY CODE §§ 39080 et seq. (West Supp. 1970).

27. 42 U.S.C. §§ 1857f-1 and 1857f-6c (Supp. V. 1965-69).

28. Reorganization Plan No. 3 of 1970, § 2(a)(3) (i), (b)(2).

29. H.R. 17,199, 17,200, 17,393, 91st Cong., 2d Sess. (1970) (bills to amend the National Emission

Standards Act and to provide for elimination of automotive pollution).

30. 42 U.S.C. § 1857d(c) (Supp. V, 1965-69).

31. Id. § 1857a(c).

32. Hearings on Air Pollution Compacts before the Subcomm. on Air and Water Pollution of the Senate Comm. on Public Works, 90th Cong., 2d Sess. 459-66 (1968) [hereinafter cited as Hearings on Air Pollution Compacts].

33. 42 U.S.C. § 1857c-1(a) (Supp. V, 1965-69).

34. Id. § 1857c-1(b)(2).

35. Act of Aug. 5, 1886, ch. 929, 24 Stat. 329.

36. Ch. 425, § 13, 30 Stat. 1152 (1899), 33 U.S.C. § 407 (1964).

37. See, e.g., United States v. Republic Steel Corp., 362 U.S. 482 (1960), rehearing denied, 363 U.S. 858 (1960); United States v. Interlake Steel Corp., 297 F. Supp. 912 (N.D. Ill. 1969).

38. 37 Stat. 309 (1912), as amended, 42 U.S.C. § 241 (1964).

39. Hines, supra note 7, at 805.

40. Act of June 7, 1924, ch. 316, §§ 1-5, 7,8, 43 Stat. 604-606 (repealed 1970). See p. 64, infra, for a discussion of recent legislation on oil pollution.

41. Hearings on H.R. 10625 Before the House Comm. on Rivers and Harbors, 71st Cong., 1st Sess. (1930).

42. For an instructive summary of these years, see Hines, supra note 7, at 805-09.

43. See S. 418, H.R. 123, H.R. 315, H.R. 470, 80th Cong., 1st Sess. (1947).

44. Act of June 30, 1948, ch. 758, §§ 2-13, 62 Stat. 1155.

45. Id. at 1155.

46. Hearings on S. 418 Before a Subcomm. of the Senate Comm. on Public Works, 80th Cong., 1st Sess. 30 (1947).

47. Act of June 30, 1948, ch. 758, § 10.

48. Act of July 17, 1952, ch. 927, 66 Stat. 755.

49. Federal Water Pollution Control Act, ch. 518, 70 Stat. 498 (1956).

50. Id. § 1.

51. Id. §§ 4-6.

52. Id. § 8.

53. Id. § 7.

54. Id. § 9.

55. 107 CONG. REC. 2585 (1961).

56. Act of July 20, 1961, Pub. L. No. 87-88, 75 Stat. 204.

57. Id. §§ 7(b).

58. 109 CONG. REC. 7304 (1963).

59. Pub. L. No. 89-234, §§ 1-8, 79 Stat. 903 (1965) (For a good summary of this process see Hines, supra note 7, at 825-29).

60. Id. § 1; Pub. L. No. 90-148, § 2, 81 Stat. 485 (1967).

61. Pub. L. No. 89-234, §§ 2,3,5, 79 Stat. 903 (196

62. Reorganization Plan No. 2 of 1966, 80 Stat. 16C

63. See Hearings Before the Subcomm. of the House Comm. on Government Operations, 89th Cong., 2d Sess. 24-26 (1966). This aim seemed quite reasonable in view

of the well known inconsistencies in the federal
effort in the water resource area, e.g.:

The Department of Agriculture has paid North
Dakota farmers to drain land while the Department
of the Interior spends money to create and protect
such wet lands for wild fowl breeding; the Department of Agriculture pays to remove land from agricultural production while the Bureau of Reclamation
spends large sums to create agricultural lands; the
Army Corps of Engineers dredges harbors in such a
manner as to increase the pollution problems that
the FWPCA is trying to abate. A. Reitze, Pollution
Control: Why Has It Failed, 55 A.B.A.J. 923, 926
(1969).

64. Reorganization Plan No. 3, § 2(a)(1).

65. See Hines, supra note 7, at 833-38.

66. Pub. L. No. 89-753, 80 Stat. 1246 (1966).

67. Id. §§ 101, 201.

68. Id. §§ 101, 211. Some controversy has developed
as to the meaning of "interstate" waters. As defined in
33 U.S.C. § 466j(e) (Supp. V, 1965-69) (repealed 1970),
interstate waters included ". . . all rivers, lakes, and
other waters that flow across or form a part of state
boundaries, including coastal waters." The obvious
difficulty arose over the term "coastal waters" which
the FWPA has attempted to give the broadest possible
definition. The issue is not yet clearly resolved.
See Bermingham, The Federal Government and Air and Water
Pollution, 23 BUS. LAWYER 473, 475 (1968).

69. "Standards are water quality norms established
for specific waters based on the present and future
uses to be made of the waters and expressed, either
descriptively or scientifically, in terms of the
accepted quality parameters required for the designated
uses." Hines, Controlling Industrial Water Pollution:
Color the Problem Green, 9 B.C. INDUS. & COMM. L. REV.
553, 557-69 (1968).

70. 33 U.S.C.A. § 1160 (1970).

71. Pub. L. No. 89-753, § 206, 80 Stat. 1461 (1966).

72. COUNCIL ON ENVIRONMENTAL QUALITY, ENVIRONMENTAL QUALITY 44 (1st annual report 1970). [Hereinafter cited as CEQ]

73. Hines, supra note 69, at 586; M. Stein, Regulatory Aspects of Federal Water Pollution Control, 45 DENVER L.J. 267, 273 (1968).

74. Hines, supra note 69, at 584-87.

75. Stein, supra note 73, at 272.

76. The sole statutory direction was provided in 33 U.S.C. § 466(c)(3) (Supp. V, 1965-69) (repealed 1970)

Standards of quality established pursuant to this subsection shall be such as to protect the public health or welfare, enhance the quality of water and serve the purposes of sections 466-466g and 466h-466k of this title.

77. U.S. DEPARTMENT OF THE INTERIOR, GUIDELINES FOR ESTABLISHING WATER QUALITY STANDARDS FOR INTERSTATE WATERS (1966).

78. Bermingham, supra note 68, at 475.

79. 2 CCH WATER CONTROL NEWS, No. 38, at 10 (Feb. 5, 1968).

80. Hines, supra note 69, at 573.

81. Id.

82. Pub. L. No. 91-224, 84 Stat. 809 (1970).

83. See H.R. Rep. No. 91-127, 91st Cong. 2d Sess. 1 (1970).

84. Pub. L. No. 91-224, § 11(b) (1970), 33 U.S.C.A. § 1161(b) (1970).

85. Id., 33 U.S.C.A. § 1161.

86. Id. § 1162.

87. Id., §§ 1164-71.

88. For a discussion of the role of the Council on Environmental Quality see p. 166, infra.

89. See e.g., S. 3500, 3507, 91st Cong., 2d Sess. (1970) (bills to amend the Federal Water Pollution Control Act to ban polyphosphates in detergents by requiring that synthetic petroleum-based detergents manufactured in the United States or imported into the United States be free of phosphorus, and to establish standards and programs to abate and control water pollution by synthetic detergents) as reflective of the recent move to deal directly with emission and effluence.

90. CEQ, at 118.

91. See, generally, Hearings on S. 306 Before a Subcomm. of the Senate Public Works Comm., 89th Cong., 1st Sess. (1965).

92. Pub. L. No. 89-272, tit. II, 79 Stat. 992 (1965).

93. Id., § 202(b).

94. L. Johnson, Special Message to the Congress on Conservation and Relocation of National Beauty, Feb. 8, 1965 in 1965 PUBLIC PAPERS OF THE PRESIDENTS 155, 163.

95. Pub. L. No. 89-272, tit. III, § 208, 79 Stat. 991 (1965). These functions were transferred to the Administrator by Reorganization Plan No. 3, § 2(a)(3)(ii)(A).

96. CEQ, at 110 et seq.

97. L. Johnson, Annual Budget Message to Congress Fiscal Year 1967, Jan. 24, 1966 in 1966 PUBLIC PAPERS OF THE PRESIDENTS 47, 61.

98. See, e.g., S. 2005, H.R. 642, H.R. 1203, 91st Cong., 1st Sess. (1969); S. 2005, 91st Cong., 2d Sess. (1970).

99. See, e.g., NEW YORK CITY CHARTER AND ADMIN. CODE § 435-5.0 (1963).

100. E.g., N.Y. VEH. AND TRAFFIC LAW § 375(31) (McKinney Supp. 1970).

101. CCH, 1965-1970 CONG. INDEX.

102. H.R. 14602, 89th Cong., 2nd Sess. (1966); H.R. 2819, H.R. 13846, 90th Cong., 1st Sess. (1967).

103. Act of July 21, 1968, Pub. L. No. 90–411, 82 Stat. 395.

104. 34 Fed. Reg. 457, 3756, 18355 (1969).

105. Pub. L. No. 91–258, 84 Stat. 219 (1970).

106. 34 Fed. Reg. 7948 (1969).

107. Urban Noise Control, 4 COLUM. J.L. & SOC. PROB. 105–6 (1968).

108. U.S. GOV. PUBLICATIONS MONTHLY CATALOG (1965–6)

109. A. D. HOSEY and C. H. POWELL, INDUSTRIAL NOISE, GUIDE TO ITS EVALUATION AND CONTROL (1967).

110. BOLT, BERANEK & NEWMAN, INC., NOISE ENVIRONMEN OF URBAN AND SUBURBAN AREAS (1968).

111. Ch. 724, 60 Stat. 755 (1946).

112. Pub. L. No. 86-373, 73 Stat. 688 (1959).

113. Reorganization Plan No. 3, § 2(a)(6).

114. J. Pastore, Law & Technology: A Challenge to Democratic Government in NUCLEAR ENERGY, PUBLIC POLICY AND THE LAW 77, 81, quoting H. P. GREEN & A. ROSENTHAL, GOVERNMENT OF THE ATOM, 272-73 (1963).

115. Blaber v. U.S., 212 F. Supp. 95 (E.D.N.Y. 1962 aff'd, 332 F.2d 629 (2d Cir. 1964).

116. 73 Stat. 688 (1959), 42 U.S.C. § 2021(h) (1964 provides that the Chairman of the NCRP shall be con- sulted by the Federal Radiation Council; H. Green, The New Technological Era: A View from the Law, 23 BULLETIN OF THE ATOMIC SCIENTIST 16 (1967).

117. Executive Order No. 10831, 24 Fed. Reg. 6669, 42 U.S.C. § 2021(h) (Supp. V, 1965-69).

118. Id.

119. Pub. L. No. 86-373, 73 Stat. 688 (1959).

120. Id., 42 U.S.C. § 2021(d)(1) (1964).

121. Id. § 2021(d)(2).

122. Letter from John W. Gofman to Dr. Janet Karlson, January 2, 1970, delivered at a meeting at McMillin Theater, Columbia University on January 8, 1970.

123. U.S. ATOMIC ENERGY COMMISSION, CIVILIAN NUCLEAR POWER--A REPORT TO THE PRESIDENT (1962).

124. N.Y. Times, Jan. 15, 1970, at 24, col. 3.

125. M. Eisenbud, Environmental Safety in the Nuclear Age, in NUCLEAR ENERGY, PUBLIC POLICY AND THE LAW, supra note 114, at 53-55.

126. In the matter of Northern States Power Co., 2 CCH 1967 ATOM. EN. L. REPORTER, ¶ 11,2641 (a report of administrative action taken by the Atomic Energy Commission in issuing a provisional permit for construction of a nuclear reactor). See id., 1970 ¶ 1076 for further developments (report approving the operation of the Monticello Nuclear Generating Plant at increased power levels).

127. E.g., N.Y. PUBLIC HEALTH LAW §§ 1264 et seq. (McKinney Supp. 1970); WIS. STAT. ANN. §§ 144.42 (Supp. 1970-71).

128. D. Greene, J. Kyle, J. Watson, The Texas Water Quality Bond, 48 TEX. L. REV. 1047 (1970).

129. Pub. L. No. 91-190, 83 Stat. 852 (1970).

130. Id.

131. Halliday, A Historical Review of Atmospheric Pollution, in AIR POLLUTION 13, 14 (World Health Organization 1961); CHARLESWORTH, LIABILITY FOR

DANGEROUS THINGS 130, 140–42 (1922).

132. E. W. GARRETT, THE LAW OF NUISANCES 125, 135 (3rd ed. 1908).

133. COUNCIL OF STATE GOVERNMENTS, SUGGESTED STATE LEGISLATION PROGRAM FOR AIR POLLUTION CONTROL 42–3 (1958); see also id., at 132 (1959).

134. Pub. L. No. 90–148, 81 Stat. 485 (1967), 42 U.S.C. § 1857 et seq. (Supp. V, 1965–69).

135. See, e.q., IDAHO CODE ANN. § 39–2901 et seq. (1961); NEV. REV. STAT. § 445.400 et seq. (1967); MICH. COMP. LAWS ANN. § 336 et seq. (1967); MINN. STAT. ANN. § 144.12 (1970); DEL. CODE ANN. tit. 7, § 7–6201 et seq. (1968).

136. See, e.q., IDAHO CODE ANN. § 39–2903 (Supp. 196 NEV. REV. STAT. § 445.445 (1967); MICH. COMP. LAWS ANN. § 336.16 (1967).

137. See, e.q., DEL. CODE ANN. tit. 3, § 7–6203 (1968).

138. See, e.q., MICH. COMP. LAWS ANN. § 336.15(m) (1967); NEV. REV. STAT. § 445.515 (1967); DEL. CODE ANN. tit. 7, § 7–6203 (1968).

139. FLA. STAT. ANN. § 403.182 (Supp. 1969).

140. COL. REV. STAT. § 66–29–6(6) (Supp. 1967).

141. E.q., PENN. STAT. ANN. tit. 35 § 4006 (Purdon's Supp. 1970).

142. E.q., ALASKA STAT. ANN. § 18–30–180 (1969); N.C. GEN. STATS. § 143–215.3(a)(11)(c) (Supp. 1967).

143. E.q., CONN. STATS. ANN. § 19–520a (Supp. 1969).

144. Council of State Governments, State Air Pollution Control Act, 26 SUGGESTED STATE LEGISLATION A3 (1967).

145. See p. 117, infra.

146. E.g., ARIZ. REV. STAT. ANN. §§ 36-1702, 37-1703 (Supp. 1969-70).

147. E.g., WYO. STAT. ANN. § 35-490 (1957); UTAH CODE ANN. § 26-24-4 (1953).

148. See, e.g., Norvell & Bell, Air Pollution Control in Texas, 47 TEX. L. REV. 1086, 1092 (1969).

149. Id. at 1120.

150. E.g., Stamford, Conn., Ordinance No. 21, June 15, 1950; WILMINGTON, DELA., CITY CODE §§ 312-315.

151. E.g., Fulton County, Ga., Board of Health Reg. No. 2, January 17, 1952.

152. E.g., St. Paul, Minn., Ordinance No. 9275, May 10, 1949.

153. E.g., Birmingham, Mich., Ordinance No. 450, April 5, 1954.

154. E.g., MIAMI BEACH, FLA., CITY CODE §§ 22.68-22.68.9 (1958).

155. E.g., AIR POLLUTION CONTROL DIST. OF LOS ANGELES COUNTY, RULES AND REGS., Reg. II, Rules 10-14, 17-25, Reg. III, Rules 40, 42-44; CHICAGO, ILL., MUNIC. CODE, ch. 17, May 1, 1959.

156. Hutchins, Background and Modern Developments in Water Law in the United States, 2 NAT'L. RES. J. 416, 422 (1962); Stein, Problems and Programs in Water Pollution, Id., at 388, 404 (1962).

157. Hutchins, supra note 156, at 420.

158. Hines, supra note 7, at 202-03.

159. E.g., ch. 18, § 1 [1864] IOWA ACTS; ch. 441, §§ 2,5 [1890] MASS. ACTS.

160. E.g., ch. 162, § 2 [1872] IOWA ACTS.

161. E.g., ch. 16, § 11 [1797] MASS. ACTS AND

LAWS; 1 LAWS OF NEW YORK 415 (Greenleaf 1787).

    162. See GRAHAM, DISASTER BY DEFAULT (1966).

    163. This ad hoc delegation of regulatory powers
to presently existing state agencies is illustrated
in Carmichael, Forty Years of Water Pollution Control
in Wisconsin, 1967 WISC. L. REV. 350, 352-59.

    164. E.g., ch. 41, § 1 [1899], N.J. SESS. LAW.

    165. Hines, supra note 7, at 203, 204.

    166. Carmichael, supra note 163, at 354.

    167. E.g., WIS. STAT. ANN., § 144 (Supp. 1969).

    168. TEX. REV. CIV. STAT. ANN. art.7621d-1, § 3.14
(Supp. 1969).

    169. Id., § 2.02.

    170. Tyler, Methods for State Level Enforcement of
Air and Water Pollution Laws, 31 TEX. BAR J. 905, 973
(1968).

    171. TEXAS REV. CIV. STAT. ANN. art. 7621d-1,
§§ 2.09, 2.10 (Supp. 1969).

    172. FLA. STAT. ANN. §§ 403.041, 403.061 (Supp. 196

    173. Id., § 403.071.

    174. OKLA. STAT. tit. 82, § 932(a) (1970).

    175. Id., §§ 932(b), 933(a), 934, 935 (1970).

    176. Ch. 7, § 4 [1960] LAWS OF N.Y. as amended,
ch. 490, § 7 [1961] LAWS OF N.Y. (repealed 1970);
ch. 666, §§ 1, 2 [1965] LAWS OF N.Y.; N.Y. PUB. HEALTH
LAW §§ 1205 et seq. (McKinney Supp. 1969-70).

    177. N.Y. ENVIRONMENTAL CONSERVATION LAW (McKinney
Supp. 1970).

    178. Comment, Water Pollution Control in New York,
31 ALBANY L. REV. 50, 60 (1967).

179. MURPHY, WATER PURITY 145 (1961).

180. Hines, *supra* note 7, at 218.

181. E.g., OKLA. STAT. tit. 82, § 932(b) (Supp. 1968).

182. E.g., N.M. STAT. ANN. § 75-39-3 (1968).

183. MURPHY, *supra* note 179, at 145.

184. Comment, Water Pollution--State Control Committee, 17 VAND. L. REV. 1364, 1369 (1964).

185. E.g., HAWAII REV. STAT. § 177-3 (Supp. 1965).

186. Bower, Some Physical, Technological, and Economic Characteristics of Water and Water Resource Systems, 3 NATURAL RES. J. 215, 219 (1963).

187. Such a grant may be broad indeed. In Application of City of Johnstown, 12 App. Div. 218, 209 N.Y.S.2d 982 (1961), the "waters of the state" were held to include all fresh water in streams, public or private, even though non-navigable.

188. PA. STAT. ANN. tit. 71, § 540(4) (1962).

189. E.g., N.M. STAT. ANN. § 40A-8-3 (1953).

190. E.g., N.Y. PUBLIC HEALTH LAW §§ 1210(1), 1220 (McKinney Supp. 1969).

191. For a representative list of powers commonly granted, see Hines, *supra* note 7, at 221.

192. PRESIDENT'S SCIENCE ADVISORY COMMITTEE (ENVIRONMENTAL POLLUTION PANEL), RESTORING THE QUALITY OF OUR ENVIRONMENT (1965).

193. N.Y. PUBLIC HEALTH LAW § 1205(2) (McKinney Supp. 1969).

194. Id., § 1205(3).

195. City of Utica v. Water Pollution Control Board, 5 N.Y.2d 164, 156 N.E.2d 301, 182 N.Y.S.2d 584 (1959).

196. City of Huntington v. State Water Committee,
137 W.Va. 786, 73 S.E.2d 833 (1953) (due process);
Madison Metropolitan Sewerage District v. Committee
on Water Pollution et al., 260 Wis. 229, 50 N.W.2d
424 (1951) (equal protection).

197. State Board of Health v. City of Greenville,
86 Ohio St. 1, 98 N.E. 1019 (1912); Board of Purification of Waters v. Town of Bristol, 51 R.I. 243, 153 A.
879 (1931).

198. NEW YORK CITY HEALTH CODE, § 143.11 (1959).

199. Id., § 143.13.

200. E.g., Solid Waste Disposal Act of 1965, Pub.
L. No. 89-272, 79 Stat. 997 (1965), 42 U.S.C. § 3251
et seq. (Supp. V. 1965-69).

201. E.g., N.Y. MUNICIPAL HOME RULE LAW §§ 10, 36,
37 (McKinney 1969); 1 NEW YORK CITY CHARTER AND
ADMINISTRATIVE CODE § 751 et seq. (Supp. 1969-70).

202. E.g., NEW YORK CITY HEALTH CODE §§ 81.37(h),
131.11 (1959); REVISED CODE OF THE CITY OF ST. LOUIS,
Ord. 51398, § 1 generally (B. B. No. 196) (1962).

203. BOCA BASIC HOUSING CODE §§ H-335.0, H-404.0,
H-405.0; HOUSING REGULATIONS OF THE DISTRICT OF
COLUMBIA §§ 2609, 2610 (1964).

204. NEW YORK CITY CHARTER AND ADMINISTRATIVE CODE
§§ B32 - 267.0, 755(2) - 6.2 (1970); N. Y. PUBLIC
HEALTH LAW §§ 1360-64 (McKinney Supp. 1969).

205. 10 CODES, RULES AND REGULATIONS OF THE STATE OF
NEW YORK § 19.2(4) (State Sanitary Code) (1962); NEW YORK
CITY HEALTH CODE § 152.23 (1959).

206. 10 CODES, RULES AND REGULATIONS OF THE STATE OF
NEW YORK §§ 19.3, 19.4 (1962). See also controversial
Local Law 14, 5 NEW YORK CITY CHARTER AND ADMINISTRATIVE
CODE § 892-1.0 et seq. (Supp. 1969-70), aimed at controlling air pollution from apartment house incinerators and oil burners. This law, one of the most
stringent and comprehensive of air pollution codes, was
upheld May 25, 1970, by the courts after a three-year

challenge by the real estate industry. Oriental Blvd. v. Heller, 58 Misc.2d 920, 297 N.Y.S.2d 431, aff'd, 34 A.D. 2d 811, 311 N.Y.S.2d 635 (N.Y. App. Div.2d Dept. 1970).

207. N.Y. Times, June 4, 1969, at 34, col. 2.

208. E.g., ARIZ. REV. STAT. ANN. §§ 36-1319-1326, ch. 11 generally (1956); MASS. GEN. LAWS ANN. ch. 40, §§ 44c, 44f (1966).

209. E.g., 4 NEW YORK CITY CHARTER AND ADMINISTRATIVE CODE § B32-267.0 (1970).

210. See p. 70, infra.

211. For a tabulation of these laws, see Kaufman, Control of Noise Through Laws and Regulations in NOISE AS A PUBLIC HEALTH HAZARD 340 (Proceedings of the Conference of the American Speech and Hearing Association, Washington, D.C., June 1968, 1969).

212. E.g., CODES, RULES AND REGULATIONS OF THE STATE OF NEW YORK, ch. V, subch. E (1963). See J. Kaufman, The Legal Aspects of Noise Control, in 115 Cong. Rec. E9031, E9041 (1969) for a compilation of state and local laws.

213. NEW YORK CITY CHARTER AND ADMINISTRATIVE CODE § 435-5.0(a) (1963).

214. Id., § 435-5.0(b).

215. CODE OF GENERAL ORDINANCES OF CITY OF PHILADELPHIA §§ 10-(401-408) (1956).

216. MUNICIPAL CODE OF CHICAGO § 99-58 (1969).

217. NEW YORK CITY ZONING RESOLUTION art. IV, §§ 42-(20-22) (1960).

218. N.Y. MULTIPLE DWELLING LAW § 84 (McKinney Supp. 1969-70); 4 NEW YORK CITY CHARTER AND ADMINISTRATIVE CODE RS12-(2-4) (1963).

219. NEW JERSEY REGS. FOR THE CONSTRUCTION AND MAINT. OF HOTELS AND MULT. DWELLINGS, art. 18, July 19, 1967. Issued pursuant to ch. 76 LAWS OF NEW JERSEY (1967).

220. For a discussion of the weak enforcement provisions of federal law see p.   , infra.

221. Pub. L. No. 88-206, 77 Stat. 392 (1963).

222. Pub. L. No. 90-148, 81 Stat. 491 (1967).

223. Id., 42 U.S.C. § 1857d(d)(1)(B) (Supp. V, 1965-69).

224. Id., § 1857d(k).

225. H.R. Rep. No. 728, 90th Cong., 1st Sess. 19 (1967).

226. S. Rep. No. 403, 90th Cong., 1st Sess. 31 (1967); H. Rep. No. 728, 90th Cong., 1st Sess. 19 (1967).

227. 81 Stat. 490 (1967), 42 U.S.C. § 1857c-2 (Supp. V, 1965-69).

228. Id., 42 U.S.C. § 1857d(c)(4).

229. Id., § 1857d(d)(1)(A).

230. Id., § 1857d(d)(1)(C).

231. United States v. Bishop Processing Co., 287 F. Supp. 624, 632 (D. Md. 1968), aff'd, 423 F.2d 469 (4th Cir. 1970), cert. denied, 398 U.S. 904 (1970).

232. 81 Stat. 495 (1967), 42 U.S.C. § 1857d(d)(2) (Supp. V, 1965-69).

233. It has been suggested that this informal procedure is a necessary result of the nature of the conference. It is basically a meeting of all the governmental agencies involved to consider a problem of common concern in the light of all the information available in order to arrive at the remedial action necessary. Edelman, Air Pollution Abatement Procedures Under the Clean Air Act, 10 ARIZ. L. REV. 30, 32 (1968).

234. 81 Stat. 495 (1967), 42 U.S.C. § 1857d(d)(3), (e), (f)(1) (Supp. V, 1965-69).

235. See 32 Fed. Reg. 5514 (1967) for the

procedures proposed by the Secretary of HEW, and
followed in the only hearing held so far.

236. 81 Stat. 496 (1967), 42 U.S.C. § 1857d(f)
(2)(3) (Supp. V, 1965-69).

237. U.S. v. Bishop Processing Co., 287 F. Supp.
624, 633 (D.C. Md. 1968), aff'd, 423 F.2d 469 (4th
Cir. 1970), cert. denied, 398 U.S. 904 (1970).

238. 81 Stat. 496 (1967), 42 U.S.C. § 1857d(g)
(Supp. V, 1965-69).

239. Id., 42 U.S.C. § 1857d(h).

240. Martin & Symington, A Guide to the Air Quality
Act of 1967, 33 LAW AND CONTEMP. PROB. 239, 266 (1968).

241. 81 Stat. 496 (1967), 42 U.S.C. § 1857d(h)
(Supp. V, 1965-69).

242. Edelman, supra note 233, at 34.

243. The history of the case can be found in 423
F.2d 469, 470 (4th Cir. 1970). Cert. was denied in
398 U.S. 904 (1970).

244. 80 Stat. 1250 (1966), 33 U.S.C.A. §§1160(a),
(d)(1) (1970).

245. Id., 33 U.S.C.A. §§1160(d)(1), (2).

246. Id., §§1160(d)(1)-(4), (e), (f), (g).

247. Stein, supra note 73 at 278. For a detailed
analysis of the forty abatement conferences held
through November 1966, see Hines, supra note 7, at 855-56.

247a. Pub. L. 89-234, § 5(a); 33 U.S.C.A. § 1160(c)(5)(1970).

248. F. P. GRAD, PUBLIC HEALTH LAW MANUAL 222
et seq. (1970) [hereinafter cited as MANUAL].

249. See, e.g., United States v. Republic Steel
Corp., 362 U.S. 482 (1960), rehearing denied, 363 U.S.
858 (1960); United States v. Interlake Steel Corp.,
297 F. Supp. 912 (N.D. Ill. 1969).

250. 30 Stat. 1151 (1899), 33 U.S.C. 401 et seq.
(1964).

251. N.Y. Times, Jan. 15, 1970, at 1; Feb. 10,
1970, at 1; Mar. 27, 1970, at 66; and Ap. 22, 1970, at 35

252. 81 Stat. 500 (1967), 42 U.S.C. §§ 1857f-3(a),
1857f-4 (Supp. V, 1965-69).

253. Reorganization Plan No. 3 of 1970, § 2(a)(3).

254. 81 Stat. 501 (1967), 42 U.S.C. § 1857f-5(a)
(Supp. V, 1965-69).

255. Id., § 1857f-5(b).

256. N.Y. Times, April 19, 1970 at 16, cols. 4-6
(quoting John Middleton, head of National Air Pollution
Control Administration).

257. In a test run by the Los Angeles Air Pollution
Control District 87% of vehicles driven over 20,000
miles failed to meet state standards. Hearings Before
the Subcomm. on Air and Water Pollution of the Senate
Comm. on Public Works, 90th Cong.,2d Sess., ser. 90-82,
pt. 1, at 225 (1967).

258. CAL. HEALTH AND SAFETY CODE §§ 39080 et seq.
(West Supp. 1970). See also p.156, infra and A.
Rosenthal, Federal Power to Preserve the Environment:
Enforcement and Control Techniques, infra at 233.

259. S. Rep. No. 1353 90th Cong., 2d Sess. (1968).

260. Allegheny Airlines v. Village of Cedarhurst,
132 F. Supp. 871 (E.D.N.Y. 1955), aff'd, 238 F.2d 812
(2d Cir. 1956); American Airlines Inc. v. Town of
Hempstead, 272 F. Supp. 226 (E.D.N.Y. 1967), aff'd,
398 F.2d 369 (1968) (holding village ordinances
explicitly and implicitly barring aircraft from lower
air, in an effort to decrease aircraft noise,invalid
as conflicting with federal law in an area of federal
preemption); 34 Fed. Reg. 18356 (1969) in which FAA
posits support of local controls stating "The judicial
decisions and legislative history of Public Law 90-411
[the Noise Abatement Act] have made it clear that the
Federal Government should not substitute its judgment

for that of the airport operator . . . and that the
Federal Government should recognize the airport
operator's right to issue regulations or establish
requirements as to the permissible level of noise
which can be created by aircraft using the airport."

261. 34 Fed. Reg. 18355 (1969) sets forth a summary
of public comments generally concluding that standards
should be changed.

262. Hearings on H.R. 3400 & H.R. 14146 before the
Subcomm. on Transportation and Aeronautics of the
House Comm. on Interstate and Foreign Commerce, 90th
Cong., 1st and 2nd Sess., at 89,91,97,100,152 (1968).

263. S. Rep., supra note 259.

264. This problem was addressed by subsection k
of the 1959 amendment which specifically reserved to
the state the authority "to regulate activities for
purposes other than protection against radiation
hazards." Pub. L. No. 86-373, 73 Stat. 688 (1959).

265. Atomic Energy Act of 1954, ch. 1073, 68 Stat.
921.

266. 73 Stat. 688 (1959), 42 U.S.C. § 2021 (1964).

267. 34 Fed. Reg. 18356 (1969).

268. E.g., N.Y. PUBLIC HEALTH LAW §§ 1100 et seq.,
1205, 1210 (McKinney Supp. 1969); ARIZ. REV. STAT.
ANN. § 36-1702 (Supp. 1969-70).

269. E.g., WIS. STAT. ANN. § 144.31(1)(c) (Supp. 1970).

270. E.g., FLA. STAT. ANN. § 403.182 (Supp. 1970).

271. E.g., MINN. STAT. ANN. § 145.01 (1970).

272. E.g., N.Y. PUBLIC HEALTH LAW § 1264 et seq.
(McKinney Supp. 1969).

273. MANUAL, at 16 et seq. For an account of a
county in search of an air pollution code see R. Cusumano
and G. Wasser, Initial Experiences with the Comprehensive
Air Pollution Survey in Nassau County, New York, 13

JOURNAL OF THE AIR POLLUTION CONTROL ASSOCIATION 281 (1963).

274. See MANUAL, at 16 et seq.

275. Id.

276. ". . . the uncertain limits of municipal power have had a stultifying effect on local initiative. Since local officials must consider whether a prospective ordinance might fall outside the area of 'property, affairs, or government,' [many will] be restrained in exercising their lawmaking functions." Note, Home Rule and the New York Constitution, 66 COLUM. L. REV. 1145, 1154 (1966).

277. MANUAL, at 20.

278. F. Grad, The State's Capacity to Respond to Urban Problems: The State Constitution in THE AMERICAN ASSEMBLY, THE STATES AND THE URBAN CRISIS at 46, 47 (A. Campbell ed. 1970).

279. E.g., NEW YORK CITY HEALTH CODE § 143.01 et seq. (1959); Brooklyn, N.Y., Rules and Regulations of the Borough President Pertaining to the Issuance of Permits for the Construction of Septic Tanks and Cesspools in Sidewalk Areas.

280. N.Y. PUBLIC HEALTH LAW § 12-b(1), (2) (McKinney Supp. 1969).

281. E.g., NEW YORK CITY HEALTH CODE §§ 143.05(a), 143.13(a) (1959).

282. Id., § 143.13(a) (1959).

283. Id., notes to § 143.11.

284. Id. § 143.11.

285. E.g., N.Y. PUBLIC HEALTH LAW §§ 1180 (New England Interstate Water Pollution Control Compact), 1190 (Ohio River Valley Water Sanitation Compact), 1299 (Tri-State Compact) (McKinney Supp. 1969).

286. E.g., id., § 1188, art. ix (New England Interstate Water Pollution Control Compact).

287. E.g., id., § 1240; KY. REV. STAT. § 224.080 (1969).

288. E.g., ALASKA STAT. § 46.05.190 (1962); GA. CODE ANN. § 17-520 (Supp. 1965); KY. REV. STAT. § 224.070 (1969).

289. E.g., ALA. CODE, tit. 22 § 140(9)(n) (Supp. 1969); FLA. STAT. ANN. § 403.121(2) (Supp. 1969).

290. N.Y. PUBLIC HEALTH LAW § 1242(7) (McKinney Supp. 1969).

291. MISS. CODE ANN. §§ 7106-127 (1968).

292. FLA. STAT. ANN. § 403.161 (Supp. 1969).

293. N.Y. PUBLIC HEALTH LAW § 1252(1) (McKinney Supp. 1970).

294. E.g., FLA. STAT. ANN. § 403.161(3) (Supp. 1970); KY. REV. STAT. § 224.990 (1969).

295. E.g., N.Y. PUBLIC HEALTH LAW § 1251 (McKinney Supp. 1970).

296. E.g., N.Y. PUBLIC HEALTH LAW §§ 1244 (McKinney Supp. 1970).

297. E.g., GA. CODE ANN. §§ 3A-120,17-513 (Supp. 1969).

298. E.g., ALA. CODE, tit. 22, § 140(9)(n) (Supp. 1967); LA. REV. STAT. § 56:1442 (1952).

299. Hearings on S. 649, S.737, S.1118, S.1183 Before a Special Subcomm. on Air and Water Pollution of the Senate Comm. on Public Works, 88th Cong., 1st Sess., at 98 (1963).

300. Hines, supra note 7, at 227.

301. State Board of Health v. City of Greenville,

86 Ohio St. 1, 98 N.E. 1019 (1912); Board of Purification of Waters v. Town of Bristol, 51 R.I. 243, 153 A.
879 (1931).

302. NEW JERSEY REGULATIONS FOR THE CONSTRUCTION
AND MAINTENANCE OF HOTELS AND MULTIPLE DWELLINGS
§ 1902.4 (Department of Community Affairs July, 1968).

303. Id., §§ 105.0, 107.0(b).

304. E.g., NEW YORK CITY HEALTH CODE § 153.23 (1959)

305. 4 NEW YORK CITY CHARTER AND ADMINISTRATIVE
CODE § 755(4)-2.0 (Supp. 1970).

306. N.Y. VEH. AND TRAFFIC LAW § 1224 generally,
and, more particularly, § 1224(9) (McKinney 1970) which
would make it possible for the New York State Dept. of
Motor Vehicles to connect an abandoned car's Vehicle
Identification Number with its last registered owner
through use of a computer.

307. City of New York, Rules and Procedures of the
Police Department §§ 3/94.0-.4 (1970).

308. E.g., N.Y. LABOR LAW §§ 21(1)(2)(8), 25, 39,
40 (McKinney 1965); id. § 213 (McKinney Supp. 1970-71).

309. E.g., N.Y. VEH. AND TRAFFIC LAW § 375(32)
(McKinney Supp. 1970). See also, Note, Urban Noise
Control, 4 COLUM. J. L. & SOC. PROB. 105 (1968) for a
general discussion of enforcement experience.

310. N.Y. VEH. AND TRAFFIC LAW § 301 et seq.
(McKinney Supp. 1970).

311. Reorganization Plan No. 3 of 1970.

312. 73 Stat. 688 (1959), 42 U.S.C. § 2021
generally (1964).

313. 4 CCH-ATOMIC ENERGY LAW REPORTER, which sets
forth the statutes of the states and territories
governing jurisdiction in the atomic energy field.

314. E.g., S.D. COMP. LAWS ANN. §§ 34-21-(18-21)
(1967).

315. N.Y. PUB. HEALTH LAW §§ 225(3), (4) (McKinney Supp. 1969).

316. E.g., CAL. HEALTH & SAFETY CODE §§ 25732, 25840 (West 1954).

317. N.Y. PUB. HEALTH LAW §§ 225(3), (4) (McKinney Supp. 1970-71).

318. 1 NEW YORK CITY CHARTER AND ADMINISTRATIVE CODE § 558 (1963).

319. 10 CODES, RULES AND REGULATIONS OF THE STATE OF NEW YORK §§ 16.40, 16.50, 16.100-.111 [hereinafter cited as State Sanitary Code]; NEW YORK CITY HEALTH CODE §§ 175.03, 175.05, 175.07, 175.21(a)(b) (1963); 12 CODES, RULES AND REGULATIONS OF THE STATE OF NEW YORK, Rules 38.0-.19 [hereinafter cited as Industrial Code] (applying to any radiation source not subject to regulatory jurisdiction of the State or City Departments of Health); N.Y. PUB. HEALTH LAW §§ 3502, 3504-10, 3512, 3514, 3515 (McKinney Supp. 1970).

320. 73 Stat. 688 (1959), 42 U.S.C. §§ 2021(c)(1)(3), 2039 (1964).

321. Industrial Code, pt. 38 generally, as amended, August 1963 and February 1964.

322. N.Y. LABOR LAW § 213 (McKinney Supp. 1969); State Sanitary Code § 1.21; N.Y. PUBLIC HEALTH LAW § 12-b (McKinney Supp. 1969).

323. NEW YORK CITY HEALTH CODE §§ 175.09(c), (d), (e) (1959).

324. 68 Stat. 930 (1954), as amended, 42 U.S.C. § 2073 (1964); 68 Stat. 932 (1954), 42 U.S.C. § 2092 (1964); 68 Stat. 933, 42 U.S.C. § 211 (1964).

325. 81 Stat. 491 (1967), 42 U.S.C. § 1857d(c) (Supp. V, 1965-69); 80 Stat. 1248 (1966), 33 U.S.C. §§ 466d(f), (g) (Supp. V. 1965-69).

326. 80 Stat. 1249-1251 (1966), 33 U.S.C. § 466e (Supp. V, 1965-69); 82 Stat. 534 (1968), 42 U.S.C. § 3102 (Supp. V, 1965-69).

327. 73 Stat. 688 (1959), 42 U.S.C. § 2021 (1964).

328. E.g., N.Y. GEN. MUNICIPAL LAW § 119-0 (McKinney 1954), §§ 111-116, 120-a, 120-t, 120-u (McKinney Supp. 1963); N.Y. TOWN LAW § 198(1)(3) (McKinney 1965).

329. E.g., N.Y. GEN. MUNICIPAL LAW § 119-0(2)(a)(c) (McKinney 1954); N.Y. TOWN LAW § 215(1-a) (McKinney 1965)

330. E.g., N.Y. GEN. MUNICIPAL LAW §§ 120t, 120v (1963).

331. E.g., N.Y. TOWN LAW § 198(4) (McKinney 1965 and Supp. 1969); ADVISORY COMMISSION ON INTERGOVERNMENTAL RELATIONS, PERFORMANCE OF URBAN FUNCTIONS: LOCAL AND AREA WIDE 92-3, 106-7 (1963). J. FESLER, THE 50 STATES AND THEIR LOCAL GOVERNMENTS 522-31 (1967); S. SIEGEL, THE LAW OF OPEN SPACE 3, 7 (Park, Recreation and Open Space Project of the Tri-State New York Metropolitan Region 1960).

332. ADVISORY COMMISSION ON INTERGOVERNMENTAL RELATIONS, METROPOLITAN COUNCILS OF GOVERNMENTS: AN INFORMATION REPORT (1966); 1968 STATE LEGISLATIVE PROGRAM OF THE ADVISORY COMMISSION ON INTERGOVERNMENTAL RELATIONS, A REPORT ON METROPOLITAN AND REGIONAL ORGANIZATION AND ADMINISTRATION 372 et seq.; PERFORMANCE OF URBAN FUNCTIONS, supra note 331 at 24-60, and FESLER, supra note 331 at 532-549.

333. E.g., SAN FRANCISCO, BY-LAWS OF THE ASSOCIATION OF BAY AREA GOVERNMENTS, in INFORMATION REPORT, supra note 332.

334. McCulloch v. Maryland, 4 Wheat. 316, 421 (1819) (dictum); West Virginia ex rel. Dyer v. Sims, 341 U.S. 22 (1951); cf. New York v. New Jersey 256 U.S. 296, 313 (1921); for a fuller discussion of this point see Grad, Federal-State Compact: a New Experiment in Co-operative Federalism, 63 COLUM. L. REV. 825, 834, 840 ff. (1963).

335. United States v. Gerlach Live Stock Co., 339 U.S. 725, 738 (1950).

336. U.S. CONST. art I, § 10.

337. ZIMMERMAN and WENDELL, THE INTERSTATE COMPACT SINCE 1925, at 3-4 (1951).

338. N.Y. UNCONSOL. LAWS § 6401 et seq. (McKinney 1961).

339. Law of Dec. 21, 1928, ch. 42, 45 Stat. 1057 (1928).

340. Ch. 779, 49 Stat. 932 (1935); CONN. GEN. STAT. REV. §§ 25-55, 25-66 (Supp. 1970); N.J. REV. STAT. §§ 32:18-1, 32:18-22 (1968); N.Y. PUB. HEALTH LAW § 1299, art. III(1) (McKinney Supp. 1969).

341. 54 Stat. 748 (1940); MD. ANN. CODE art. 43, § 407 (1965); PA. STAT. tit. 32, § 741 et seq. (1967); VA. CODE § 28.1-203 (1963); W.VA. CODE § 29-1C-1 (1966).

342. CONN. GEN. STAT. REV. § 25-68 (1958); ME. REV. STAT. ANN. tit. 38, § 491 et seq. (1964); N.H. REV. STAT. ANN. § 488:1 et seq. (1968); N.Y. PUB. HEALTH LAW § 1180 (McKinney Supp. 1970-71); R.I. GEN. LAWS ANN. § 46-16-1 (1956); VT. STAT. ANN. tit. 10, § 991 et seq. (1959).

343. Potomac Valley Pollution and Conservation Compact.

344. 54 Stat. 752 (1940); ILL. REV. STAT. ch. 111 1/2, § 117 (1967); IND. ANN. STAT. § 68-601 (1961); KY. REV. STAT. § 224-190 (1969); N.Y. PUB. HEALTH LAW § 1190 (McKinney Supp. 1969-70); OHIO REV. CODE ANN. § 6113.01 (page 1954); PA. STAT. tit. 32, § 816.1 (1949); TENN. CODE ANN. § 70-401 (1955); W.VA. CODE ANN. § 29-1D-1 (1966).

345. The Commission was not confronted with a situation that prompted use of its enforcement power until nine years after its formation. Since 1967 there have been only six cases of formal intervention. E.g., the Terre Haute case, ORSANCO, SECOND ANNUAL REPORT, Appendix A, at 40 (1950); the Gallipolis case, ORSANCO, NINTH ANNUAL REPORT 12 (1957). In the meantime, compliance has been secured informally from hundreds of municipalities and industries. E. J. CLEARY, THE ORSANCO STORY 117 (1967).

346. Pub. L. No. 87-328, 75 Stat. 688 (1961); DEL. CODE ANN. tit. 23, § 901m (1953); N.J. REV. STAT. § 32:11D-1 et seq. (1963); N.Y. CONSERVATION LAW § 801 (McKinney 1967); PA. STAT. tit. 32 § 815.01 (Supp. 1966).

347. ANN. CODE OF MD. art. 96A, § 59 et seq. (Supp. 1969); N.Y. CONSERV. LAW § 835 (McKinney Supp. 1970-71).

348. N.Y. PUB. HEALTH LAW § 1299-m (McKinney Supp. 1969).

349. 81 Stat. 485 (1967), 42 U.S.C. § 1857a (Supp. V, 1965-69).

350. W.VA. CODE § 29-1G-1 et seq. (Supp. 1969).

351. IND. STAT. ANN. §§ 35-4621 et seq. (Burns 1969)

352. N.Y. PUB. HEALTH LAW § 1299, art. III(1) (McKinney Supp. 1969).

353. PENJERDEL AIR POLLUTION CONTROL COMPACT IN REGIONAL CONFERENCE OF ELECTED OFFICIALS, AIR POLLUTION SURVEY REPORT, GOVERNMENT ASPECTS Pt. 3 (Government Studies Center, Fels Institute of Local and State Government, University of Pennsylvania 1968) [hereinafter cited as PENJERDEL]. (The author performed legal analysis and technical assistance in the preparation of the draft compact.)

354. H. Rep. No. 916, 90th Cong., 1st Sess. 1986 (1967).

355. 81 Stat. 485 (1967), 42 U.S.C. § 1857a(c)(2) (Supp. V, 1965-69).

356. Hearings, supra note 32, at 459-66.

357. SENATE COMMITTEE ON PUBLIC WORKS, RECOMMENDATIONS TO THE COMMITTEE ON THE JUDICIARY REGARDING THE CONDITIONAL CONSENT OF THE CONGRESS TO VARIOUS INTERSTATE AIR POLLUTION CONTROL COMPACTS, 90th Cong., 2d Sess. (1968).

358. Hearings, supra note 32.

359. Recommendations, supra note 357, at 3, 4 and Appendix A.

360. Id.

361. H.R. Rep. No. 728, 90th Cong., 1st Sess. 24 (1967).

362. H.R. Rep. No. 728, 90th Cong., 1st Sess. 24 (1967).

363. The Supreme Court has held the contract clause of the Constitution applicable to a state's capacity to legislate with respect to interstate compacts (see West Virginia ex rel. Dyer v. Simms, 341 U.S. 22 (1951); Olin v. Kitzmiller, 259 U.S. 260 (1922); Virginia v. West Virginia, 246 U.S. 565 (1918); Pennsylvania v. Wheeling & Belmont Bridge Co. 54 U.S. (13 How.) 518, 566 (1852); Green v. Biddle, 21 U.S. (8 Wheat.) 1, 13 (1823), and has strongly indicated that the federal government, despite the absence of an explicit Constitutional provision, is similarly restrained (Lynch v. United States, 292 U.S. 571, 579 (1934). Apart from this restriction, state law would apply both to the state's enabling legislation and laws passed in furtherance of such legislation. (See, generally Grad, supra, note 334 at 848.)

364. Hearings, supra note 32 at 464, 466.

365. Pub. L. No. 87-328, 75 Stat. 688 (1961); N.Y. CONSERV. LAW § 801 (Preamble) (McKinney Supp. 1967).

366. W. VA. CODE ANN. § 29-IG-1-5d (Supp. 1969). The major changes include authorization to the President of the United States to designate a federal representative who can cast the deciding vote if there is a tie (Art. II), to the Interstate Commission to develop and implement air quality standards, carry on monitoring activities, enter on property, and enjoin air pollution which violates standards or causes imminent danger (Art. IV), and a statement that nothing in this compact authorizes a lower level of air quality than those adopted by the commission (Art. VI).

367. PENJERDEL 151, 158.

368. Id. at 159, 160.

369. Id. at 163.

370. MARTIN, BIRKHEAD, BURKHEAD & MUNGER, RIVER BASIN ADMINISTRATION AND THE DELAWARE 132 (1960); Stein, supra note 73, at 167.

371. Grad, supra note 334, at 853; Stein, supra note 73 at 167.

372. Stein, supra note 73, at 167.

373. 81 Stat. 485 (1969), 42 U.S.C. § 1857c-1 (Supp. V, 1965-69).

374. See, e.g., 23 U.S.C. § 103 (1964) and § 103 (d) (1)-(3) (Supp. V, 1965-69). See also 49 U.S.C. (1964) generally for additional policy statements and details of administrative organization.

375. 68 Stat. 921 (1954), 42 U.S.C. § 2011 (1964); 78 Stat. 602 (1964), 42 U.S.C. § 2012 (1964).

376. R. CURTIS & E. HOGAN, PERILS OF THE PEACEFUL ATOM 183 (1970), citing a report by J. G. Terrill, Jr. to the American Society of Civil Engineers.

377. Eisenbud, supra note 125; M. Peterson, Environmental Contamination from Nuclear Reactors, 8 SCIENCE AND CITIZEN 1 (1965); Letter from John Gofman to Dr. Janet Karlson, supra note 122; N.Y. Times, March 16, 1970, at 57, col. 1.

378. 33 U.S.C., ch. 12 generally (1964); 82 Stat. 625 (1968), 16 U.S.C. § 1221 et seq. (Supp. V, 1965-69). See p.145, infra for a discussion of the problems of the lack of a constituency and equal sovereignty.

379. CEQ at 37.

380. 78 Stat. 329 (1964), 42 U.S.C. § 1961 et seq. (1964); e.g., 61 Stat. 913 (1947), 30 U.S.C.A. §§ 351-54 (Supp. 1970).

381. "The state governments' attitude toward pollution control parallels that of the Federal Government. A

profusion of conflicting state agencies dealing with these problems is common. Even more common are the lack of effective power and the miniscule budgets." A. Reitze, Jr., _supra_ note 63, at 926.

382. See, _e.g._, New Jersey v. New York, 283 U.S. 805 (1931), _modified_, 347 U.S. 995 (1954).

383. E.g., N.Y. CONST. art. IX, §§ 1, 9, 12.

384. E. Rusco, Municipal Home Rule: Guidelines for Idaho 38 _et seq._ (Bureau of Public Affairs Research, University of Idaho, Res. Mem. No. 1 (1960)).

385. P.117, _supra_. See _also_ Rosenthal, p. 235, _infra_.

386. E.g., Ohio River Valley Water Sanitation Compact, art. IV, OHIO REV. CODE ANN. § 6113.01 (1954).

387. DEL. CODE ANN., tit. 23, § 901m (1953).

388. E.g., _id._

389. The prime example of this is the New York Port Authority. An interstate compact agency between the states of New York and New Jersey, concerned with many aspects of the movement of goods and people in the metropolitan area, the Port Authority is one of the most affluent governments in the metropolitan area. Its enormous political influence is apparent in the Authority's sponsorship, in the face of major political opposition, of such projects as the World Trade Center. Yet, in spite of the importance of its role, the Authority is not obliged to contribute to the solution of transportation and development problems in the metropolitan area as a whole. The Court of Appeals has held that the Authority does not even owe a duty of disclosure to Congress. Tobin v. U.S., 306 Fed. 270, _cert. denied_, 371 U.S. 902 (1962).

390. Note, _The Air Quality Act of 1967_, 54 IOWA L. REV. 115, 135-137 (1968); O'Fallon, _Deficiencies in the Air Quality Act of 1967_, 33 LAW & CONTEMP. PROB. 275 (1968).

391. E.g., MICH. COMP. LAWS ANN. § 257.707 (1967); N.H. REV. STAT. ANN. § 263:46 (1966).

392. Halliday, _supra_ note 131, at 13, 14.

393. Pub. L. No. 91-190, 83 Stat. 852 (1970).

394. States Loosen Restrictions on Use of Highway Revenues 5 STATE GOVERNMENT NEWS, May, 1970, at 2.

395. E.g., OKLA. STAT., tit. 82, § 932(a), (b) (Supp. 1968).

396. E.g., FLA. STAT. ANN. § 403.011 et seq. (Supp. 1970-71).

397. E. & J. Hanks, An Environmental Bill of Rights: The Citizen Suit and the National Environmental Policy Act of 1969, 24 RUTGERS L. REV. 230 (1970).

398. Pub. L. No. 91-190, tit. II, 83 Stat. 852 (1970)

399. Id. § 202.

400. Id. § 204.

401. COUNCIL ON ENVIRONMENTAL QUALITY, ENVIRONMENTAL QUALITY (First Annual Report transmitted to Congress August 1970).

402. CF LETTER, April 1970.

403. Id.

404. Section 207 authorized a $300,000 appropriation for fiscal 1970, $700,000 for fiscal 1971 and $1,000,000 for each fiscal year thereafter.

405. Pub. L. No. 91-224, 84 Stat. 91 (1970).

406. See H.R. REP. No. 91-765, 91st Cong., 1st Sess. 9-10 (1969), commenting on the change in the House bill which did not include this language.

407. Pub. L. No. 91-190, § 102, 83 Stat. 853 (1970); Pub. L. No. 89-554, 80 Stat. 383 (1966); Pub. L. No. 90-23, § 1, 81 Stat. 54 (1967), 5 U.S.C. § 552 (Supp. V, 1965-69).

408. Exec. Order No. 11,514 (March 5, 1970).

409. 35 Fed. Reg. 7390 (1970).

410. Hearings Before the Subcomm. on Fisheries and Wildlife Conservation of the House Comm. on Merchant Marine and Fisheries, 91st Cong., 2d Sess. 69 et seq. (1970). As of August 12, 1970, 26 final and 45 draft statements had been received by the Council. Id. at 71.

411. See D. Sive, Some Thoughts of an Environmental Lawyer in the Wilderness of Administrative Law, 70 COLUM. L. REV. 612, 619 et seq. (1970) for a discussion and suggestion for change in the scope of judicial review in environmental cases.

412. See CF LETTER, supra note 402. Soon after the passage of the Act the Army Corps of Engineers held a press conference to announce the formation of an environmental advisory board to carry out the requirements of the Act. N.Y. Times, April 5, 1970, pt. I, at 91.

413. CF LETTER, supra note 402; Allakaket v. Hickel, C.A. No. 706-70 (D.D.C. April 3, 1970); Texas Committee on National Resources v. United States, No. A-69-CA-119 (W.D. Tex., Feb. 5, 1970). The Act had been cited in at least 17 other court cases and 5 administrative proceedings as of August 1, 1970. Hearings Before the Subcomm. on Fisheries and Wildlife Conservation, supra note 410, at 163.

414. Pub. L. No. 91-190, § 101(c), 83 Stat. 852 (1970)

415. H.R. Rep. No. 91-765, 91st Cong., 1st Sess. 8 (1969).

416. E.g., FLA. STAT. ANN. § 403.011 et seq. (Supp. 1970-71); N.Y. ENVIRONMENTAL CONSERVATION LAW (McKinney Supp. 1970).

417. Reorganization Plan No. 3; Reorganization Plan No. 4 of 1970, H. DOC. NO. 91-365, 91st Cong., 2d Sess. (1970).

418. Reorganization Plan No. 2 of 1965, 30 Fed. Reg. 8819 (1965).

419. Reorganization Plan No. 3 of 1970, § 1.

420. Id. § 4.

421. Id. § 2(a).

422. Id. § 2(a)(5), (b).

423. 116 CONG. REC. H6,525 (daily ed. July 9, 1970.

424. E.g., N.J. STAT. ANN §§ 13:10-1 et seq. (Supp. 1970-71).

425. H. Perry, Air Pollution from Powerplants and Its Control, and J. Middleton, Air Conservation and the Protection of Our Natural Resources 101, 166 PROCEEDINGS, NATIONAL CONFERENCE ON AIR POLLUTION (1963)

426. Pollution is a consequence of using a cheap, convenient waste disposal method. The alternative, no longer to treat air and water as free goods, is impressively expensive. Consider that in 1966, for example, the total budget for all governmental air pollution control programs combined was $20 million; the estimated need was $72 million. Comment, Equity and the Ecosystem: Can Injunctions Clean the Air?, 68 MICH. L. REV. 1254, 1260 n. 33 (May 1970). The electric power industry, in addition to its air pollution problems, faces the problem of thermal pollution (caused by discharge of water for cooling purposes). The Department of Interior estimates that by 1980 the electric power industry will require about one-sixth of the total available fresh-water runoff in the entire nation for cooling purposes. Remarks by Max Edwards, Assistant Secretary of the Interior for Water Pollution Control, before the Natural Resources and Public Utilities Sections of the annual meeting of the American Bar Association, Philadelphia, Pa., Aug. 6, 1968, at 1. The forecasted building cost for cooling towers to control the consequent thermal pollution over the next five-year period is $2 billion. The Cost of Clean Water and its Economic Impact, 1 FEDERAL POLLUTION CONTROL ADMINISTRATION, Jan. 10, 1969, at 158. In the more conventional areas of air pollution control, the costs remain equally impressive. A combined mechanical and electrostatic installation (device to catch cinders and fly ash particles) for a 360,000-kilowatt unit, cost about

$5 million, as early as 1963, representing an invest-
ment of about $14 for each kilowatt of customer
demand. These costs do not include research expenditures. Needless to say, costs in 1970 are even
higher. Hearings on S. 432, S. 444, S. 1009,
S. 1040, S. 1124 and H.R. 6518 Before a Special Sub-
Comm. on Air and Water Pollution of the Senate Comm.
on Public Works, 88th Cong., 1st Sess. 373-75
(1963). A discussion of the costliness and difficulties of removing sulfur-bearing compounds from
coal or oil may be found in PROCEEDINGS, supra note
425.
   Conversely, the costs of pollution are also
staggering. The CEQ estimates the economic costs of
pollution at billions of dollars annually. Evidence
of the damaging effects of air pollution has been
accumulating since 1963. Paint deterioration, higher
cleaning bills, reduced crop yields, and increased
medical bills are some of its costs. On a more
long-term basis, major ecological changes may take
place, including major climatic changes. CEQ, at
17-18. Gerhardt, Incentives to Air Pollution Control,
33 LAW & CONTEMP. PROB. 358 (1968).

   427. Evidence of this contest may be found in the
proliferation of cases involving the Federal Power
Commission's licensing operations. E.g., Udall v.
Federal Power Commission, 387 U.S. 428 (1967); Scenic
Hudson Preservation Conference v. Federal Power Com-
mission, 354 F.2d 608 (2d Cir. 1965), cert. denied,
348 U.S. 941 (1966); Federal Power Commission v.
Union Electric Co., 381 U.S. 90 (1965).

   428. OUR CROWDED PLANET: ESSAYS ON THE PRESSURES
OF POPULATION (Osborn ed. 1962); THE POPULATION
DILEMMA (Hauser ed. 1963); POPULATION BULLETIN, A
SOURCEBOOK ON POPULATION (Nov. 1969) (a bibliography
on population problems of every dimension).

   429. E.g., N.Y. SESSION LAWS, ch. 127 (1970),
amending N.Y. PENAL LAW § 125.05(3) (McKinney 1967).

   430. See Hearings on S. 1676 Before the Subcomm.
on Foreign Aid Expenditures of the Comm. on Government Operations, 89th Cong., 1st Sess. 2013-86 (1965)
(materials on state legislation collected by Sen.
Gruening).

431. Presidential Message to Congress on Population Growth, July 18, 1969, 115 CONG. REC. 20,025 (1969).

432. 22 U.S.C. § 2201, authorizes funds for research into population growth in less developed countries. The states' police power--to protect the public health and safety--has long provided the basis for health legislation generally. Jacobsen v. Massachusetts, 197 U.S. 11 (1904). Laws regulating the performance of abortions, based on the police power, have recently been subjected to a number of limitations, on due process and other constitutional grounds. United States v. Vuitch, 305 F. Supp. 1032 (D.D.C. 1969); Babbitz v. McCann, 310 F. Supp. 293 (E.D. WISC. 1970).

433. Griswold v. Connecticut, 381 U.S. 479 (1965). The Court held that a Connecticut statute that prohibited the use of contraceptives violated the right of marital privacy, a right found within the "penumbra" of other specific guarantees of the Bill of Rights.

434. The problem which such balancing involves, with its juggling of the "value-need" ratio, is illustrated by the 1968 amendments of the Federal Highway Act in response to pressure from conservationist groups. S. REP. NO. 1340, 90th Cong., 2d Sess. 5 (1968).

435. E.g., fully one-third of San Francisco Bay has already been filled in and developers are asking for more. E. Drew, Dam Outrage: The Story of the Army Engineers, 225 ATLANTIC, April 1970, at 60.

Albert J. Rosenthal

Federal Power to Preserve the Environment: Enforcement and Control Techniques

It is the purpose of this paper to examine various ways in which the federal government can compel or induce compliance with environmental standards. Accordingly, some provocative areas of inquiry, such as those pertaining to the substantive standards to be set or the process by which such decisions are to be made, have not been discussed. Since the focus is the enforcement role of the federal government, it also seems necessary to forego consideration of many interesting questions pertaining to the possible role of private litigation in protecting the environment.[1]

Introduction: the Constitutional Power
of the Federal Government

It is sometimes said that the constitutional structure of the United States, with only limited powers
accorded to the federal government, restricts its
ability to act on a nation-wide basis in preserving
the environment and requires it to accomplish its
goals through enlisting the cooperation of state and
local governments.[2] It is suggested that this nation,
unlike those with centralized governments such as
Great Britain, is precluded by law from taking the
steps needed for an all-out national effort to protect
the environment from every challenge. Whatever might
have been the prevailing notions one or two generations
ago, most students of constitutional law would assert
today that this is simply not true. Political considerations calling for restraint in the exercise of
federal power may cause a choice to be made, wisely
or unwisely, in favor of local programs and local
enforcement; it may be that the sheer size and
geographical diversity of our country--unlike Great
Britain--argue for a large measure of local control
as a matter of policy; but such elections should be
frankly recognized as resting upon conscious choice
and not compelled by any constitutional barrier.

SOURCES OF FEDERAL AUTHORITY

The federal government, unlike the states and most
centralized foreign governments, is one of enumerated
powers and can act only within the area of its

218

authority. Yet these powers have been so broadly
extended by a succession of Supreme Court decisions
that virtually any conceivable measure reasonably
intended to protect the environment can readily be sustained under one or more of the grants of authority to
Congress. Regulations forbidding or restricting
activities that contribute to pollution or otherwise
despoil the environment, a wide range of criminal
and civil sanctions to ensure   adherence to these
regulations, and the spending of government funds for
research, as well as incentives for desired conduct,
are all within the power of the federal government
if it chooses to act.

The Commerce Power

Direct federal regulation, including outright prohibition where it is deemed appropriate, of virtually
every activity tending to contaminate the environment
may be sustained under the federal power over interstate and foreign commerce. Federal authority to
forbid water pollution need not be limited to interstate or boundary streams or to navigable waters.
Federal authority to protect the quality of the air
need not depend on the argument that the movement of
contaminating gases or particles is a form of commerce.
Pesticides need not be traced across state lines
before federal power may be invoked. Solid wastes
may remain in the state where they are dumped without
conferring immunity from federal control. Congress
can act in all of these areas if it sees fit.

The commerce power has been by far the most widely

used--and upheld--regulatory weapon in the congressional arsenal. From its initial definition by John
Marshall in <u>Gibbons</u> v. <u>Ogden</u>,[3] "commerce" has been
given an extremely broad construction and once it is
found that interstate commerce is involved, the power
of Congress "may be exercised to the utmost extent
and acknowledges no limitations other than those
prescribed in the Constitution."[4]

Thus, anything which may be properly characterized
as "interstate commerce" may be regulated, or indeed
forbidden by Congress. But that is not all. The
power to regulate or protect interstate commerce
extends to include the power to control those things
which are not commerce or are purely intrastate commerce, provided that such control is reasonably deemed
by Congress to be of assistance in the regulation or
fostering of interstate commerce itself.

For example, while the production of goods intended
to move in interstate commerce may not, in itself, be
deemed "commerce," Congress may regulate the circumstances of that production, including the wages, hours[5]
and labor relations[6] of those employed in it. Nor need
goods move, or even be intended to move, in interstate
commerce to be subject to federal regulation. A trivial
amount of wheat produced by a small farmer entirely
for use on his own farm was held to be an integral
part of the supply of a commodity, some of which moves
in interstate commerce, and therefore subject to
congressional regulation in order to control the interstate price.[7] Even though the effect of a single
person's conduct "may be trivial by itself," Congress

is entitled to consider the total impact of "his contribution taken together with that of many others
similarly situated."[8]

Thus, such essentially local activities as the
refusal of a restaurant, a motel, or even an amusement
area, to serve a black customer have been held subject
to proscription, on the basis of the congressional
finding that such refusals inhibit the interstate
transportation of food, or entertainment equipment, or
the interstate movement of travelers.[9]

Moreover, the fact that the power of Congress is
sought to promote a social objective unrelated to
business is no bar to its exercise.[10] Thus, the Court
has upheld the application of the commerce power to
prohibit the interstate transportation of lottery
tickets.[11] It is interesting that in reaching its
decision the Court characterized the decision of
Congress as one that "such commerce shall not be
polluted by the carrying of lottery tickets from one
state to another."[12] Other instances of Court-approved
use of the commerce power for purposes not related to
business include prohibitions of the transportation of
persons for purposes of prostitution,[13] or even
amateur immorality,[14] and the interstate transportation of a kidnapped person.[15]

In addition, in upholding the federal power over
wages and hours in employment, the Court in United
States v. Darby[16] sustained prohibition of interstate
transportation of goods manufactured through use of
labor employed contrary to the federal standards,
and, as a means of implementing this, Congress was

permitted to forbid their manufacture as well.[17] The
Court has therefore, it would seem, drawn up the blue-
print for almost any exercise of congressional power.
Something--anything--is prohibited from movement in
interstate commerce, and then to make this prohibition
effective, that something cannot be produced at all.

Therefore, if Congress wishes to forbid a manufacturing process which pollutes the air or the water,
or the manufacture of a product which itself will be
damaging--e.g., detergents containing phosphates--it
may forbid the movement in interstate commerce of the
product and then to implement this prohibition forbid
its manufacture as well. Indeed, the power of Congress
to forbid the manufacture need not rest upon its exercise of the power to forbid the interstate movement;
if the manufacture itself may affect interstate commerce
it may be regulated or prohibited even though Congress
elects not to forbid interstate transportation of the
product.[18]

Alternatively, Congress can, after appropriate
hearings, reach the factual conclusion that air pollution, or water pollution (even of intrastate, non-
navigable, streams), hurts interstate commerce by
injuring crops, farm animals or fish, impeding aerial
or possibly even surface transportation, discouraging
travel for employment or recreation, etc. On the basis
that even the acts of one small polluter, whose
effluence alone would be insignificant, looms large
when taken in conjunction with those of thousands of
others, a rationale for total control may be readily
put forward.[19]

In many situations there are alternate grounds for congressional exercise of the commerce power to control the waterways or the airways as highways for commerce.[20] If it were necessary, arguments could be made that not only interstate waterways, but even intrastate navigable waterways used or susceptible of use by interstate commerce, fall within the regulatory power of Congress.[21] Alternatively, it might be asserted that the pollutants themselves were articles in commerce, the movement of which could be regulated.[22] These approaches might, however, fail to provide a basis for regulation of pollution of a non-navigable, purely intrastate body of water;[23] while every river reputedly finds its way into the sea, there must be some lakes, and streams feeding lakes, the entire systems of which are entirely within the borders of a single state.

The air, of course, is subject to no such confining process and it must be assumed that every molecule ultimately finds its way to every part of the world.[24] Hence, if particles or gases emitted into the air are regarded as themselves articles of commerce, there would be no doubt of their inclusion in interstate streams of air; their movement, as air pollutants, across a state line would constitute interstate commerce. Even offensive odors have been held to be air pollution moving in interstate commerce.[25] Alternatively, if visibility is affected by concentrations of particles, or possibly gases, even if they did not cross a state line, their interference with interstate air navigation would seem to be a sufficient basis for federal control.[26] But again, there are other grounds for asserting federal control, suggested above, falling much more closely within established constitutional doctrines.

The Power to Tax and Spend

The power to spend money is an important device available to Congress for accomplishing many purposes. Some of its possible uses for purposes of protecting the environment will be explored below. Expenditures generally do not give rise to constitutional issues, at least in the absence of a violation of one of the negative commands of the Constitution such as that forbidding the establishment of religion. The spending power may be used only for the "general welfare,"[27] as distinguished from narrower purposes, but it is difficult to believe that the protection of the national environment would not be sufficiently general to pass any test, even assuming that there were a litigant with standing to challenge the expenditure.[28] After all, the environment is the epitome of what is "general."

The taxing power is equally broad, and except for a few limitations not here pertinent, may be regarded as substantially untrammeled.[29] If a tax is primarily a camouflaged regulation rather than a revenue-raising measure, there is still little likelihood of successful challenge to it. First of all, the Supreme Court has been extremely willing to adopt the characterization given by Congress and accept the tax at face value.[30] But if, in a rare case, the Court regarded the "tax" as not a revenue measure at all but a purely regulatory one, it would still uphold it if it could be sustained under one of Congress' regulatory powers--for example, its power over interstate commerce.[31]

These considerations are pertinent when the question of the effluent charge[32] is raised. This is a suggested device, discussed below, whereby a polluter (generally of water) is taxed an amount measured by the cost of cleaning up the quantity and type of effluent he emits, with the proceeds used for such treatment operations. Whether the charge be regarded as a revenue-raising measure, or more like a protective tariff aimed at discouraging rather than raising money, it nevertheless would stand up. If the charge is part of a scheme, modeled perhaps on that in use in the Ruhr Valley in Germany,[33] of earmarking money taken from polluters for financing the processes of purification, a possible attack might be made on the basis of United States v. Butler,[34] but it may be confidently predicted that the Court would uphold the plan.

In Butler, a tax on processors of certain agricultural products was specifically earmarked for payments to the farmers who had grown the crops. The Court, during the high water period of judicial invalidation of New Deal economic measures, held that the processor had standing to attack the tax imposed on himself, and could then bring into question the entire scheme; since the awarding of benefits to farmers was intended to purchase adherence to a regulatory scheme then regarded as beyond the powers of Congress, the Court invalidated the entire program. Subsequent decisions cast doubt upon the continued force of this precedent,[35] but in any event

at least two distinctions would make it inapplicable
to the effluent charge: (1) The proposal does not
involve any buying of cooperation; and (2) the entire
program could be sustained independently under the
commerce power, which at the time of the <u>Butler</u>
decision was not deemed sufficient to uphold the
agricultural program there involved.[36]

The Treaty Power

If these grants of power are not sufficient, there
are still further grounds for federal authority in
the area. Under the treaty power, for example, the
President can enter into an agreement with another
nation whereby both agree to engage in or refrain
from designated conduct; thereafter, Congress can
implement this treaty through legislation which in
the absence of the treaty it might not have had the
power to enact.[37] For example, an attempt by Congress
in 1913 to legislate protection over migratory birds
had been held unconstitutional by two lower courts,
which did not deem the commerce power to be applicable.[38]
(It is doubtful whether that result would be reached
today.) In 1916, the President, with the consent of
two-thirds of the Senate, then entered into a treaty[39]
with Great Britain[40] providing for mutual protection of
the birds by the United States and Canada. Following
this, Congress in 1918 enacted legislation forbidding
the killing, capture or sale of such birds. Assuming
<u>arguendo</u> that such legislation would not have been
within the power of Congress in the absence of the
treaty, in <u>Missouri</u> v. <u>Holland</u> [41]the Court nevertheless
upheld it as an implementation of the treaty.

Thus the United States could enter into a treaty with Canada whereby both nations agreed not to pollute the air or the water.[42] Especially between neighboring countries, there would be no problem as to the validity of such a treaty. To the extent that air pollution crossed the international boundary, the mutual interest of the two nations would be clear, and it may be assumed that even though prevailing winds are generally from West to East there is a sufficient possibility of North-South movement to sustain any implementation deemed desirable by Congress. Even as to the pollution of waters which do not serve as or move across international boundaries, the effect on the total continental ecology (through killing of wildlife, etc.) would appear ample to sustain similar broad legislation.

But the validity of such a treaty or of legislation intended to implement it would not seem to depend on the proximity of the signatory nations; protection of the environment would seem to be a most appropriate subject for international agreement.[43] Doubts as to validity would arise only if the use of the treaty power were a clear subterfuge intended to permit Congress to do something which it could not otherwise do. If, for example, we entered into a water pollution treaty with a remote nation with which we had virtually no physical or commercial relationship or interest-- e.g., Vietnam?--the treaty might be deemed so flagrant an attempt to raise the federal power by its own bootstraps as to be treated as nugatory.[44] In such an improbable event, federal power would

have to rest upon some other basis; even so, there
would seem to be no difficulty.[45]

POSSIBLE LIMITATIONS

Thus far we have discussed the affirmative bases
for federal authority, without considering such
limitations as there may be upon a grant of authority
which is applicable prima facie but might nevertheless
run afoul of some other constitutional prohibition.
By way of analogy, Congress can certainly regulate
interstate railroads, but it could not forbid Democrats
to travel on them.

Just Compensation

The Fifth Amendment proscribes the taking of
private property for public use except upon payment
of just compensation. Presumably, the argument can
be made in some states that one who owns land abutting
a stream has certain "property" rights incidental to it,
which may be regarded traditionally as including the
right to dump waste products into the stream; under the
law of other states, analogous claims may be based
upon "appropriation" of water through prior use of it.
A large body of law has evolved concerning rights to
discharge wastes into waterways, the relative posi-
tions of upstream and downstream users, the development
of prescriptive rights and the doctrines of appropriation and res communes.[46] But all of these asserted
rights, if they can be elevated to the status of
"property" at all,[47] are presumably subject to the
police power of the appropriate state or local

government[48] and its analogue, the regulatory power
of the federal government.[49] Certainly, as to navigable
waterways the authorities appear clear that the property rights of abutting owners are subject to federal
regulation.[50] And to the degree that the federal power
may extend to non-navigable intrastate waters as well,
the same reasoning could also subordinate any asserted
property right to such regulatory authority.

The police power--meaning, in effect, the right of
government to legislate in the public interest[51]--when
used for a legitimate purpose has frequently tended to
qualify otherwise existing property rights.[52] "Most
regulations of business necessarily impose financial
burdens on the enterprise for which no compensation
is paid. These are part of the cost of our civiliza-
tion."[53]

Air and water pollution may properly be characterized as a nuisance; if there is a property right to
continue to commit such a nuisance, it is certainly
subject to legislative abridgement, without compensation, in the interest of the public welfare.[54] Indeed,
a state may, if it wishes, destroy one industry if it
finds it essential in order to protect another.[55] The
federal government, wherever one of its grants of
power gives it reach, may do much the same things as
the states may under their more generalized police
power.[56]

Even more clearly, there is no "property right" to
pollute the air. While the property owner was once
thought to have rights to the air above his land up
to the heavens, this is very much qualified by the

right of aircraft to traverse his air space[57] and, moreover, would not necessarily include the right to emit particles or gases which would quickly pass into the air space over someone else's property.[58]

While the dividing line between valid regulation under the police power or other grants of legislative authority on the one hand, and a taking of private property for public use for which the Constitution requires compensation, is not easily defined,[59] regulation of pollution would seem to fall clearly within the area where compensation is not required.

Due Process of Law

Federal legislation, even if enacted pursuant to a constitutional grant of authority, must still be consistent with the prohibition against taking life, liberty or property without due process of law, found in the Fifth Amendment. From a procedural standpoint, this may require that the proceedings of regulatory or other administrative agencies meet standards of basic fairness.

At an earlier period of constitutional interpretation, the due process clause was also used to strike down legislation on the ground that it was substantively unfair or unreasonable.[60] The Supreme Court has, in recent years, veered away from this approach;[61] there have been almost no instances in which the Court has invalidated either federal or state legislation on grounds of substantive due process,[62] and apparently none at all in cases of economic regulation.[63] The types of environmental control measures currently in contemplation could scarcely be regarded as likely to give rise to serious objections on substantive due process grounds, even assuming the present vitality of the doctrine.

It is possible, however, to conceive of a later era, in which the environmental situation has become so critical that much more drastic measures, sharply curtailing individual liberty, are seriously contemplated; in such a case constitutional problems might indeed arise. If, for example, no satisfactory answer to environmental problems can be found so long as population continues to grow at its present pace, we are likely to consider elimination of tax exemptions for children after the second, or third. If that fails to reduce the birth rate to a sufficient degree, the next step might be the imposition of an additional tax upon the more fecund, and, ultimately, suggestions for limitations upon the number of babies a couple is permitted to have, compulsory contraception, or the eventual proposal that parents of two or more children be sterilized.[64] If and when that issue comes to the fore, there will undoubtedly be a serious debate as to the constitutional, as well as the ethical, religious, and practical overtones of this kind of emission control; however, it would seem premature to explore it at this time.[65]

Political Limitations

Much more significant than the limitations imposed by the Constitution in a legal, judicially enforced,

sense are the practical political factors which have
thus far restricted the federal role in the protection
of the environment and may be expected to have a
restraining influence in at least the near future.
As pointed out by Professor Wechsler: "National
action has always been regarded as exceptional in
our polity, an intrusion to be justified by some
necessity, the special rather than the ordinary case
. . . .The tradition plainly serves the values of our
federalism insofar as it maintains a burden of persuasion on those favoring national intervention."[66]

We have undoubtedly reached the point at which, in
the judgment of many students of environment, that burden has been met and need for a much larger federal role
has become manifest. Even so, there are serious doubts
whether in a nation as vast as ours, complete centralization of control over environmental protection would
be wise, even if it were politically feasible.[67]

Caution as to Preemption

Congressional action under a grant of power such as
the commerce clause may displace state law, under the
Supremacy Clause of the Constitution.[68] Frequently, however, Congress prefers to permit all or certain kinds of
state regulation to coexist with its own requirements.
If it expresses its intention to preempt or not to preempt with sufficient clarity, its expression should be
decisive. But federal laws are often less than clear
in this respect, and the courts are left with the difficult task of ascertaining the "intention" of Congress
on questions which it had probably not considered.

Until recently, federal statutes on water and air pollution expressly left large areas of responsibility to the states.[69] With the apparently inevitable increased assumption of responsibility by the federal government in these fields, however, questions of how much authority is left to the state and local governments will have to be faced. Where state regulations are more permissive than federal, there should, of course, be no difficulty in striking them down. But when a state seeks to insist on standards of environmental protection more stringent than those imposed by federal authority, decisions will have to be reached as to whether the interest in having a single comprehensive plan and in achieving nationwide uniformity of regulation is sufficiently great to justify forbidding the state from so acting.[70]

Congress will, therefore, probably have to give more attention in the future to avoiding the unwitting exercise of its power in such fashion as to strike down under the Supremacy Clause state laws intended to protect the environment.

* * * *

Assuming, therefore, almost plenary power in the federal government to legislate for the protection of the environment, we must turn to the techniques which can be used to accomplish this purpose, the various carrots and sticks available to induce or compel compliance with the government's decisions in this area.

It should be recognized at the outset that good intentions will not be sufficient to save the environment.

233

Pollution will not be ended through individual housewives rejecting detergents containing phosphates, col-
lege students refusing to buy beer in throwaway cans,
motorists insisting on lead-free gasoline. Nor is
any major contribution to the solution likely to be
found in voluntary measures on the part of public-
spirited business concerns. In most situations, under
current rules of the game, it pays to pollute, and
the company that increases its expenses substantially
to avoid doing so will generally find itself at a competitive disadvantage; on the other hand, if all competing firms were subjected to the same regulations,
all would have an incentive to comply, especially if
we succeed in making it sufficiently expensive to harm
the environment, or sufficiently cheap to preserve it,
or a combination of both.

Direct Regulation

TYPES OF SANCTION

Thus far we have had only a trickle of enforcement,
as contrasted with torrents of pollution. While no
devices to compel compliance can succeed in the absence
of a national commitment to save the environment, there
is reason to hope that such a commitment may be forthcoming; it is therefore important to explore ways in
which it can be turned to most effective use.

The most obvious way to discourage any kind of
conduct deemed undesirable is to prohibit it and to

make it painful for anyone who violates the prohibition. There are a number of traditional legal devices which can be used for this purpose.[71] When sought to be applied in cases of damage to the environment, however, some of these sanctions may not work well.

Criminal Prosecution

Perhaps the most direct sanction is to make violation a crime. Despite the emphasis in state anti-pollution legislation on criminal, as opposed to other types of sanction,[72] criminal prosecutions have seldom been used effectively in the enforcement of environmental protection laws. There are several possible explanations.

First of all, if anything more than a small fine (analogous to that given for a parking violation) is to be imposed, tradition,[73] perhaps reinforced by a constitutional mandate,[74] may require that there be a showing of some kind of mens rea. To impose a substantial prison term, willfulness, or at least negligence, would probably have to be proved beyond a reasonable doubt.[75] Since the most important polluters are likely to be large business concerns, it will often be impossible to prove the personal culpability of individual officers or employees. (Corporations can, of course, be fined but can scarcely be imprisoned.) And in a criminal prosecution, the government will have to prove its case beyond a reasonable doubt, and because of the privilege against self-incrimination it may have to do so without the benefits of discovery of information known to the defendant; moreover, if it loses in the trial court, it may not appeal.[76]

235

There is also the difficulty of establishing a level
of punishment which will be effective. One may well
doubt the effectiveness of our criminal law as a whole,
as well as find difficulty in evaluating its actual
deterrent effect. But at least where there is a strong
public revulsion toward the offense and the offender,
there can generally be a wider range of punishment which
may be severe enough to have whatever deterrent value
punishments ever have and yet not be so harsh as to
deter a judge from imposing them or a jury from con-
victing.

This degree of latitude may not be available,
however, where criminal sanctions for pollution are
concerned. It is doubtful that public opinion has yet
reached the point, in spite of rapidly growing interest
in the protection of the environment, that one who
murders a lake would be regarded as comparably culpable
to one who murders a person.[77] At the other end of the
spectrum is the fact that small fines[78] simply will not
deter large corporations. It is quite clear, for
example, that the attempts by Consolidated Edison to
reduce its pollution of New York City's atmosphere
have not been the result of the occasional $25 or $100
fines imposed upon it.[79]

As long as the context appears to the public to be
a commercial one, and the net damage done by any one
act on the part of one polluter is not clearly discern-
ible, the situation may continue to resemble that which
has obtained in connection with enforcement of the antitrust laws. In that area, the criminal sanction has
played a negligible part,[80] while the injunction, the

divestment order and the private treble damage action have all been of much greater significance.[81]

Civil Penalties

The imposition of monetary penalties in a non-criminal proceeding may be an effective substitute for a prosecution[82] if the latter is merely for the sake of levying a fine. Such penalties may have substantial deterrent value, particularly if they can be imposed administratively.[83] The National Air Quality Standards Act of 1970, if enacted in the form in which it passed the Senate, would provide for civil penalties of up to $10,000 per day, as well as criminal penalties of up to $25,000 per day [84]--sums large enough to give even major corporations considerable pause. Much can also be said for the technique, previously proposed in a different context,[85] of establishing mandatory cumulative penalties as a means of providing a reasonable and credible sanction.

There is fairly clear authority for the characterization of such penalties as civil. This characterization would allow them to be imposed without the usual safeguards in criminal proceedings, such as trial by jury and proof beyond a reasonable doubt.[86] Nevertheless, there can never be assurance that a sanction so nearly criminal in all but name will not be so regarded by the courts.[87]

Injunctions

The most effective remedy against a business concern violating a law, and certainly the most widely used,

is the injunction. As a civil remedy it may be granted
upon a mere preponderance of the evidence, and although
scienter or willfulness may be relevant,[88] neither
should be a prerequisite to relief from environmental
wrongs. While there may, on the one hand, be one or
possibly two levels of appeal, on the other hand a
temporary restraining order is also possible, as well
as a preliminary injunction. If a stay pending appeal
is refused, the questioned practices may be brought
to an immediate halt.

There is some doubt, however, whether courts will
grant such immediate relief when the practice sought
to be enjoined is one which has been going on for years
and the enforcement attempt is directed toward improvement in the quality of the environment.[89] There is
obvious tension between the possibility of immediate
injunctive relief, before trial or even ex parte, and
the practice of granting stays of injunctions pending
appeal. It may be resolved on the basis of whether the
relief sought is against a long-standing abuse, such
as the continued pollution of a river, or a projected
new affront, such as the dramatic and irreversible
desecration of a mountain. Courts are more likely to
interpose an immediate barrier to a new rape than they
are to a long-continued defilement.[90] Even greater
difficulty in achieving quick injunctive relief will
probably be encountered if the defendant can show the
prospect of serious loss, and perhaps a sharp curtail-
ment of employment in the affected plant.[91]

One would at least hope, however, that enforcement
authorities will be permitted to institute injunction

proceedings as quickly as possible. A recent threat to
start an action against the Penn Central Railroad if
after six months it was continuing to pollute the
Hudson River[92] seems startling; if six months is a
reasonable period in which correction may be completed,
it would appear appropriate to sue immediately and ask
that the court order compel the defendant to eliminate
the offending practice within six months.[93] Similarly,
the shocking delay of about five years from the time
of institution of charges to final effectiveness of
a court order in the single federal air pollution case
brought to judgment[94] suggests that serious attention
must be given to the time factor as a major deter-
minant of the effectiveness of the sanction.

There is therefore substantial likelihood that if
the injunction is to be the principal weapon relied
upon, polluters may find it economically advantageous
to give no more than lip service toward correction and
to keep on polluting until the last order of the last
court is finally affirmed and rehearing denied. Procedures calling for protracted conferences and consul-
tations before litigation may commence[95] must be modified
in the interest of speed. If this is done, the injunction
can become a truly effective enforcement technique.

Actions for Damages

The civil action for damages sometimes serves as an
effective enforcement device. An action for damages
brought by the federal government might run into difficulties in establishing what monetary damage the
government itself--as distinguished from its citizens--

had suffered. In many cases, it might be difficult to prove this to have been substantial. Another approach might be to permit the government to recover for all damage inflicted upon private persons except to the extent that the private persons themselves brought suit. An analogue might be found in the Emergency Price Control Act of 1942,[96] which permitted the government to recover up to treble damages in cases of sales above maximum price levels. Where the sale was for use in trade or business the government's right was immediate; where it was to a private consumer the government could sue only if the consumer failed to bring suit within a specified period. Courts at the time were divided on the question of whether such treble damage actions by the government were to be characterized as "remedial" or "penal,"[97] but there was ultimately no dispute that what was involved was a civil action and that the special requirements imposed in criminal prosecutions were not applicable.[98]

Even assuming creation of a sanction of this kind, there still remains the problem of proof of damage. When under the price control laws a seller charged $2,000 for an automobile whose ceiling price was $1,700, there was no difficulty in computing single damages of $300 and hence treble damages of $900. How does one measure, however, the harm done to the inhabitants of New York City, or of other downwind areas, coming from a power plant whose stacks gush sulfur dioxide or noxious particles, an automobile emitting hydrocarbons or carbon monoxide, or an apartment house incinerator casting up large quantities of

soot? Assuming that such legislation can affirma-
tively create causes of action for pollution-caused
injuries, the problems of proof of causation and
damages remain extremely difficult.[99] The civil
penalty, on the other hand, may be imposed without
such proof; in most instances it would be a far
more effective remedy, requiring only a showing that
the prohibited acts had occurred or that prescribed
acts had been omitted.

Licensing

Another possible device for enforcement would be
a program of licensing of businesses, with a forfeiture of license to be imposed upon violation of
regulations or perhaps upon a second violation after
one warning. Across the board licensing was employed
by the Office of Price Administration pursuant to an
authorization in the Emergency Price Control Act of
1942;[100] all sellers were declared subject to licensing,
all were automatically given a license, and licenses
were to be suspended for up to a year upon a second
offense.[101] This device was not used with any frequency as a mechanism for controlling prices, and was
presumably not thought to be as effective as the civil
and criminal penalties also available.[102] Its very
harshness probably tended to make the sanction unpal-
atable to the regulators and rendered the threat
incredible to the regulated. Moreover, loss of a needed
facility such as a power plant, or the economic fallout from closing down a major industrial establishment,
would in many cases be so great as to discourage any
effort to invoke such a power.

Nevertheless, isolated instances of closedown to meet the growing environmental crisis can be found[103] (although not in a licensing context), and such action may be a barometer of a changing public climate and judicial response. The licensing device with its suspension features may find favor as the crisis deepens.[104]

Seizure and Forfeiture

Another technique available to the federal government is to take possession of an offending plant and operate it in such fashion as to comply with environmental law. Seizure of property in the public interest has occasionally been employed, most notably in order to compel continued production despite a strike.[105] The same approach could be followed in the case of a particularly flagrant polluter, with the government taking over the plant, correcting the offending process, and then returning the plant, with the question of compensation deferred for later litigation in the Court of Claims.[106] To the extent that production could be continued during the changeover, it would be possible to avoid the community resentment which follows upon loss of jobs.

A more drastic form of seizure would be the forfeiture of the offending plant to the government, with no compensation and no return. Laws exist, authorizing forfeiture of property used in committing certain kinds of violations:[107] boats employed in smuggling, automobiles used in the dope traffic, distilleries violating the alcohol tax laws, all are subject to seizure under

such statutes.[108] Since forfeiture is considered
a drastic remedy, not favored by the courts, the
cases have tended to construe such statutes strictly.[109]
Similar powers are authorized in the Sherman Act,[110]
but apparently have never been utilized.[111] Judge
Taft (in the only case to consider this provision)[112]
interpreted the Sherman Act provisions to mean that
antitrust forfeiture proceedings should follow the
procedures used under the revenue laws.[113]

Safeguards required in criminal cases may not be
applicable in forfeiture proceedings. In The Palmyra,[114]
the Supreme Court stated that "The thing is here primarily considered as the offender, or rather the
offence is attached primarily to the thing. . ." and
in Dobbins[115] it said: "Nothing can be plainer in
legal decision than the proposition that the offence
therein defined is attached primarily to the distillery. . .without any regard whatsoever to the personal
misconduct or responsibility of the owner. . ."

Thus, the forfeiture proceeding has traditionally
been regarded as a civil proceeding in rem rather than
criminal. Its basis is grounded in the primitive
anthropomorphic notion of endowing objects with
personality and attributing responsibility to them.[116]
Certainly, an environmental offense might then be said
to attach to the factory or plant and, conceivably,
forfeiture might be invoked by the government, which
would take it over with no constitutional obligation
to compensate the owners.[117] The burden of managing
such a plant might not be one easily assumed by the
government, although such responsibility has been

accepted from time to time, as in the seizure of
alien enemy property in wartime.[118] Thus, forfeiture
would serve as a serious threat hanging over the heads
of polluting companies (perhaps augmented by officers'
and directors' fear of stockholders' actions), but
would not result in the loss of the plant's economic
contribution to the community.

There is doubt, however, whether the characterization of forfeiture cases as civil actions in rem
automatically insulates them from at least some of
the constitutional safeguards with which criminal
proceedings are invested.[119] Further refinements in
their characterization may be expected.[120]

POINT OF APPLICATION

Apart from the question of the kind of sanction to
be employed, there are a wide range of possible stages
at which they might be applied. The question of the
point at which to concentrate enforcement is closely
related, of course, to the question of what aspects
of the problem are best subject to regulation. This
paper is concerned with the latter only to the extent
that it relates to the former.

For example, while prohibition of emission of certain
matter into the air or the water is one way to curtail
it, it is not the only way. Regulation, together with
enforcement sanctions, may in some circumstances be
applied at an earlier stage of a process. For example,
control of the sulfur content of fuel oil used in
power production has been employed effectively to
reduce the emission of sulfur oxides into the atmosphere

in New York City[121] and elsewhere. Where such a
"toll gate" on the stream of pollution is available,
proof of non-compliance is comparatively easy, and
almost any of the criminal or civil sanctions referred
to above might well prove effective. Sanctions against
actual emissions do not have to be dropped--the two
techniques are not mutually exclusive--but a limited
enforcement budget may well go many times as far if
there is available a "pressure point" of this sort
toward which they can be directed.

As a substantive matter, it is of course most
desirable that regulations offer the potential polluter the widest possible range of choices of methods by
which to avoid damaging the environment, allowing him
to reach the decision most in accordance with his own
self-interest and therefore presumably least wasteful
economically.[122] This principle probably has to be
sacrificed, however, in some situations where limited
enforcement budgets dictate the application of controls
at those points in the process at which enforcement is
most feasible and least expensive. Ideally, regulatory
decisions should be made first without regard to
enforcement problems and the enforcement techniques
only then applied to ensure their application. At
times, however, it may be necessary to consider the
ease or difficulty of enforcement as a relevant factor
in shaping the regulatory technique.

Where the source of pollution is not a manufacturing
process but a manufactured product, there is again the
possibility of control of what is manufactured as an
addition or an alternative to control over the use of

the product. For example, it seems easier to prohibit the manufacture of detergents containing phosphates than to forbid housewives to use them or to require municipalities to install sewage treatment plants to control their effects.

Several such techniques are available in connection with the automobile. Regulation of the design of newly manufactured cars to reduce their pollution of the air affords a partial solution. But since cars that start clean may become dirty and since there are well over 80 million old cars already on the highways,[123] enforcement at the manufacturing level obviously provides no complete answer. Nevertheless, in conjunction with other techniques,[124] it may contribute toward a solution.

Again, control over the fuels used in automobiles--for example, forbidding gasoline containing lead--might further help reduce automobile pollution. In drawing up regulations, the technology of both the fuel and the engines would have to be considered. Once decisions were made, however, it might be possible to enforce them by applying sanctions to violations in the manufacture or sale of forbidden fuels; in the manufacture, sale or use of automobiles with forbidden engine design; in the use of an automobile violating emission standards; or in a combination of several of these.

A range of possible enforcement devices is available in connection with the problems created by packaging materials. Paper wrappings or metal, glass or plastic containers which are not returnable could be forbidden or, to the extent that technological developments permit, those which are not rapidly degradable could be barred. The prohibition could be applied to their use at the source, to their transportation in interstate commerce, or (probably less effectively) over the disposition of the product by the last user. Such materials are a primary source of solid waste, but since they are also often disposed of in air or water, they give rise to other types of pollution as well. Industry-wide prohibitions might diminish the reluctance, for competitive reasons, of a single manufacturer to eschew harmful packaging materials; for example, soft drink and beer companies might cheerfully abandon throwaway cans and bottles if their competitors were obliged to do the same.[125]

Perhaps this approach need not be limited to packaging or fuel controls. In some circumstances, regulation of all of the materials used or processes employed in an entire activity, such as a manufacturing operation or the generation of power, might afford the best, or possibly even the only effective method of minimizing environmental damage.[126]

The classical technique of federal regulation is to forbid the movement of objectionable items in interstate commerce. This could be applied to those goods whose inherent properties are not objectionable, but whose process of manufacture causes damage. It could also include goods which could be expected to do harm at a later stage--such as the throwaway beer bottle or the automobile which could be expected to pollute the atmosphere.[127]

The most obvious point of impact in most instances,
however, is likely to be the emission of pollutants
themselves. This is a difficult and expensive area
to monitor and it may not be easy to ascertain what
effect the individual polluter may have upon the
total character of the air quality region or watershed.
Thus, where the nature of the problem is such that
other points of application are feasible, they should
be given serious consideration. There will probably
remain, however, a large number of situations in which
control over emissions will be the only effective mode
of enforcement.

Subsidies, Incentives and Charges

GRANTS

While federal enforcement efforts are still limited,
the principal contribution of the federal government
has been the granting of money to finance pollution
treatment[128] and the use of its fiscal resources, rather
than its regulatory power, to prod the nation in the
direction it wishes it to move.[129]

The most frequent form of these grants is to governmental bodies, state and local, for construction, contro
and research--in particular, the award of money for
municipal sewage treatment plants and similar devices.[13
Grants may be conditioned on compliance with federal
standards. Funds made available on a matching basis[131]
reduce the net cost to the recipient governmental

authority. They also strengthen the hand of those favoring construction of the plants, not only in making them less expensive, but also in permitting use of the argument that these attractive federal funds are ready and waiting and should not be allowed to remain unused or, worse still, go to another community.

Grants may also be made directly to private enterprise[132] in order to assist in the purchase or construction of facilities to reduce their pollution.[133] In most cases, economies of scale would make preferable the awarding of grants to public authorities rather than to private polluters in the same area. This factor may be pertinent in connection with water pollution and solid waste disposal, but it is unlikely to have any relevance to the air pollution problem.

Giving grants to private concerns to encourage them to cure their own damaging processes raises many other problems. If a finite amount of money is to do the most good, presumably it has to be used to encourage future improvement rather than to reward past accomplishments. Yet, this tends to give a seemingly unfair advantage to the recalcitrant company which has resisted public demands that it cease polluting and to penalize the public-minded company which expended large sums of money to correct its processes before it was either legally compelled or offered any bribes to do so.[134] More important, there is serious doubt as to the desirability of having the public finance the cost of correcting the effluence of industrial polluters.[135] Presumptively, such costs should be borne by the users of the products which give rise to them, although there may be instances when it would be appropriate for the public as a whole to bear part or all of these expenses.

A possible use of subsidies in the private sector which might be less vulnerable to the foregoing objections would be the granting of incentives to concerns which could reclaim the waste products of others but only at a loss. If the cost would be less than that involved in any other satisfactory method of disposal, such a subsidy might be justified. At the same time, government-sponsored research might find ways in which the reclamation process could be made profitable and the subsidies discontinued.[136]

There may well be some plants which cannot be made to conform to reasonable environmental standards at any economically feasible price. As previously shown,[137] it is not believed that there is any Constitutional requirement to compensate such enterprises for putting them out of business. Nevertheless, there may be valid arguments for taking over such plants, compensating the owners and providing for generous termination pay, retraining programs, or both, for the displaced employees. It will probably be found that for a somewhat smaller expenditure, most plants can be made to produce cleanly or if necessary be converted into a different type of operation, either under the same ownership and management or pursuant to a government takeover.

TAX WRITE-OFFS AND CREDITS

An indirect form of subsidy which has proliferated

in recent years due to its political attractiveness is
the awarding of favorable tax treatment. While the
impact of the various forms of taxation imposed by
state and local governments[138] upon business enterprises is usually insufficient to play a major part
in business planning or, certainly, to induce construction of what would otherwise be an uneconomical
pollution control apparatus, the large federal
corporate income tax (or in cases of individual or
partnership enterprises, personal income tax) is of
an entirely different dimension.

But such plans as are advanced, as well as those
already in effect, offer only modest incentives. The
principal forms of tax assistance are either an
"investment credit" of the order of seven per cent[139]
or a provision for accelerating depreciation.[140] The
former would be pleasant to receive, but will only in
rare cases be decisive in the arrival at a business
decision.[141] Accelerated depreciation, theoretically
at least, means no more than deferment of the time
when part of a tax obligation is due, rather than complete elimination of it. This is the equivalent of
an interest-free loan for the amount of tax deferred
over the period of deferment, but, again, it is not
too likely to serve as a major incentive. If, through
sale or otherwise, the deferred tax may be ultimately
avoided entirely or reflected only in a capital gain,
the value of the device is augmented for the taxpayer,
but it still may not, except in rare cases, induce
action which would not be forthcoming anyway.[142]

Moreover, tax relief is a most inefficient way of

giving subsidies.[143] The expertise necessary for
careful tailoring of incentives to induce the precise
action needed is far less likely to be found in the
Senate Finance Committee, the House Ways and Means
Committee or the Internal Revenue Service than in the
Congressional committees and agencies of the
Executive Branch that have been directly concerned
with the substantive problem. Less, rather than more,
efficient programs may be encouraged. Many concerns
will undoubtedly secure tax relief for action they
would have taken in any event. And the value of the
benefit will be proportionate to the company's marginal
tax bracket, a seemingly irrelevant factor. To a company operating at a loss a deduction or tax credit may
be completely worthless; yet, some polluters most in
need of financial assistance may be in just this
category.

The device, as a whole, appears quite unlikely to
secure the maximum benefit to the environment from the
minimum number of dollars. The only argument in favor
of it is that, through concealment of its true nature,
a subsidy through tax relief is often politically more
saleable than an unmasked device.[144]

LOANS

Government loans may be a helpful device to encourage businesses to expend funds to control their pollution.[145] If the company's credit were such that it
had ready access to capital markets, such a program
would add nothing, unless the government were willing
to offer lower interest rates; in that case, what we

would have is little more than another form of subsidy,
measured by the interest differential. Where, however,
the company does have difficulty securing private
financing, government loans would be useful in filling
this vacuum. The loan programs of the Small Business
Administration, [146] the Export-Import Bank, [147] and other
government agencies, [148] make use of a small portion
of the vast power of the federal government to accumu-
late and disseminate funds for purposes regarded as
socially useful.

RESEARCH PROGRAMS

Much of the federal air and water quality legislation has authorized research to find ways of controlling pollution. [149] In appropriate cases, research may
be conducted in house by the staffs of the various
government departments themselves. More typically, it
is contracted to universities, private research organizations or companies involved in the substantive areas
under consideration.

Research may be shaped in several directions. Better
and less expensive forms of air and water treatment
are an obvious objective. There may also, however, be
other less traditional directions in which research can
be channeled with even more attractive long term
potential.

A very large proportion of waste products that pollute the water, the land or the air are inevitable
consequences of industrial life. To some degree, the
creation of such wastes can be reduced or avoided;
for example, control over fuels used for power production

253

can eliminate or at least reduce emissions of sulfur
compounds into the air. While research in those
directions is important, there is inevitably going
to be an irreducible minimum of emissions of pollutants about which something will have to be done.
Much of the effort thus far has been devoted to
finding ways of disposing of such products in the
least harmful fashion. Garbage is towed out to sea
and there dumped, rather than dropped into rivers.[150]
Nuclear wastes are buried deep in the ground.[151] The
unuseable heat from nuclear power production is dissi-
pated into the atmosphere rather than injected into
lakes and rivers.[152] In some cases, little more is
accomplished than the substitution of one form of
pollution for another, without always even the
certainty that the new is less damaging than the
old.[153] Some of our other efforts are based on the
notion that we still have infinite, rather than finite,
receptacles for our waste in the oceans and under
ground. This may be true for the short run, but it
is certain that it will not remain true forever.
To treat the ocean today as a forever-patient dump
for wastes to the end of time is the precise analogue
of the notion a few decades ago that the air and the
lakes and the rivers could take any amount of waste
products. Sooner or later this must cease; although
the role of the ocean in the entire structure of life
on this planet is not fully understood, the possibility of a disaster of unprecedented dimension through
upsetting of its life balance ought not to be
ignored.[154]

If, therefore, it is conceded that, as our gross
national product becomes grosser and grosser, no place
on earth will exist where we will be able eternally
to dispose of our waste, the choices would seem
inevitably to narrow down to two. We can stop all
growth--of population, industrial and agricultural
production, everything. Or, we can give highest
priority to the recycling of wastes. To stop growth
would give rise to serious ethical problems as well
as acute political difficulties. With a large part
of the population of even this unprecedentedly prosperous country living below a decent standard of
living, it would be callous indeed to adopt a policy
of no further economic growth. When the problem is
viewed in the context of much larger populations
elsewhere in the world, surviving at or below the
subsistence level, a decision to put an end to economic
development would indeed be difficult to defend. Difficult, that is, unless there were clear and convincing
evidence that all life might be terminated if such
drastic measures were not instantly adopted. And the
knowledge of global ecology has not yet advanced
to the point where such predictions could be made
with confidence, convincingly, and in time.

But even if it were ethically justifiable to make
such a decision, it is impossible to imagine that it
would be politically feasible. Those not sharing in
the bounty of modern industrial progress can scarcely
be expected to accept a permanent barricade against
the opportunity ever to raise their standards of
living, unless the more affluent were willing to bring

255

their own level down to that of the poor--a decision
which, on any wide scale, is utterly without historical precedent. Even if the United States were willing
to put a moratorium on its own growth, the rest of
the world would go its own course.

The alternative would seem to be a high priority
on research into ways in which waste products can be
recycled and, particularly, how this can be done at a
tolerable cost.[155] Most of the products which pollute the air and the water, as well as the solid
wastes, have at least some potential commercial
value.[156] Although they are not worth the cost of
recapturing them, neither are they utterly valueless.
Many of them, in addition, contain elements in
comparatively short supply which one day will undoubtedly be needed.[157] If someone were tomorrow to develop
a way in which we could shoot all of our polluting
wastes into outer space (perhaps using nuclear waste
as the fuel?) despite the immediate attractiveness of
the idea, cooler heads would probably quickly decide
that the irrevocable loss of these materials to
humanity ought to be avoided.

Reclamation of some pollutants has been economically successful. Municipal sewage has been turned into
saleable fertilizer.[158] Fly ash gathered from smokestacks has been made into cinder block and other useful
construction materials.[159] Solid wastes have been
compressed into useful land fill[160] (though at times
creating fresh problems involving water pollution and
marine ecology).[161] Old steel, aluminum, glass and
paper can all be used to make new. The sulfur emitted

in paper manufacturing might be regarded as a low grade ore, refinement of which is too costly to be economically feasible under present technology, but might become reclaimable at a profit at some later stage of technological development.[162]

Thermal pollution from power plants involves the dissipation of heat of too low a grade to be commercially useable, thus presenting the unpleasant choice of either spoiling our rivers, changing the local atmospheric climate or curtailing total power production. Research devoted to finding ways to utilize this heat for economically viable purposes might afford the opportunity to escape having to choose among any of these unattractive alternatives.

Even if the research did not lead to a profitable use of the waste, if it gave rise to a use which was only marginally unprofitable it could permit the institution of subsidies at a much lower level than would otherwise be required.[163] Furthermore, research should not be limited to technological areas; related studies of potential markets, labor supplies and the like are also needed.

In short, there are a number of different aspects of the pollution problem on which research would be appropriate and where results outweighing by many times the cost of the research might reasonably be hoped for. While the proposition that the problems generated by technology may be cured by more technology is far from self-evident, increased use of research appears to offer the only reasonable alternative to the extremely unattractive choice of answers to our present

environmental crisis suggested above.[164] And in our
society, the federal government is by far the largest
potential source of the funds needed for this purpose.

ARTIFICIAL GOVERNMENT MARKETS FOR WASTE

Related to the foregoing suggestion is the idea
that the financial power of the federal government
be employed to provide markets for waste products
unless and until ways are found to dispose of them
profitably.[165] In many circumstances, the cost to the
government of buying and processing these products
and disposing of them as best it can would be substantially less than either the cost of replacing the
process completely or of slowing down a significant
portion of the economy. Moreover, depending upon
geographical considerations and the expense of
transportation, a government marketing program might
afford economies of scale which could not be matched
by the individual enterprises involved, reducing the
loss in disposing of the products or conceivably even
turning a loss into a profit.

EFFLUENT AND SIMILAR CHARGES

Considerable attention has been given in recent years
to the notion of charging those users of the environ-
ment--especially water--for the pollution they cause.[166]
The theory is, that while most costs of production are
reflected in the profit and loss figures of the producer
and must therefore be given appropriate attention in
a cost analysis of a given program, it has been traditional to treat the cost of polluting the environment

as zero, with the entire loss borne either by persons downstream or downwind or by society as a whole. The effluent charge is an attempt to find a device for internalizing these costs and imposing them upon the polluter in the same fashion as the more traditional costs of production must be borne by him.

This has been the basis of the program in effect for a number of years in the Ruhr Valley in Germany and has apparently been marked by considerable success in that area.[167] Charges which may be regarded as taxes are scaled in proportion to the quality and quantity of what is emitted and the proceeds used for large scale purification plants. A concern which finds its own particular circumstances are such that it could more cheaply purify its own wastes than pay for its share of the large scale operation would be free to do so. This, in turn, would presumably be desirable since the total charge on the economy would be less.

Such a program obviously involves many problems. It would work more easily with a small river, which could be dammed and gathered into a purification plant and then discharged below. It is not clear that at the present level of technology the lower Hudson or the Mississippi would be appropriate for any such process.

Certain kinds of solid wastes could also be the subject of a charge of this kind, perhaps at so much per pound, modified where the substances involved were especially easy or difficult to dispose of.[168]

It would be more difficult to employ an effluent charge on air pollution. The air cannot be artificially

259

laundered, and it is unlikely that it will be feasible
to connect all the smokestacks in a large area into
one central receiving vessel in which purification
could somehow take place.

It should also be noted that the imposition of an
effluent charge on one type of pollution, such as that
of the water, without a corresponding control (through
tight regulation if a charge is inappropriate) on other
forms of pollution, such as that of the atmosphere,
would serve simply to divert the damage from the one
medium to the other without any necessary gain. If
paper mills, for example, were charged for polluting
streams but left free to burn their debris in the air,
little would be gained from the use of the effluent char.

Even in the one circumstance where effluent charges
are most likely to be useful, in the control of water
pollution in river basins, many problems remain. There
are difficulties in measuring quantities and composition of discharge. Certain types of damage, such as
destruction of the river or lake bottom or the introduction of toxic compounds of mercury and other metals,
may be beyond the reach of any curative process, so
that no charge would be high enough to reflect the
harm done. Moreover, river basins suffer not only
from waterside industrial plants and sewage systems,
but also from many activities far inland, such as
the running off of agricultural fertilizers, organic
wastes and pesticides. Problems of measuring the
nature and amount of those run-offs from farms,
animal feeding grounds and the like would seem to
be extremely difficult. Perhaps the notion of the

effluent charge could be modified to make it work in such situations, by abandoning the attempt to tie the amount to be paid to the cost of correcting the payer's effluence.

None of the foregoing, however, is intended to suggest that effluent charges may not be a good solution to at least some of our problems, especially those involving water pollution. Much more research clearly has to be done.[169] It is not necessary to accept the enthusiastic conclusions of the supporters of the effluent charge, some of whom regard it as virtually a total solution for major problems.[170] In many instances, it can play a significant role, not in competition but in conjunction with other more traditional regulatory devices. In fact, in some contexts, if effluent charges are going to work at all, they will have to be coupled with effective prohibitions of alternative courses of conduct.

In short, the case for effluent charges has been neither proved nor refuted. Until Vermont adopted them last year,[171] they had not been tried in this country, and we do not really know whether experience with them abroad will offer conclusive proof. Their proponents claim that direct enforcement has been tried and proved a failure and that this remains the only meaningful alternative; the premise of this argument may, however, be questioned, since it can scarcely be argued that we have ever really given vigorous enforcement a try.[172]

* * * *

261

The ultimate question in much of this is who will
bear the cost? Economic and political, as well as
ethical, considerations probably have to be taken into
account in reaching an answer. Ideally, the users
of a product should pay for whatever it costs to make
it, including such costs as the effect on the environment which until recently have been masked. There are
problems of vested interests, however, not all of an
invidious nature. Industries and employment are often
dependent upon an existing permissive legal structure,
and governmental assistance to cushion the shock of
change has many precedents. [173] There may also be
activities whose role in the national life is regarded
for collateral reasons as sufficiently important that
some of the cost should be borne by the public at large.
In terms of ability to pay, one cannot generalize as to
all industries in determining whether it is better
that expenses be borne by the taxpayers or by the
consumers of the products of the industry. [174] Perhaps
the environmental costs of food production, for example,
should be borne by those who eat it in proportion to
their consumption, rather than by essentially the same
people, but pursuant to a graduated income tax; but
this proposition is certainly not self-evident. In
any event, the loss should not be permitted through
inattention and inaction to fall upon a group of
downstream or downwind victims nor should the total
quality of life for everyone, or indeed the likelihood of survival, be permitted to continue to
deteriorate. Political decisions of the highest
order are required in the selection among these

alternatives. The wider the range of possible devices
for deflecting these costs in different directions,
the better the basis upon which such decisions may
be predicated.

Use of the Purchasing Power
of the Federal Government

The federal government, with an annual budget of
$200 billion, consumes about a fifth of the gross
national product.[175] Correspondingly, it therefore
is the customer for a fifth of the nation's products
and services. This is, of course, a national average;
in many industries the fraction is substantially
higher and in a few it is negligible.

As the economic effect of the federal government's
purchases grew, observers recognized that the way in
which the government procured might play a large part
in shaping many aspects of American life. Even before
it was clear that the regulatory power of the federal
government could enforce minimum wage levels in the
economy generally or even in products crossing state
lines,[176] Congress enacted the Walsh-Healey Act[177]
imposing such standards in the performance of government purchase contracts.

Another instance of conscious attention to government procurement policies to affect collateral objectives may be found in the continuing effort to prevent
distortions in the economy induced by what appears to
be a natural tendency for government purchases to be
made from big business. Starting with World War II,
various government programs have sought to increase the

263

proportionate share of small business concerns in
sales to the government.[178] This has been done through
a number of devices: the administrative inclusion of
"boiler plate" clauses in government contracts requiring prime contractors to subcontract to small
business concerns wherever possible;[179] administrative rules inserted in the Armed Service Procurement
Regulation requiring contracting officers to deal with
small business concerns to the greatest extent possible;[180] and statutory requirements together with
creation of an independent agency in the Executive
Branch (the Smaller War Plants Corporation in World
War II,[181] the Small Defense Plants Administration
during the Korean War,[182] and the Small Business
Administration[183] since).

In these programs for increasing the role of small
business in government procurement, the emphasis has
been less on imposing requirements upon a contractor
already selected (as under the Walsh-Healey Act) as
in influencing the selection of the contractor to do
the work or to sell the goods to the government.

Still another collateral use of the contracting
power is found in the attempts to prohibit racial
and other invidious forms of discrimination in employment. Again starting in World War II, with the Fair
Employment Practices Commission,[184] there have been a
series of executive orders[185] requiring all government
contractors and first-tier subcontractors to avoid
discrimination, not only in the performance of the
particular contract in question but throughout their
entire operations.[186]

The original motivation for creation of this program was undoubtedly the assumption that it would be impossible to put a fair employment program through Congress, in the face of a threat of a Southern filibuster. The hope was that a sufficiently large proportion of the nation's employers would find it necessary or at least desirable to do business with the government that the executive order, bolstered by the contract clauses, would have a major impact on employment practices throughout the nation.

Interestingly, however, in 1964 when regulatory legislation to ensure fair employment was finally adopted by the federal government,[187] the contracts program was not abandoned, and indeed, superficially at least, has since even showed some signs of being strengthened.[188] An exploration of the reasons for this may be of some value in the assessment of the usefulness of contract provisions as a substitute for or an adjunct to direct regulatory control of pollution.

The shortcomings of Title VII of the Civil Rights Act of 1964 as an adequate federal remedy for employment discrimination do not spring from constitutional limitations upon federal control over local employment, but rather from inherent weaknesses in the statute. For one thing, a cumbersome administrative proceeding was required as a prerequisite to the institution of a civil action for enforcement;[189] moreover, in the first few years of the statute, some lower court decisions,[190] since reversed,[191] made it appear that the administrative barriers were even more difficult to surmount than has proved to be the case. Secondly,

the statute offers no criminal sanctions, but merely
injunctive relief together with such ancillary relief
as back pay where appropriate.[192] Finally, the main
litigation burden was imposed upon aggrieved individuals, which generally meant poor black workers in the
South, so that in practice the major enforcement
effort was undertaken not by the federal government but
by civil rights organizations, in particular the NAACP
Legal Defense Fund.[193] With limited resources, such
agencies could concentrate only on fighting a selected
group of test cases that might result in favorable
precedents, rather than engaging in a vigorous nationwide enforcement program. To be sure, the statute permitted the Attorney General to bring his own action if
there were a "pattern or practice" of discrimination,[194]
but this authority has been sparingly used.[195] Some
assistance has also been rendered to private litigants
by the Equal Employment Opportunity Commission, through
the release of investigative data, and through submission of amicus curiae briefs.[196] Despite these governmental efforts, however, the program has been relegated
in the main to private enforcement.[197]

The federal contract compliance program, on the other
hand, does offer at least the potential of a government-
staffed enforcement program. Moreover, it offers an
array of sanctions far more effective than the injunction (even if sweetened with back pay) provided by the
statute. One who violates the executive order--and,
at the same time, breaches his contract--is subject to
the normal array of remedies for breach of contract,
such as cancellation of the contract and an action for

damages, or for specific performance.[198] Even more important, the executive order permits the blacklisting of a violating employer from further government business.[199] In theory, the _in terrorem_ effect of these threats ought to frighten into meticulous compliance all government contractors doing any appreciable amount of business with the government.

No citation of authority is necessary, however, to demonstrate that employment discrimination has not been defeated. For that matter, neither has the share of government contracts awarded to small business concerns been substantially enhanced during the long period in which government contracting officials have supposedly been moving in this direction.[200] Further studies of the functioning of these programs for employing the government's contracting power would undoubtedly be of help in determining whether, and in what fashion, that power could be used in order to protect the environment. At least one explanation, however, leaps to the fore as a clue to the apparent failure of both the small business and fair employment programs. This is the "mission orientation" of the government contracting officer, and particularly the contracting officer in the military establishment. Whenever there is a need, sometimes urgent, to procure weapons or other equipment or even to construct a building quickly, the contracting officer will be regarded as having done his job best if he awards the necessary contracts as rapidly as possible and to concerns whose size and financial responsibility afford assurance of prompt and satisfactory performance.

The injection of what he considers extraneous factors
into the contract-awarding process causes the contracting officer considerable anguish, and his natural incli-
nation is to concentrate narrowly on his primary mission
and pay lip service to the other elements which supposed
should enter into his decision. Unless strong pressure
from higher echelons compels him to favor a small business concern or refuse to deal with a discriminating
employer, he is not likely to do it. If his superiors,
and their superiors all the way up, are similarly moti-
vated to get on with the job of procuring the best for
the least money with a minimum of delay, and if there
is no threat of reprimand or other sanctions against the
contracting officer who ignores what he regards as collateral considerations, he is unlikely to heed them.
When the Deputy Secretary of Defense insisted on awarding procurement contracts to Southern textile mills
which had been discriminating against blacks and had
not even complied with the regulation requiring them to
enter into written agreements to take corrective
measures,[201] what lesson was likely to be learned by the
contracting officer many echelons below?

It should be noted that the effectuation of this
program has no longer been left entirely to the mercy
of the contracting officer or the procuring department.
A separate Office of Federal Contract Compliance, under
the Secretary of Labor, has been assigned responsibility
for assuring compliance.[202] Nevertheless, it seems
quite clear that racial discrimination in employment
has not been eliminated or even sharply curtailed in
this country, even among government contractors.

With this history in mind, we can approach the question of the use of the contracting power for preservation of the environment. A contract clause could provide, for example, that in the performance of the contract no federal regulation pertaining to emission into the air or water, or other appropriate substantive rule, was to be violated.[203] It could go a step further and follow the fair employment pattern of requiring the contractor to agree to adhere to these rules in all of its operations, whether related to the specific contract or not.[204] The same array of horrendous consequences, as theoretically applicable in cases of employment discrimination, could be detailed as punishments for contractors who broke their word.

The doubt persists, however, as to whether it would work. Contracting officers disposed to ignore, or pay mere lip service to, small business or anti-discrimination requirements should not be expected to be more zealous in their protection of the environment. In view of the great difficulties in getting federal agencies to pay adequate attention to the environmental damage they themselves are perpetrating,[205] there is no reason to be sanguine as to the degree of vigor with which they would pursue violations by their contractors. Much, of course, would depend upon the degree of dedication at the very highest levels of the federal government. If, in fact, the present surge of interest in protection of the environment were to lead to an intense and sustained commitment at the top to take all appropriate steps, enforcement of contract provisions of the type suggested might become meaningful. It is

possible that the drive against pollution will have a
more solid national consensus supporting it than ever
was committed to protection of small business or to
ending racial discrimination in employment.

If the contracting power is used in this fashion
for environmental protection, there are strong reasons
to place enforcement of the contract provisions in an
agency with responsibility and expertise in the area,
such as the Environmental Protection Agency or the
Council on Environmental Quality. Contracting officers
of procuring agencies, apart from probably lacking
wholehearted devotion to environmental goals, are also
not likely to have sufficient expertise to do the
job well.

If enforcement through contract compliance is going
to succeed, it is probably also important that the
process of determining whether the contractor is in
violation be made as simple as possible. The comparative success of the Walsh-Healey Act minimum wage
regulations as contrasted with the failure of the
employment discrimination program, may be explained at
least in part by the simplicity of ascertaining what
wages an employer is paying, as opposed to the difficulty of proof of racial discrimination in employment.
Anti-pollution provisions are likely to fall somewhere
between these extremes.

Use of the contracting power in this sense, in
addition to providing stringent remedies, offers the
attractive possibility of operating fairly rapidly
with little or no delay for judicial review,[206] with
no need to prove violations beyond a reasonable doubt,

and with sanctions sufficiently strong to serve as a possible deterrent. If, however, even the apparently non-urgent need for textiles was sufficient to cause the federal government at its highest levels to ignore its own requirements as to racial discrimination, then a major change in mood will have to occur before an anti-pollution clause will be enforced against a manufacturer of guns or planes thought to be urgently needed for the defense of the nation.

There are other possible uses of the government's contracting power beyond the regulatory applications discussed above. For example, the government can, and frequently does, enter into contracts in order to stimulate development of various kinds. A substantial portion of the procurement activities of the defense establishment are in the area of research and development. A manufacturer, for example, is paid to attempt to create a new weapon or other device. In addition to the profits on the particular "R & D" contract, there is sometimes the hope of a subsequent production contract to make and sell the product to the government if the exploration of its feasibility proves successful.

While contracts of this sort are usually employed in connection with the regular procurement activities of the federal government as means of developing the various devices it hopes to be able to purchase for itself, there is no inherent reason to limit research and development contracts in this fashion. It would be entirely appropriate for the government to award such a contract for the production of a mechanism to be made available to non-governmental users--for

271

example, a device for water purification or for control
of emissions at the smokestack.

There are additional possible uses for this technique.
For example, the government could enter into contracts
for research and development leading to production of
a pollution-free automobile or an automobile powered by
some device other than the internal combustion engine.
The purpose could be either to encourage the development of such automobiles for general public sale, their
development even at non-competitive prices for sale to
the government itself, or a combination of both.   Similarly, contracts could be let for development of cheaper
methods of producing lead-free fuels, again with the
purpose of ultimate sale to the government, to the
public, or both.

Still another use of this technique would be for
the government itself to undertake to build and operate
model plants in industries notorious for the harm they
do to the environment. Government-sponsored research
might lead to the design of a paper mill, for example,
which polluted neither the air nor the water. Depending on whether the end product was a design or a plant,
ownership could remain in the government if deemed
desirable, or it might ultimately be sold to private
industry and the techniques learned made available
to others in the private sector.

The extent to which the government should incur
expense of this kind, as distinguished from engaging
in vigorous regulation and leaving it to industry to
do its own research to find the ways in which it can
comply, would have to depend upon judgments as to the

appropriate allocation of expenditures among the several sectors of society, referred to above.[207]

It should be noted that there is no sharp dividing line between government research and development contracts of this kind and government-sponsored research referred to above.[208] The latter may be handled by way of either contract or grant, depending on circumstances. Whatever the theoretical form of the technique employed, the government would, in effect, be using its financial resources to assist in the discovery of new ways of protecting the environment.

Still another way in which the government can influence the environment through its contracting power would be simply to insert specifications in appropriate procurement contracts which obliged the seller to meet government standards, even if it entailed an increase in cost. This device could also be used in the procurement of automobiles, for example.[209] As a minimum, those automobiles owned by the government would pollute to a lesser extent. Moreover, the creation of that large a market for a pollution-free car might possibly tip the scales and make financially attractive to industry the production of such a car for the mass market where without such government orders this would be economically unfeasible.

Thus, the government's contracting power offers no panacea. In and of itself, it probably cannot play the major role in fighting pollution. Nevertheless, particularly in conjunction with direct enforcement techniques, there are ways in which it may be effectively used.[210]

273

A Word on Private Litigation

While redress for private injury resulting from conduct harmful to the environment has for generations
been sought through legal actions brought by those
suffering especial damage, a new breed of environmental
litigation has burgeoned in the last few years. Cases
are now being brought by individuals, often as class
actions, or by organizations dedicated to the preservation of environmental values, for the purpose of protecting an entire community, ranging in dimension from
a village to the world. In some cases, the defendants
are agencies of government--federal, state or local--
charged either with conduct actively harmful or with
failure to regulate to prevent harm by others. In
other cases, the defendants are private, typically
companies engaged in or threatening actions detrimental
to the environment.

Such litigation can serve as a valuable device sup-
plementary to those used by the government for the
enforcement of laws and regulations.[211] It can also
fill the void where public enforcement authorities
are remiss.[212] And where the government itself is the
offender, it can be an extremely useful antidote
to the lack of sensitivity to environmental values on
the part of some government officials. In addition,
such actions may serve to direct badly needed public
attention to the importance of environmental protection.

The magnitude of the task of enforcing the government's own regulations, however, suggests that for the

job to be done effectively the main burden must be assumed by the government itself; private persons and groups lack the resources to act on more than a sporadic, case-by-case basis. And where private actions by-pass the legislative and administrative process, seeking to induce the courts to create a common law of the environment in disregard of laws and regulations already promulgated or in the process of formulation,[213] they may prove to be counterproductive. Courts lack the opportunity, which is available both to Congressional committees and to the agencies charged with implementation of federal statutes, to devote continued attention to environmental problems, to view them from a nationwide perspective, or to acquire the technical expertise so necessary for effective creation of policy.

As indicated above,[214] this discussion does not purport to analyze in depth the actual or potential contribution of the various kinds of private litigation brought to protect the environment; it is intended only to suggest some of the factors pertinent to an evaluation of such litigation in the context of the overall problem of developing ways in which the federal government can effect compliance with environmental standards.

International Action

Just as the widening impact of pollution has tended to shift responsibility from municipalities and states to the federal government, the danger has become sufficiently global to be beyond the control of the

United States acting alone. But here the analogy ends; much as we may need one, we have no World Government. The next best thing would be the use of multilateral agreements for this purpose.

If, however, such agreements are sufficiently well drafted to promise meaningful improvement, they may run into serious difficulties. Less developed countries may regard environmental concern as a luxury they cannot afford. They might well regard us as "overdeveloped" in terms of the comparative affluence we have bought at the price of the most extensive despoilment of nature, and have little patience with efforts initiated by us to achieve international agreement to protect the oceans and the atmosphere. Their objections might be softened if, along with other prosperous nations, we offered to assume the bulk of the financial burdens involved, including the cost of the major research program suggested above. A United Nations conference on the human environment, at which the United States might advance its proposals, has been scheduled for 1972. In view of the urgency of the problem, however, it would seem undesirable to wait that long.

Conclusion

The techniques which have been considered, to compel or induce compliance, are not necessarily mutually exclusive; in many situations they can be used in combination. Moreover, it is desirable to have available a broad range of remedies, so as to permit selection of the appropriate one or ones in each case. Doubts,

such as have been mentioned, as to the effectiveness
of some of them should not preclude their adoption.
We need to experiment with every reasonable device
we can invent, in order to develop the strongest possible arsenal of legal weapons; what we are seeking to
protect is nothing less than the survival of the human
race.

Notes

1. See p. 274, _infra_.

2. _Compare_ Bermingham, The Federal Government and Air and Water Pollution, 23 BUS. LAWYER 467, 478-81, 487-89 (1968), with Edelman, Federal Air and Water Control: The Application of the Commerce Power to Abate Interstate and Intrastate Pollution, 33 GEO. WASH. L. REV. 1067, 1072-73 (1965); Hines, Nor Any Drop to Drink: Public Regulation of Water Quality, Part III: The Federal Effort, 52 IOWA L. REV. 799, 800 (1957).

3. 9 Wheat. 1 (1824).

4. _Id._ at 196.

5. United States v. Darby, 312 U.S. 100 (1941). The Supreme Court refused to look at Congressional motive so long as the action fell within a power conferred by the Constitution.

6. National Labor Relations Board v. Jones & Laughlin Steel Corp., 301 U.S. 1 (1937). The Court held that respondent's labor relations were subject to Congressional control because suspension of its manufacturing operations could impede interstate commerce. The Court later applied this reasoning to smaller enterprises, holding that the commerce power does not depend on the volume of commerce affected. National Labor Relations Board v. Fainblatt, 306 U.S. 601 (1939).

7. Wickard v. Filburn, 317 U.S. 111 (1942). Here, the Court applied Congressional power under the commerce clause to local activity which clearly could not be deemed commerce, asserting that whether the subject of regulation in question was "production," "consumption," or "marketing" was not material; that the activity is local is also not material; it may still be reached by Congress if it affects interstate commerce, and this "irrespective of whether such

effect is what might at some earlier time have been
defined as 'direct' or 'indirect.'" Id. at 125. The
Court held that home-consumed wheat would have a substantial influence on price and market conditions
since to the man who grew it it supplied a need which
would otherwise have to be met by purchases on the
open market.

8. Id. at 127-28.

9. Heart of Atlanta Motel v. United States, 379
U.S. 241 (1964); Katzenbach v. McClung, 379 U.S. 294
(1964); Daniel v. Paul, 395 U.S. 298 (1969).

10. E.g., Covington & C. Bridge Co. v. Kentucky,
154 U.S. 204 (1894) (non-commercial travel by persons
using an interstate bridge held to be interstate commerce); United States v. Hill, 248 U.S. 420 (1919)
(transportation of property on one's person across
state line held interstate commerce although destined
for personal use); United States v. Darby, 312 U.S.
100 (1941).

11. Champion v. Ames, 188 U.S. 321 (1903).

12. Id. at 356 (emphasis supplied).

13. Hoke v. United States, 227 U.S. 308 (1913).

14. Caminetti v. United States, 242 U.S. 470
(1917). Other kinds of recreational facilities have
been held subject to Congressional regulation on the
alternative basis of: (i) the out-of-state origins
of food served and equipment used, and (ii) the
service of out-of-state patrons. Daniel v. Paul, 395
U.S. 298 (1969).

15. Gooch v. United States, 297 U.S. 124 (1936).

16. 312 U.S. 100 (1941).

17. Id. at 117.

18. Thus, Congress may forbid unfair labor practices
which affect interstate commerce, on the part of manufacturers, without forbidding the transportation of
their products. National Labor Relations Board v.

Jones & Laughlin Steel Corp., 301 U.S. 1 (1937). An
additional, although not essential, basis for such
power would be found in instances in which a manufacturer not meeting specified standards might be
able to compete advantageously in national markets
with one which complied. Darby, 312 U.S. at 122. On
this basis, Congressional action which sought to deny
competitive advantage to those concerns which had vio
for example, air or water pollution standards would
be valid.

19. Wickard v. Filburn, 317 U.S. 111 (1942).

20. Cf. Edelman, Federal Air and Water Pollution
Control and Bermingham, The Federal Government and
Air and Water Pollution, supra, note 2.

21. The interstate commerce power has been held
to apply to rivers presently impeded by obstructions
that once were navigable, though only by canoe (Unite
States v. Holt State Bank, 270 U.S. 49 (1926)) and
streams that could be made navigable only through improvement (United States v. Appalachian Electric Powe
Co., 311 U.S. 377 (1940)), as well as a non-navigable
tributary of a navigable stream so long as it in some
way affects navigation (Oklahoma v. Atkinson, 313 U.S
508, 529 (1941)). The touchstone would seem to be th
navigability, rather than the interstate character of
the stream, and the mere fact that a stream crosses a
state line or serves as a boundary might not, without
more, be sufficient for federal control. See Berming
supra note 2, at 478-79. Yet the Water Quality Act c
1965 (Pub. L. No. 89-234, 79 Stat. 903, now 33 U.S.C.
§ 1157 (1970)), provided for abatement of pollution c
"interstate or navigable waters."
In relinquishing to the states title to "land
beneath navigable waters," Congress was careful to re
tain the navigational servitude of the United States
Submerged Lands Act, 67 Stat. 32 (1953), 43 U.S.C.
§ 1314 (1964). This reservation has been held to pre
serve the federal power to protect wildlife in naviga
waters from harm caused by environmental changes.
Zabel v. Tabb, 430 F.2d 199, 206 (5th Cir. 1970).
There is another possible constitutional basis for
federal regulation of navigable waters, whether inter
state or not, entirely distinct from the commerce
clause. The judicial power (U.S. CONST. art. 3, § 2

extends, *inter alia*, "to all Cases of Admiralty and Maritime Jurisdiction"; bolstered by the necessary and proper clause, this provision has been held to give Congress the power to enact substantive law. It is not clear, however, how far this power can be extended beyond matters closely related to the subject-matter of admiralty jurisdiction. Cases arising thus far have been well within such traditional limits. *See*, *e.g.*, Panama R.R. v. Johnson, 264 U.S. 375 (1924) (upholding a change of rules relating to the liability of a maritime employer for injuries to his employees); In re Garnett, 141 U.S. 1 (1891) (upholding statute imposing limited liability for loss of cargo).

22. *See* Edelman, *supra* note 2, at 1070-73.

23. *See* Bermingham, *supra* note 2, at 478-79. *See also* Brown & Duncan, *Legal Aspects of a Federal Water Quality Surveillance System*, 68 MICH. L. REV. 1131, 1133 (1970); but *cf*. *id*., note 7.

24. *See* S. REP. NO. 638, 88th Cong., 1st Sess. 3 (1963).

25. *See* United States v. Bishop Processing Co., 287 F. Supp. 624, 629 (D. Md. 1968). *See also id*., 423 F.2d 469 (4th Cir. 1970), *cert*. *denied*, 398 U.S. 904 (1970). An analogy might be seen in cases holding that the movement of electrical impulses by wire or through the air is commerce. Pensacola Telephone Co. v. Western Union Telegraph Co., 96 U.S. 1 (1877); Federal Radio Commission v. Nelson Bros., 289 U.S. 266 (1933).

26. *See* Edelman, *supra* note 2, at 1083-87.

27. United States v. Butler, 297 U.S. 1, 65 (1936), construing art. 1, § 8 of the Constitution. On the state level, *see*, *e.g*., CAL. HEALTH & SAFETY CODE § 24370:2 (West 1967).

28. *Cf*. Frothingham v. Mellon, 262 U.S. 447 (1923); Flast v. Cohen, 392 U.S. 83 (1968).

29. The power to tax "is given in the Constitution, with only one exception and only two qualifications. Congress cannot tax exports, and it must impose direct

taxes by the rule of apportionment, and indirect taxes by the rule of uniformity. Thus limited, and thus only, it reaches every subject, and may be exercised at discretion." Chief Justice Chase, in License Tax Cases, 5 Wall. 462, 471 (1867).

30. See, e.g., Veazie Bank v. Fenno, 8 Wall. 533, 548 (1869); McCray v. United States, 195 U.S. 27, 154-59 (1904); United States v. Doremus, 249 U.S. 86, 93 (1919); United States v. Kahriger, 345 U.S. 22, 26-31 (1953). But cf. Bailey v. Drexel Furniture Co., 259 U.S. 20 (1922); Carter v. Carter Coal Co., 298 U.S. 238 (1936).

31. The tax would simply be the means selected by Congress as necessary and proper for the exercise of its power to regulate interstate commerce. "The power of taxation, which is expressly granted, may of course be adopted as a means to carry into operation another power also expressly granted." United States v. Butler, 297 U.S. 1, 69 (1936).

32. See pp.258-63, infra; G. Rathjens, National Environmental Policy--Goals and Priorities, p.30 supra. For the use of this device at the state level, see VT. STAT. ANN., tit. 10 § 910(A) et seq. (Supp. 1970).

33. See Hearings before a Special Subcomm. on Air and Water Pollution of the Senate Comm. on Public Works, 89th Cong., 1st Sess. (1965).

34. 297 U.S. 1 (1936).

35. Cf. Steward Machine Co. v. Davis, 301 U.S. 548 (1937); Helvering v. Davis, 301 U.S. 619 (1937).

36. Cf., e.g., Carter v. Carter Coal Co., 298 U.S. 238 (1936); Schechter Poultry Corp. v. United States, 295 U.S. 495 (1935).

37. Congress's powers are derived not only from specific grants of authority but also from the clause authorizing Congress "to make all laws which shall be necessary and proper for carrying into execution the foregoing powers, and all other Powers vested by this Constitution in the Government of the United States, or

in any Department or Officer thereof." U.S. CONST.,
art. I, § 8, cl. 17 (emphasis supplied).

38. United States v. Shauver, 214 Fed. 154 (D.
Ark. 1914); United States v. McCullagh, 221 Fed. 288
(D. Kans. 1915).

39. 39 Stat. 1705 (1916).

40. Acting, as it did at that time, on behalf of
Canada in its foreign relations.

41. 252 U.S. 416 (1920).

42. There is in fact a Boundary Waters Treaty of
1909 with Great Britain (acting on behalf of Canada),
containing a provision (in Art. IV) that the boundary
waters "shall not be polluted on either side to the
injury of health or property on the other." 36 Stat.
2448, 2450 (1909). While an international joint commission has been established, its powers are limited,
and there is no other implementing legislation. See
Erichsen-Brown, Legal Implications of Boundary Water
Pollution, 17 BUFF. L. REV. 65 (1967).

43. P. 275, infra.

44. The Supreme Court has never held a treaty
invalid on any grounds. It has, however, held an
executive agreement invalid as violative of express
constitutional restraints on the federal government.
In Reid v. Covert, 354 U.S. 1 (1957), the Court held
that the Status of Forces Agreements could not validly
authorize the trial by court-martial of civilian de-
pendents of American soldiers overseas, since the
Constitution guarantees them a jury trial. The Court
indicated by dictum that the treaty power is similarly
limited. Id. at 16.
The distinction should be kept in mind, however,
between attacks based on violations of express constitutional restraints on federal action, and those based
on 10th Amendment considerations; Missouri v. Holland
(252 U.S. 416 (1920)) would presumably dispose of the
latter unless it proved possible to persuade the Court
that the purported treaty was a sham.

45. Another possible basis for Congressional authority to preserve the environment is the national defense power (found chiefly in art. I, § 8, cls. 11-16), and in fact federal control over the environmental as well as other aspects of atomic energy is generally regarded as predicated on that power. The relationship of other types of pollution to defense can probably also be demonstrated; but at most the links would seem to be no stronger than those to interstate commerce, and the much larger body of pertinent precedent in the latter area would suggest that greater reliance should continue to be placed upon the commerce clause.

It has sometimes been asserted that there is a constitutional right under the Ninth Amendment to a decent environment, and at least something of a hint in one Supreme Court case that the Ninth Amendment may serve as a further source for creation of individual rights not hitherto recognized. See Griswold v. Connecticut, 381 U.S. 479, 484 (1965) (majority); id. at 488 et seq. (concurring opinion of Goldberg, J. B. PATTERSON, THE FORGOTTEN NINTH AMENDMENT (1955); Sive, The Environment--Is it Protected by the Bill of Rights?, CIVIL LIBERTIES, April 1970, at 3. If there is such a right under the Ninth Amendment, and if it is part of the fundamental rights carried over or "incorporated" as limitations upon the states by the Fourteenth Amendment, it could be argued that the congressional power to implement the Fourteenth Amendment might include authority to protect these rights. By way of analogy, it was held in Katzenbach v. Morgan 384 U.S. 641 (1966), that Congress could forbid the requirement of literacy in English as a voting qualifi cation when imposed upon Spanish-speaking citizens of Puerto Rican origin. The Court held that this could be done under either of two theories--that the literac requirement, although not in itself a violation of the Fourteenth Amendment, might interfere with the asser tion by residents of Puerto Rican origin of their rights to equal treatment--such as in the allocation of public services which were guaranteed by the Four teenth Amendment; or, alternatively, that even if the courts would not themselves find that such a literacy requirement violated the equal protection clause, nevertheless, a reasonable judgment by Congress to that effect would be accepted by the Court.

One problem, however, with the use of the Fourteenth Amendment is that it applies only to state action, and might not be applicable to conduct by nongovernmental organizations injuring the environment of others. Since there are so many better grounds for finding a constitutional basis for federal regulation than this one, it may not be worth pursuing further, except perhaps as an intellectual exercise.

46. In most of the eastern states, rights to water are based on ownership of adjacent, or "riparian," land. In some of these states, allocation is based on "natural flow," in others on "reasonable use." In the West, where water is scarcer, rights are based on "appropriation"; the first user, regardless of land ownership, acquires rights which continue unless he fails to utilize them. See J. SAX, WATER LAW, PLANNING AND POLICY: CASES AND MATERIALS 1-3 (1968) for an exceptionally clear outline of the various theories of water rights. See also Note, Private Remedies for Water Pollution, 70 COL. L. REV. 734 (1970).

47. "Rights, property or otherwise, which are absolute against all the world are certainly rare, and water rights are not among them. Whatever rights may be as between equals such as riparian owners, they are not the measure of riparian rights on a navigable stream relative to the function of the Government in improving navigation. Where these interests conflict they are not to be reconciled as between equals, but the private interest must give way to a superior right, or perhaps it would be more accurate to say that as against the Government such private interest is not a right at all." United States v. Willow River Power Co. 324 U.S. 499, 510 (1945).

48. The police power enables a state to regulate for the comfort, health, safety, and welfare of its citizens; its scope is limited only by provisions in the federal or applicable state constitution. See, e.g., Jacobson v. Massachusetts, 197 U.S. 11, 25 (1904) Town of Shelby v. Cleveland Mill and Power Co., 155 N.C. 196, 200, 71 S.E. 218, 220 (1911). The typical state pollution control act would seem in theory to present a classic example of a legitimate exercise of the police power: protection against significant

danger to public health and welfare; consequently, such legislation has been uniformly upheld. See, e.g., Hatcher v. Board of Supervisors, 165 Iowa 197, 145 N.W. 12 (1914); Huron Portland Cement Co. v. Detroit, 362 U.S. 440, 442 (1960).

49. "[I]t is no objection to the exertion of the power to regulate interstate commerce that its exercise is attended by the same incidents which attend the exercise of the police power of the states." United States v. Carolene Products Co., 304 U.S. 144, 147 (1938).

50. Such control over the property rights of abutting owners is based on the federal government's control over navigable waterways, and is not deemed a taking of the riparian owner's property for which he must be compensated; the property is deemed always to have been held subject to the lawful exercise of just such power. United States v. Willow River Power Co., 324 U.S. 499, 510 (1945), note 47 supra; see also United States v. Chicago M, St. P & P. R. Co., 312 U.S. 592 (1941); United States v. Appalachian Electric Power Co., 311 U.S. 377 (1940). This power may be employed not only for navigation, but also to protect environmental values. Zabel v. Tabb, 430 F.2d 199 (5th Cir. 1970).
In other areas of federal activity as well, the fact that regulation may reduce the value of property does not in itself defeat its constitutionality or necessitate compensation. Federal Power Comm. v. Hope Natural Gas Co., 320 U.S. 591, 601 (1944); Bowles v. Willingham, 321 U.S. 503, 517-18 (1944).

51. See Lawton v. Steele, 152 U.S. 133, 136, 137 (1894); C. B. & Q. v. Illinois, 200 U.S. 561, 592-94 (1906).
See also Huron Portland Cement Co. v. Detroit, 362 U.S. 440, 442 (1960), referring to the Detroit Smoke Abatement Code: "The Ordinance was enacted for the manifest purpose of promoting the health and welfare of the city's inhabitants. Legislation designed to free from pollution the very air that people breathe clearly falls within the exercise of even the most traditional concept of what is compendiously known as the police power."

52. Id.

53. Day-Brite Lighting, Inc. v. Missouri, 342 U.S. 421, 424 (1952).

54. See Euclid v. Ambler Realty Co., 272 U.S. 365, 387-88 (1926).

55. Miller v. Schoene, 276 U.S. 272 (1927); but cf. Pennsylvania Coal Co. v. Mahon, 260 U.S. 393 (1922).

56. See United States v. Darby, 312 U.S. 100, 114 (1941); Hamilton v. Kentucky Distilleries & Warehouse Co., 251 U.S. 146, 156 (1919).

57. The ancient doctrine that the landowner's property rights to the air above his land extend to the heavens has been discarded. United States v. Causby, 328 U.S. 256, 261 (1945). But it has also been held that the landowner 'owns' "at least as much of the space above the ground as he can occupy or use in connection with the land." Id. at 264. The Court in Causby recognized that airspace is a "public highway" and the federal authority to regulate air commerce and to control the navigable air space rests securely on the commerce clause and has never been doubted. See Braniff Airways v. Nebraska State Bd. of Equalization, 347 U.S. 590, 596-97 (1954). Yet the Court in Causby found it necessary to qualify this power, which unqualified would have consequences not attending the exertion of Congress's plenary power over navigable waters: ". . . the flight of airplanes, which skim the surface but do not touch it, is as much an appropriation of the use of the land as a more conventional entry upon it" (328 U.S. at 264). See also Griggs v. County of Allegheny, 369 U.S. 84, 87 (1962).

58. United States v. Bishop Processing Co., supra note 25.

59. See Michelman, Property, Utility, and Fairness: Comments on the Ethical Foundations of 'Just Compensation' Law, 80 HARV. L. REV. 1165 (1967), Sax, Takings and the Police Power, 74 YALE L. J. 36 (1964).

60. E.g., Lochner v. New York, 198 U.S. 45 (1905).

61. E.g., West Coast Hotel Co. v. Parrish, 300 U.S. 379 (1937). But many state courts have continued to

invalidate state legislation on grounds of substantive
due process under the due process clauses of state
constitutions. See Paulsen, The Persistence of Substantive Due Process in the States, 34 MINN. L. REV.
91 (1950); Hetherington, State Economic Regulation and
Substantive Due Process of Law, 53 NW. U. L. Rev. 13,
226 (1958).

62. See Greenawalt, "Uncontrollable" Actions and
the Eighth Amendment: Implications of Powell v. Texas,
69 COLUM. L. REV. 927, 972 (1969); Kent v. Dulles,
357 U.S. 116 (1958); Griswold v. Connecticut, 381 U.S.
479, 486 (1965) (concurring opinions).

63. For examples of the Court's tolerance of
legislation in the economic area, see, e.g., Williamson
v. Lee Optical Co., 348 U.S. 483 (1955); Day-Brite
Lighting, Inc. v. Missouri, 342 U.S. 421 (1952).

64. The last mentioned proposal would at least
avoid the "intrusion into the bedroom" problems that
would arise if the alternative of compulsory contraception were adopted. Cf. Griswold v. Connecticut,
381 U.S. 479 (1965).

65. Compare Buck v. Bell, 274 U.S. 200 (1927), with
Skinner v. Oklahoma, 316 U.S. 535 (1942).
A few other constitutional limitations on federal
action might prove pertinent.
Laws unreasonably classifying those subject to
their command might run afoul of principles of equal
protection, which are applied to the federal govern-
ment through the due process clause of the Fifth
Amendment. Bolling v. Sharpe, 347 U.S. 497 (1954).
But regulation of business is seldom invalidated on
equal protection grounds these days. Compare Ry. Express
Agency v. New York, 336 U.S. 106 (1949) with Morey v.
Doud, 354 U.S. 457 (1957); cf. Shapiro v. Thompson, 394
U.S. 618 (1969), and Mr. Justice Harlan, dissenting, at 655.
Inspection of plants to determine whether pollution
regulations were being obeyed might have to be made
pursuant only to warrant in order to avoid violation of
the Fourth Amendment's prohibition of unreasonable
searches and seizures. See Camara v. Municipal Court,
387 U.S. 523 (1967).

66. Wechsler, The Political Safeguards of Federalism--

The Role of The States in the Composition and Selection of the National Government, 54 COLUM. L. REV. 543, 544–45 (1954).

67. _See_ Grad, _supra_ p. 160 _et_ _seq._

68. Art. VI, § 2.

69. _See_ Grad, _supra_ p. 51 _et_ _seq._

70. Congress expressly considered the preemption problem in connection with its authorization to the Secretary of Health, Education and Welfare to prescribe emission standards for new motor vehicles and decided to bar state controls except where a state had adopted a higher standard before March 30, 1966--in effect, barring all state regulation except that of California. Air Quality Act of 1967, Pub. L. No. 90-148, § 2, 81 Stat. 490, U.S.C. §§ 1857f-1 _et_ _seq._ (Supp. V, 1965-69) Since the federal statute relies upon a woefully inadequate regulatory technique, _i.e._ clearance of all new cars or engines of a given model if a test vehicle passes the test (_see_ Grad, _supra_ p. 54), preemption serves to preclude meaningful action at any level of government.

Cases raising questions of whether federal legislation barred state or local controls have occasionally involved environmental regulation. In Huron Portland Cement Co. v. City of Detroit, 362 U.S. 440 (1960), Detroit's Smoke Abatement Code was held validly applicable to a ship using its waters, despite compliance of the ship's boilers with federal boiler inspection laws. The Court relied heavily on Congressional statements which at the time declared air pollution to be primarily a matter of state and local concern. In American Airlines, Inc. v. Town of Hempstead, 272 F. Supp. 226 (E.D.N.Y. 1966), _aff'd_, 398 F.2d 369 (2d Cir. 1968), _cert._ denied, 393 U.S. 1017 (1969), a municipal ordinance attempting to ban excessive noise from jet aircraft was invalidated on grounds of federal preemption. _See also_ Allegheny Airlines, Inc. v. Village of Cedarhurst, 132 F. Supp. 871 (E.D.N.Y. 1955), _aff'd_, 238 F.2d 812 (2d Cir. 1956). Interestingly, federal aircraft noise regulations apparently do not preclude airport operators from imposing more stringent standards, and this is true even where the airport is operated by an agency of state or local government. _See_

Port of New York Authority v. Eastern Air Lines, Inc., 259 F. Supp. 745 (E.D.N.Y. 1966); S. REP. NO. 1353, 90th Cong., 2d Sess. 4 (1968); 34 Fed. Reg. 18355-56 (1969).

Litigation is now pending which raises the question of whether a state may impose more stringent regulations on disposal of nuclear waste than those promulgated by the Atomic Energy Commission. Northern States Power Co. v. Minnesota, D. Minn., filed Aug. 26, 1969.

71. For a survey of the enforcement techniques most generally employed by the states in this area, see Grad, supra p. 117 et seq.

72. F. Grad, PUBLIC HEALTH LAW MANUAL 138 (2d ed. 1970).

73. See, e.g., People v. Zerillo, 34 Cal. 2d 222, 223 P.2d 223 (1950); Brown v. State, 23 Del. 159, 74 Atl. 836 (1909); 22 C.J.S. § 1(e); AMERICAN LAW INSTI-TUTE, MODEL PENAL CODE §§ 1.12, 2.02 (1962). Apart from constitutional considerations, this tradition weighs heavily in persuading courts to read such a requirement into criminal statutes in which it does not appear explicitly.

74. See Greenawalt, supra note 52, at 934 et seq.; Packer, Mens Rea and the Supreme Court, [1962] SUP. CT. REV. 107; Dubin, Mens Rea Reconsidered: A Plea for a Due Process Concept of Criminal Responsibility, 18 STAN. L. REV. 332, 378 (1966). But see Gribetz & Grad, Housing Code Enforcement: Sanctions and Remedies, 66 COL. L. REV. 1254, 1279 (1966). Where fines are small, tests of constitutionality are likely to be rare.

While the Supreme Court has indicated that mens rea is not constitutionally required as an element of a crime (United States v. Balint, 258 U.S. 250 (1922); Fisher v. United States, 328 U.S. 463 (1946); Leland v. Oregon, 343 U.S. 790 (1952)), there have been more recent indications of inroads into that principle. Cf. Lambert v. California, 355 U.S. 225 (1957); Robinson v. California, 370 U.S. 660 (1962).

There is considerable controversy as to the propriety of a doctrine of "strict liability" in the criminal field. Actions detrimental to public welfare have been characterized as "in the nature of neglect where the

law requires care; inaction where it imposes a duty.
. . . ." Morrissette v. United States, 342 U.S. 246,
255 (1952). The dividing line may well be the degree
of severity of punishment: "The defendant asks us to
test the meaning of this statute by standards applicable to statutes governing infamous crimes. The
analogy, however, is deceptive. The element of conscious wrongdoing, the guilty mind accompanying the
guilty act, is associated with the concept of crimes
that are punished as infamous. . . ." Cardozo, J., in
Tenement House Dept. v. McDevitt, 215 N.Y. 160, 168,
109 N.E. 88, 90 (1915); see also MODEL PENAL CODE
§ 2.07(2).

75. Some degree of participation by higher levels
of management may also be required, for a corporation
to be liable for a crime. See MODEL PENAL CODE § 2.07
(1962); Note, Antitrust Enforcement against Organized
Crime, 70 COL. L. REV. 307, 319 et seq. (1970).
There are additional problems peculiar to corporate
defendants. Increasingly, corporations have been
entering into agreements with their officers and directors to indemnify the latter against certain types of
claims brought against them. While the corporation
cannot sit in prison in place of a vice president who
deliberately or carelessly helped to poison a river,
might it, consistently with public policy, agree to
indemnify him for any fine he has to pay? Even if
such a practice were not upheld, it would be virtually
impossible to prevent the corporation from indirectly
reimbursing its officer for fines he had paid or even
for the discomfort of a time in jail, by raising his
salary or awarding other fringe benefits after a
decent interval had elapsed.
Stockholders may be able to assert a derivative
cause of action against officers or directors whose
illegal conduct caused the corporation to be fined or
otherwise suffer loss. Here, too, questions arise as
to the validity of an indemnification agreement in
this circumstance, as well as to the possibility of
a corporation paying the premiums for insurance against
such a liability. See Dykstra, The Revival of the
Derivative Suit, 116 U. PA. L. REV. 74 (1967).

76. See Antitrust Enforcement against Organized
Crime, supra note 75, at 319-20.
The privilege against self-incrimination could not, o

course, be used by a corporation, nor could an employee
refuse to testify on the ground that he might incriminate the corporation or another employee. Corporate
records could not be withheld on Fifth Amendment grounds.
Nevertheless, the possibility that a witness might
incriminate himself would in many situations permit him
to keep silent.

77. Cf. Gribetz and Grad, Housing Code Enforcement,
supra note 74, at 1279. The authors point out that inadequate sentencing practices in housing cases arise
out of the unwillingness of criminal courts to recognize housing violations as true "crimes," and that the
same odium does not attach to the offense malum prohibit um as to the offense malum in se. The difficulty
is not confined to prosecutions for housing violations,
but extends to virtually all municipal prosecutions for
health and safety offenses. There are grounds for
apprehension that the same attitudes may prevail in
prosecutions for environmental offenses.

78. It is significant that when a fine of $10,000
was recently levied against a New Jersey firm, the
United States Attorney described it as the largest
ever imposed for water pollution in the United States.
N.Y. Times, July 18, 1970, at 27, col. 1.

79. Small fines may, of course, be effective to
deter the small-scale private polluter, such as the
casual litterer, the careless motorist or power-boat
operator, etc.

80. See LANE, THE REGULATION OF BUSINESSMEN, 21
et seq. (1954); Sutherland, Is "White Collar Crime"
Crime?, 10 AM. SOC. REV. 132, 136 (1945); Flynn,
Criminal Sanctions under State and Federal Antitrust
Laws, 45 TEX. L. REV. 1301, 1304, 1305 (1967); Note,
70 COL. L. REV. 307, 319 et seq. (1970).
This is not to say that the ripples which spread
out from the prison terms given to some electrical
industry officials a few years ago did not have some
deterrent effect upon corporate officers and employees
generally. Perhaps a study might profitably be made
of the impact of these sentences. There was not
apparently, however, a sufficient impression of general
success to give rise either to an intensified campaign
on the part of federal enforcement officials to request

prison sentences or to a widespread tendency on the part of judges to impose them.

81. See Timberg, The Case for Civil Antitrust Enforcement, 14 OHIO ST. L. J. 315 (1953); Note, 71 YALE L. J. 280, 282 et seq. (1961), which presents the view that the criminal fine as presently administered is but "a reasonable license fee" for engaging in prohibited conduct. On a state level, see, e.g., MINN. STAT. ANN. § 115.07(6) (1964).

82. Criminal and civil proceedings are not necessarily mutually exclusive. See, e.g., Standard Sanitary Manufacturing Co. v. United States, 226 U.S. 20, 52 (1912). On a state level, see, e.g., CONN. GEN. STAT. ANN. § 19-516 (1969).

83. Cf., e.g., Federal Trade Commission Act, 38 Stat. 719 (1914), 15 U.S.C. § 45(b)(1) (1964); Clayton Act, 38 Stat. 734 (1914), 15 U.S.C. § 21(b)(1) (1964).

84. S.3546, 91st Cong., 2d Sess., § 10(b), (c). (1970).

85. See Gribetz and Grad, supra note 74, at 1281 et seq., especially 1283.

86. See Frankfurter & Corcoran, Petty Federal Offenses and the Constitutional Guaranty of Trial by Jury, 39 HARV. L. REV. 917 (1924); Gribetz and Grad, supra note 74, at 1284; United States ex rel. Marcus v. Hess, 317 U.S. 537 (1943); Helvering v. Mitchell, 303 U.S. 391 (1938); cf. Duncan v. Louisiana, 391 U.S. 145, 159 (1968).

87. See Note, Trial by Jury in Criminal Cases, 69 COL. L. REV. 419, 427-29 (1969).
It should be noted that a sanction, the severity of which is out of all proportion to the offense or the necessity, may be challenged on due process grounds. Cf. Life & Casualty Co. v. McCray, 291 U.S. 566, 571 (1934); Chicago & N. W. Ry. v. Nye Fowler Schneider Co., 260 U.S. 35, 44-45 (1922); St. Louis, I. M. & So. Ry. Co. v. Williams, 251 U.S. 63, 66-67 (1919); Missouri Pacific Ry. v. Tucker, 230 U.S. 340, 350-51 (1913); Chicago & Alton R. R. v. People ex rel. Koerner, 67 Ill. 1 (1873). Attack on the basis of the cruel and

unusual punishment clause of the Eighth Amendment is also possible. Cf. Douglas, J., concurring, in Robinson v. California, 370 U.S. 660, 676 (1962). There is no reason to believe, however, that penalties of the dimension suggested and in the circumstances referred to herein would run into constitutional difficulties of these kinds.

88. The mental state of the defendant could be pertinent in two respects: (a) if it is an element of the nuisance or other tort sought to be enjoined (this would not normally be so in environmental cases); (b) as an indication of whether the defendant is likely to continue or repeat the offense, thus necessitating injunctive relief. On a state level, see, e.g., MONT. REV. CODE ANN. § 69-3921 (Supp. 1969).

89. See, e.g., Boomer v. Atlantic Cement Co., 26 N.Y. 2d 219, 257 N.E. 2d 870, 309 N.Y.S. 2d 312 (1970), in which the New York Court of Appeals refused to enjoin operation of a plant which injured plaintiffs' property through its emissions of dirt, smoke and vibration, on the grounds that the technology permitting operation without pollution had not yet been developed and that the defendant's investment and its contribution to the economy of the community were large. Damages for permanent reduction in value of plaintiffs' property were awarded instead.

It should also be noted that the courts are unlikely to construe a statute requiring issuance of an injunction in case of actual or threatened violation as eliminating their discretion to refuse such relief if on balance they deem it undesirable. See Hecht Co. v. Bowles, 321 U.S. 321 (1944). See also Seadade Industries, Inc. v. Florida Power and Light Co., 232 So.2d 46 (D.C. App. Fla., Feb. 18, 1970). The court based its findings that the power company had not been guilty of gross abuse of discretion in discharging heated waters into Biscayne Bay on the fact that "a number of power generating plants are doing this at the present time," and refused to consider whether such discharge would adversely affect the area's environment and ecology.

90. E.g., Parker v. United States, 309 F. Supp. 593 (D.C. Colo. 1970). The court ordered a preliminary injunction to continue indefinitely, barring the

Secretary of Agriculture from selling lumber rights
in a relatively untouched area.

91. For example, a state court fined a major
polluter $10,000 for failing to halt the discharge of
industrial waste into the Buffalo River, but refused
to enjoin its continued illegal operations because of
the adverse effect its closing would have on business
in the community. N.Y. Times, Oct. 6, 1970, at 44,
col. 3.

Present federal laws also encourage denials of in-
junctions in the event of economic hardship. See,
e.g., 33 U.S.C.A. § 1160(h) (1970); Barry
The Evolution of the Enforcement Provisions of the
Federal Water Pollution Control Act: A Study of the
Difficulty in Developing Effective Legislation, 68
MICH. L. REV. 1103, 1106, 1120 (1970).

An advantage attending the injunctive process is
the retention of jurisdiction by the court of equity.
This enables the court to issue future orders in aid
of its initial judgment, to modify its provisions,
and to enforce compliance with or punish violations
of the judgment. See, e.g., United States v. Florida
Power and Light Co., 311 F. Supp. 1391 (S.D. Fla.,
1970). The court did not find irreparable damage at
the time the government requested that the utility be
required to submit a plan to cool discharged water;
but the court retained jurisdiction and implied such
plan might be required later, stating "I am concerned
about the large amount of heated water the units will
discharge . . . in 1971 and 1972. Therefore, I do
plan to receive evidence on this point at hearings to
be scheduled at a later date" (311 F. Supp., at 1392).

While the usual maxims of equity are generally
applied in injunction actions, where water quality is
notoriously poor, a judge might be persuaded to waive
the requirement that the plaintiff come into court
with clean hands.

92. Penn Central is allegedly violating water
quality standards by discharging oil from its Harmon,
N.Y., yards into the Hudson River. Abatement hearings
have been scheduled under § 10 of the Federal Water
Pollution Control Act, 80 Stat. 1250 (1966), 33 U.S.C.A.
§ 1160 (1970). Current Developments, 1 ENVIRONMENT
REP. 101 (1970).

93. Such a procedure was employed in Schwarzenbach
v. Oneonta Light & Power Co., 207 N.Y. 671, 100 N.E.
1134 (1911).

94. In United States v. Bishop Processing Co., (423
F.2d 469 (4th Cir. 1970), cert. denied, 398 U.S. 904 (1970))
administrative proceedings dragged on from 1965 until 1968,
when suit was finally initiated to abate interstate
pollution pursuant to the Clean Air Act (81 Stat. 485
(1967), 42 U.S.C. § 1857 et seq. (Supp. V, 1965–69)).
On July 28, 1968, the District Court denied defendant's
motion to dismiss the government's suit, and an order
to cease operations was affirmed by the Fourth Circuit
on March 3, 1970. Certiorari was denied by the
Supreme Court on May 18, 1970.

95. See Grad, supra, p. 107 et seq.

96. 56 Stat. 33 (1942) (repealed 1947).

97. E.g., Testa v. Katt, 71 R.I. 472, 47 A.2d 312
(1946), rev'd on other grounds, 330 U.S. 386 (1947);
Miller v. Municipal Court of Los Angeles, 22 Cal.2d
818, 142 P.2d 297 (1943); Stevenson v. Stoufer, 237
Iowa 513, 21 N.W.2d 287 (1946) (characterizing such
actions as "penal"); and Overnight Motor Transport Co.
v. Missel, 316 U.S. 572, 583-84 (1942) (double damage
action under Fair Labor Standards Act); Lambros v.
Brown, 184 Md. 350, 41 A.2d 78 (1945); Schaffer v.
Leimberg, 318 Mass. 396, 62 N.E.2d 193 (1945) (calling
them "remedial").

98. Bowles v. Willingham, 321 U.S. 503, 512 (1944);
Porter v. Warner Holding Co., 328 U.S. 395, 398-99
(1946); cf. Helvering v. Mitchell, 303 U.S. 391 (1938);
United States ex rel. Marcus v. Hess, 317 U.S. 537 (1943).

99. This is true even with respect to actions for
damages brought by private plaintiffs. "The greatest
single impediment in civil actions for damages has
been proving that the defendant's pollution is the
direct cause of the plaintiff's legal injury." Note,
Private Remedies for Water Pollution, 70 COL. L. REV.
734, 745 (1970).

100. 56 Stat. 23 (repealed 1947).

101. Licensing Order No. 1, 8 Fed. Reg. 13240
(1943). This provision of the statute and its implementation were upheld in Gordon v. Porter, 155 F.2d
949 (9th Cir. 1946), cert. denied, 329 U.S. 763 (1946).
It should be noted that this action was taken under
the war power. Peacetime licensing would normally
have to rest upon another source of Congressional
authority, such as the commerce power, and might therefore not be applied so all-inclusively.

102. 56 Stat. 23, § 205(b) (repealed 1947) which
provided for a fine of not more than $5,000 or im-
prisonment for not more than one year, or both; § 205(e)
provided for damages of the greater of $50 or treble
the excess amount charged; § 205(a) authorized injunctions against violations. On a state level, see, e.g.,
CAL. HEALTH & SAFETY CODE § 242631 (West 1967).

103. An eight-man investigating team, dispatched
by the National Air Pollution Control Administration,
in pursuance of its emergency inspection program, re-
ported an American Cyanimide plant to be in violation
of emission standards. Consequently, the plant has
been forced to close pending replacement of its
sulfuric acid producing units. Current Developments,
1 ENVIRONMENTAL REP. 55 (1970).

104. Licensing is being used by the Federal Power
Commission in an experiment of possible substantial
significance. The Commission has been attempting to
condition licensing of the use of navigable rivers for
power production with provisions that would invest it
with continuing authority to appraise the public
importance of the uses being made by the licensee,
and, when desirable, to require the resource involved
to be shifted to another use, such as comprehensive
waterway development and conservation. These provisions were considered in Rumford Falls Power Co. v.
Federal Power Commission, 355 F.2d 683 (1st Cir. 1966),
and found to be within the Commission's authority to
exact; the case was remanded for clarification so that
the licensee might know what it might have to surrender
or what compensation might be paid to it in the event
of such diversion.
Previous attempts to retain control over private
rights granted in natural resources have been largely
ineffective. While the user may be regarded as a

trustee of the public interest, that interest has
generally been left vague and undefined. In particular, courts have been reluctant to find a departure
from the public interest where it would undermine the
user's large investment. See Sax, Licenses--Restricting
Private Rights in Public Resources, 7 NAT. RES. J. 339
(1967).

105. See United States v. United Mine Workers of
America, 330 U.S. 258 (1947); United States v. Pewee
Coal Co., 341 U.S. 114 (1951); but cf. Youngstown
Sheet & Tube Co. v. Sawyer, 343 U.S. 579 (1952).

106. The extent of the government's liability for
compensation in such circumstances is unclear. See
United States v. Pewee Coal Co., 341 U.S. 114 (1951).
Another variation might be a procedure for an
equitable receivership of the offending plant. The
federal government would retain possession and conduct
operations for as long as it was necessary to install
corrective equipment or otherwise remove the cause of
the violation and charge the expenses against the
plant. Cf., e.g., the use of this technique as a
remedy for housing violations. N.Y. MULT. DWELL. LAW
§ 309; Gribetz and Grad, supra note 74, at 1272-75.

107. E.g., 26 U.S.C. §§ 4745, 7301 et seq. (1964)
(internal revenue violations); 49 U.S.C. § 781, 782
(1964) (transportation of contraband).

108. Illustrative cases applying these statutes
include: United States v. Windle, 158 F.2d 196 (8th
Cir. 1946) (automobile, used by owner to carry on
wholesale liquor business without paying required tax,
forfeited); United States v. One 1962 Ford 2-Door
Sedan, 234 F. Supp. 798 (W.D. Va. 1964)(automobile
used to transport customers to point of sale of illegal
whiskey, forfeited); Ted's Motors v. United States,
217 F.2d 777 (8th Cir. 1954) (libel for forfeiture of
automobile used for transporting narcotics); The
Harpoon, 71 F. Supp. 1022 (D. Mass. 1947) (action to
obtain forfeiture of boats carrying contraband firearms);
and Dobbins's Distillery v. United States, 96 U.S. 395
(1877) (distillery subject to forfeiture where lessee
conducts business with intent to defraud revenue).

109. E.g., United States v. Windle, 158 F.2d 196, 199

(8th Cir. 1946); United States v. One 1950 Ford Half-
Ton Pickup Auto. Truck, 195 F.2d 857, 859 (6th Cir.
1952); United States v. One 1951 Cadillac Coupe De
Ville, 125 F. Supp. 661, 663 (D. Mo. 1954).

110. 26 Stat. 210 (1890), 15 U.S.C. § 6 (1964).

111. Antitrust Enforcement Against Organized Crime,
supra note 75, at 327-28.

112. United States v. Addyston Pipe & Steel·Co.,
85 F.271 (6th Cir. 1898), modified, 175 U.S. 211 (1899).

113. Id. at 295-96.

114. 12 Wheat. 1, 14 (1827).

115. Dobbins's Distillery v. United States, 96
U.S. 395, 401 (1877). See also Hartman v. Bean, 99
U.S. 393, 397 (1878); United States v. Stowell, 133
U.S. 1, 14 (1899); Goldsmith-Grant Co. v. United
States, 254 U.S. 505, 511 (1920); and, applying these
principles to the states, Van Oster v. Kansas, 272
U.S. 465, 468 (1926).

116. This is the basis of the doctrine of deodand,
which decreed that any chattel causing a person's
death be forfeited to the crown. The Supreme Court
narrates a short history of forfeiture in Goldsmith-
Grant Co. v. United States, 254 U.S. 505, 510-11 (1920).

117. Cf. Dobbins's Distillery v. United States,
96 U.S. 395 (1877); Goldsmith-Grant Co. v. United
States, 254 U.S. 505 (1920); United States v. One Ford
Coupé Automobile, 272 U.S. 321 (1926).

118. See Silesian-American Corp. v. Clark, 332
U.S. 469 (1947). Domestic property has also been
seized by the Federal Government in certain situations.
See United States v. United Mine Workers of America,
330 U.S. 258 (1947).
There may be some circumstances in which seizure of
something less than the entire offending property
might be appropriate. For example, where the threat
to environment is aesthetic rather than tangible, a
scenic easement or other limited property right might
be seized in order to avoid offenses to the eye.

119. In One 1958 Plymouth Sedan v. Pennsylvania, 380 U.S. 693, 697 (1965), the Supreme Court held that evidence obtained in violation of the Fourth Amendment cannot be the basis for sustaining a forfeiture. See also Boyd v. United States, 116 U.S. 616, 633-34 (1886): "We are also clearly of the opinion that proceedings instituted for the purpose of declaring the forfeiture of a man's property by reason of offenses committed by him, though they may be civil in form, are in their nature criminal. . . ."

120. Cf. United States v. United States Coin and Currency Co., 393 F.2d 499 (7th Cir. 1968), cert. granted, 393 U.S. 949 (1968), reargument ordered, 395 U.S. 918 (1969). See also Edwards, Forfeitures--Civil or Criminal?, 32 TEMP. L. Q. 191 (1970); Metallic Flowers, Inc. v. City of New York, 4 A.D.2d 292, 164 N.Y.S.2d 227 (1957), modified, 5 N.Y.2d 246, 157 N.E.2d 170, 183 N.Y.S. 2d 801 (1959).

121. N.Y.C. AIR POLLUTION CODE, § 9.07 (1964).

122. See Rathjens, supra, p. 29 et seq.

123. In 1968, 83,698,100 automobiles were registered in the United States. NEW YORK TIMES ENCYCLOPEDIC ALMANAC 672 (1970).

124. Such as the periodic inspection of old vehicles, admittedly a difficult and expensive task.

125. There are other devices, apart from direct regulation, which may be useful in the packaging field, such as the use of deposits, bounties, user charges, etc.

126. This might be accomplished by direct regulation, or through one of the other techniques discussed above, such as licensing. See p. 241 supra.

127. As to the constitutionality of such regulatory techniques, see p.219 supra.

128. 42 U.S.C. §§ 1857b, 1857b-1, 1857c (Supp. V, 1965-69); 33 U.S.C.A. §§ 1153(c), 1155-58, 1164-70 (1970).

129. See W. ANDERSON, THE NATIONS AND THE STATES, RIVALS OR PARTNERS? 175-81 (1955); W. ANDERSON, INTERGOVERNMENTAL RELATIONS IN REVIEW 43-45 (1960). On a

state level, see, e.g., MONT. REV. CODE ANN. § 69-3920
(Supp. 1969).

130. Clean Water Restoration Act of 1966, 80 Stat.
1248, 33 U.S.C.A. § 1158 (1970).
It should be noted that a grant for a municipal
sewage treatment plant is in part a subsidy for industrial users of it, unless the municipality imposes
appropriate charges upon such users. In some cases it
may therefore be appropriate to condition the award
upon the imposition of such charges.

131. See Report of the Joint Committee on Reduction
of Nonessential Expenditures, Federal Grant-in-Aid to
States and Payment to Individuals 605-10 (1957); U.S.
Advisory Comm'n on Intergovernmental Relations, The
Role of Equalization in Federal Grants; a Commission
Report (1964).

132. Id. For a cogent criticism of subsidies to
private enterprise, see ABT ASSOCIATES, INC., ECONOMIC
ANALYSIS OF INDUSTRIAL INCENTIVES FOR POLLUTION CON-
TROL: IMPLICATIONS FOR WATER QUALITY 46-48 (1967)
[hereinafter cited as "ABT"].

133. See note 128 supra.

134. See Hines, Controlling Industrial Water
Pollution: Color the Problem Green, 9 B.C. IND. & COM.
L. REV. 553, 598 (1968). The same might be said with
respect to grants to slow-moving state and local
governments.

135. See Rathjens, p.33, supra.

136. A tire manufacturer has stated that it can use
discarded tires in the making of new ones, but not on
a break-even basis, and has suggested that a government
subsidy or improvements in the process would be necessary if it were to be financially practicable. N.Y.
Times, Sept. 27, 1970, § 3, at 1, col. 1. See also
pp.258-67, infra.

137. Pp.230-1, supra.

138. For a discussion of state tax relief to induce
pollution control, see McNulty, State Tax Incentives

to Fight Pollution, 56 A.B.A.J. 747 (1970).

139. Int. Rev. Code of 1954, §§ 38, 46-48.

140. Int. Rev. Code of 1954, § 169, as amended by § 704 of the Tax Reform Act of 1969, Pub. L. No. 91-172.

141. See generally, Surrey, Tax Incentives as a Device for Implementing Government Policy, 83 HARV. L. REV. 705, 713-15 (1970).

142. See Hines, supra note 134, at 599-601.

143. For a cogent criticism of tax incentives, see Surrey, supra note 141. For criticisms directed specifically at the use of tax incentives for pollution control, see ABT 41-46; Roberts, River Basin Authorities: A National Solution to Water Pollution, 83 HARV. L. REV. 1527, 1530-37 (1970).

144. But cf. Surrey, supra note 141, at 732-34. On a state level, see, e.g., MASS. ANN. LAWS, ch. 59, § 5(39) (Supp. 1969).

145. The Small Business Administration and the Economic Development Administration are presently making loans for this purpose. See ABT 24, 48-50. On a state level, see, e.g., CAL. HEALTH & SAFETY CODE § 24370.4 (West 1967).

146. 13 C.F.R. § 120.2 (1970).

147. 12 C.F.R. § 402.1 (1970).

148. E.g., Bureau of Indian Affairs, 25 C.F.R. § 91.19 (1970); Federal Housing Administration, 24 C.F.R. § 201.6 (1970); Veterans Administration, 38 C.F.R. § 36.4 et seq. (1970).

149. 42 U.S.C. §§ 1857b, 1857b-1 (Supp. V, 1965-69); 33 U.S.C.A. § 1155 (1970). On a state level, see, e.g., MONT. REV. CODE ANN. § 69-3909(9) (Supp. 1969).

150. NATIONAL ACADEMY OF SCIENCES, WASTE MANAGEMENT CONTROL 12-13, 186-90 (1966).

151. Id. at 14, 39-40.

152. Id. at 54-55, 82; see also Kneese, Pollution and a Better Environment, 10 ARIZ. L. REV. 14 (1968).

153. H. BOSSEL, SOLID WASTE: PROBLEMS AND SOLUTIONS 34 (1970); see generally R. LINTON, TERRACIDE (1970).

154. See NATIONAL ACADEMY OF SCIENCES, supra note 150, at 18-21; N.Y. Times, Oct. 8, 1970, at 1, col. 4 (recommendation of Council on Environmental Quality for national policy limiting dumping of waste into oceans).

155. Additional authority for federal expenditures for research in this area is contained in the Solid Waste Disposal Act of 1965, 79 Stat. 998 (1965), 42 U.S.C. § 3253 (Supp. V, 1965-69). Further steps have just been taken in the Resource Recovery Act of 1970, adopted Oct. 27, 1970 (CCH 1970 CONG. INDEX 1737).

156. See H. Bossel, supra note 131, at 16-17; Adams, Who Will Pay for Recycling Those "Disposables"?, 11 J. OF SOLID WASTES & SOIL, Jan.-Feb., 1970, at 12.

157. See 148 CHEMICAL & ENGINEERING NEWS, March 2, 1970, at 14; 148 CHEMICAL & ENGINEERING NEWS, April 6, 1970, at 38.

158. S. A. Hart, W. J. Flocker & G. K. York, Refuse Stabilization in the Land, 11 J. OF SOLID WASTES & SOIL, Jan.-Feb., 1970, at 14. See also H. Bossell, supra note 153, at 35-36.

159. H. Bossel, supra note 153, at 61-62.

160. Id. at 31-33.

161. See also COUNCIL ON ENVIRONMENTAL QUALITY, ENVIRONMENTAL QUALITY 114 (1st Ann. report 1970).

162. See, e.g., N.Y. Times, Mar. 15, 1970, § 4, at 10; N.Y. Times, July 8, 1970, at 24, col. 5 (project to recover saleable chemicals from power plant smoke); B. EASTLUNE & W. GOUGH, U.S. ATOMIC ENERGY COMM'N, THE FUSION TORCH: CLOSING THE CYCLE FROM USE TO REUSE.

163. Cf. note 136, supra.

164. See, e.g., Handler, Science Policy: Federal
Support and Scientific Purpose, NATIONAL ACADEMY OF
SCIENCES NEWS REP., Aug.-Sept., 1970, at 8.

165. See generally R. VAUGHN, BUREAU OF SOLID
WASTE, SOLID WASTE MANAGEMENT: THE FEDERAL ROLE.

166. See especially A. KNEESE, THE ECONOMICS OF
REGIONAL WATER QUALITY MANAGEMENT 82-98 (1964). See
also, Rathjens, supra p. 29.

167. Id. at 160-67.

168. 116 CONG. REC. S6841 (daily ed., May 7, 1970)
(remarks of Senator Proxmire); S.3665, 91st Cong., 2d
Sess. (1970).
There remains, however, doubt whether there can be
a way of disposing of solid wastes without hurting
something. Burning them gives rise to one problem,
grinding them up and depositing them in the water
another. Carting them out into the ocean will help
for a while, but as mentioned above this expedient
will not last forever.

169. See Hearings on S. 2987 Before the Subcomm.
on Air and Water Pollution of the Senate Comm. on
Public Works, 89th Cong., 1st Sess., pt. 3 (1966);
S. 2987, 89th Cong., 2d Sess. § 104(b) (1966).
The Council on Law Related Studies is presently
sponsoring research in the workings of the Ruhr Valley
program.

170. See Kneese, supra note 166, at 82-98; see
also Delogu, Effluent Charges: A Method of Enforcing
Stream Standards, 19 MAINE L. REV. 29 (1967).

171. VT. STAT. ANN., tit. 10, § 910(A) et seq.
(Supp. 1970).

172. Combinations of several of these methods may
be most effective in dealing with certain problem
areas. For example, required deposits together with
payment of bounties might be useful in dealing with
such different aspects of solid waste management as
the throw-away beer or soda container and the junked
automobile.

305

173. An early example was the protective tariff, to safeguard "infant industries."

174. See Roberts, River Basin Authorities: A Natural Solution to Water Pollution, 83 HARV. L. REV. 1527 (1970).

175. N.Y. TIMES ENCYCLOPEDIC ALMANAC 178 (U.S. Budget), 674 (Gross National Product) (1970).

176. Cf. Hammer v. Dagenhart, 247 U.S. 251 (1918); Schechter Poultry Corp. v. United States, 295 U.S. 495 (1935); Carter v. Carter Coal Co., 298 U.S. 238 (1936). United States v. Darby, 312 U.S. 100, upholding federal regulation of wages and hours, was decided in 1941.

177. 49 Stat. 2036 (1936), 41 U.S.C. §§ 35-45 (1964). The statute also prescribes maximum hours, forbids child or convict labor, and requires safe and sanitary working conditions, in the performance of government contracts. Pursuant to the last of these provisions, regulations have recently been issued limiting noise levels in plants of government contractors. 34 Fed. Reg. 7948 (1969); see Grad, p. 72 supra.

178. 56 Stat. 351 (1942);72 Stat. 384 (1958), as amended, 15 U.S.C. § 631 (1964); 70A Stat. 127 (1956), 10 U.S.C. § 2301 (1964); 63 Stat. 393 (1949), as amended, 41 U.S.C. § 251(b) (1964).

179. 4 CCH GOVT. CONT. REP. ¶ 33,638.70 (1970); id. at ¶ 33,722.45; id. at ¶ 33,755.22; id. at ¶ 33,760.20; id. at ¶ 33,771.60, ¶ 33.825. See also Standard Clause for Small Business Concerns, 7-104.14 set out in id. at ¶ 33,638.70 (1970). See generally for policy id. at ¶ 1020 (1970).

180. 70A Stat. 127 (1956), 10 U.S.C. § 2301 (1964); 32 C.F.R. §§ 1.700 et seq. (1970).

181. Act of June 11, 1942, ch. 404, §§ 1-12, 56 Stat. 351 (1942).

182. Defense Production Act of 1950, 64 Stat. 798 (1950), 50 U.S.C. App. § 2061 (1964).

183. Small Business Act, 72 Stat. 384 (1958), as amended, 15 U.S.C. § 631 et seq. (1964).

184. Exec. Order No. 8802, 6 Fed. Reg. 3109 (1941); Exec. Order No. 9346, 8 Fed. Reg. 7183 (1943). See also M. SOVERN, LEGAL RESTRAINTS ON RACIAL DISCRIMINATION IN EMPLOYMENT 9-17 (1966).

185. Exec. Order No. 10308, 16 Fed. Reg. 12303 (1951); Exec. Order No. 10479, 18 Fed. Reg. 4899 (1953); Exec. Order No. 10557, 19 Fed. Reg. 5655 (1954). Exec. Order No. 10925, 26 Fed. Reg. 1977 (1961); Exec. Order No. 11246, 30 Fed. Reg. 12319 (1965); Exec. Order No. 11375, 32 Fed. Reg. 14303 (1967). See also Sovern, supra note 184, at 103-142, app. G.

186. 4 CCH GOVT CONT. REP. ¶ 33,638.70 (1970); id. at ¶ 33,695.25; id. at ¶ 33,722.45; id. at ¶ 33,755.22; id. at ¶ 33,760.20; id. at ¶ 33,771.60; id. at ¶ 33,825; id. at ¶ 33,831.60. See also Standard Clause for Equal Opportunity, 7-103.18 set out in id. at ¶ 33,636.90 (1970). See generally for policy 2 CCH GOV'T CONT. REP. ¶ 15,771 (1970). The appropriate "boiler plate" language, embodying these requirements, must be included in government contracts and subcontracts.

187. Civil Rights Act of 1964, 78 Stat. 253 (1964), 42 U.S.C. §§ 2000(e)-2000(e)-12 (1964).

188. Exec. Order No. 11246, 30 Fed. Reg. 12319 (1965), 42 U.S.C. § 2000(e) (Supp. III, 1967), as amended, Exec. Order No. 11375, 32 Fed. Reg. 14303 (1967). See also Note, 44 N.Y.U. INTRA. L. REV. 590 (1969), for a fuller discussion.

189. A charge of violation of the act must first be filed with the Equal Employment Opportunity Commission, which serves a copy on the respondent and investigates it. If it determines after investigation that there is reasonable cause to believe the charge is true, it is to endeavor to eliminate the practice by informal methods of conference, conciliation and persuasion. If it fails to achieve voluntary compliance, it so notifies the charging party, who may then bring an action in the Federal District Court, where the charges are considered de novo. Civil Rights Act of 1964, 78 Stat. 253 (1964), § 706, 42 U.S.C. § 2000e-5 (1964).

190. The small staff of the Equal Employment Opportunity Comm'n (E.E.O.C.) was swamped with thousands of cases and found itself unable to undertake informal methods of conciliation. It adopted the practice of notifying the charging party of its inability to effect compliance where such inability sprang from lack of capacity even to commence conciliation proceedings. It was held in Dent v. St. Louis-San Francisco Railway Co. (265 F. Supp. 56 (N.D. Ala. 1967)) and a few other cases that the institution of efforts at conciliation was a jurisdictional prerequisite to the institution of an action in court, thus leaving the aggrieved party remedyless.

If the lower court decision in Dent was the Scylla facing the aggrieved Southern Negro employee, Miller v. International Paper Co. (290 F. Supp. 401 (S.D. Miss. 1967)), was the Charybdis. There it was held that the charging party had to institute his action in the District Court within sixty days of his filing of charges with the E.E.O.C., regardless of the latter's progress or lack of it in processing the charges; otherwise the case was forever barred.

191. Dent was reversed in 406 F.2d 399 (5th Cir. 1969) as was Miller, 408 F.2d 283 (5th Cir. 1969). See also Johnson v. Seaboard Coast Line R.R. 405 F.2d 645 (4th Cir. 1968) and Choate v. Caterpillar Tractor Co., 402 F.2d 357 (7th Cir. 1968).

192. 78 Stat. 253 (1964), 42 U.S.C. § 2000e(5)(g) (1964); see generally Walker, Title VII: Complaint and Enforcement Procedures and Relief and Remedies, 7 B.C. IND. & COMM. L. REV. 513-21 (1966).

193. Title VII, Civil Rights Act of 1964: Present Operation and Proposals for Improvement, 5 COL. J. OF LAW AND SOC. PROB. 1 (1969). See also EQUAL EMPLOYMENT OPPORTUNITY COMMISSION, 4th ANN. REP. 11 et seq. (1970), summarizing judicial decisions construing the scope of the statute. Almost all of the cases cited were actions brought by aggrieved individuals and most of them by the N.A.A.C.P. Legal Defense Fund.

194. 78 Stat. 253 (1964), 42 U.S.C. § 2000(e)(6) (196

195. Title VII, Civil Rights Act of 1964, supra note 193, at 39.

196. See, e.g., Johnson, Miller and Dent, supra note 191. The problem of who speaks for the government, E.E.O.C. or the Attorney General's Office is discussed in Title VII, Civil Rights Act of 1964, supra note 193, at 39. See generally CCH EMPL. PRAC. GUIDE ¶ 16,900.001 (1968) and Berg, Title VII: A Three-Year's View, 44 NOTRE DAME LAWYER 311 (1969).

197. E.g., compare the 35 suits brought by the N.A.A.C.P. Legal Defense Fund alone through 1968 with the total of 10 by the Justice Department during the same period. Title VII, Civil Rights Act of 1964, supra note 193, at 39, 43. See also N.Y. Times, Oct. 13, 1970, at 44, col. 1.

198. Exec. Order No. 11246, 30 Fed. Reg. 12319 (1965), 42 U.S.C. § 2000(e) (Supp. III, 1967), as amended, Exec. Order No. 11375, 32 Fed. Reg. 14303 (1967).

199. Id., § 209(a)(6); 58 LAB. REL. REP. 127, 165 (1965). This has been done precisely once, and then only for a brief period. Sovern, supra note 184, at 115.

200. The small business share of Department of Defense procurement actually dropped from 25.1% to 19.4% from 1954 to 1967. Its share of total government procurement has increased between 1960 and 1967 from 18.3% to 20.1%. S.B.A., SEMI-ANNUAL REPORTS (1956-61); S.B.A., ANNUAL REPORTS (1962-67).

201. See Hall v. Schultz, Civil No. 893-69 (D.D.C., filed Mar., 1969) (suit voluntarily dismissed following belated government compliance). See also N.Y. Times, Feb. 1, 1969, at 23, col. 1.

202. 41 C.F.R. § 60-1 et seq. (1970); see also for order of the Secretary of Labor, 30 Fed. Reg. 13441 (1965) and Exec. Order No. 11246, 30 Fed. Reg. 12319 (1965).

203. See H.R. 17222, 91st Cong., 2d Sess. (1970).

204. See clause 7-103.18 set out in 4 CCH GOV'T CONT. REP. ¶ 33,636.90 (1970) and 2 CCH GOV'T CONT. REP. ¶ 15,771 (1970).

205. Compare the careless disregard or conscious

subordination of environmental factors in a wide range
of federal activities. Among some of the more obvious
examples are the federal highway program, the Department of Agriculture's encouragement of almost indis-
criminate use of pesticides and fertilizers, and the
insistence on proceeding with the new supersonic
transport plane. Attempts to bring this process under
control can be found in the National Environmental
Policy Act of 1969, § 102, Pub. L. No. 91-190, and
Executive Order No. 11507, 35 Fed. Reg. 2573 (Feb. 4,
1970).

206. See Perkins v. Lukens Steel Co., 310 U.S. 113
(1940).

207. See p. 262 supra.

208. See pp. 253-8 supra.

209. This approach, however, is a questionable one
and has not met with great success. Both the Federal
Government and the County of Los Angeles have met
severe opposition in attempting to procure anti-
emission devices. Hearings Before the Subcomm. of
the Senate Select Comm. on Small Business, 90th Cong.,
2d Sess., at 341, 555 (1968).

210. The government's contracting power may be
used in other ways as well. For example, federal
leases to drill for offshore oil may contain clauses
permitting revocation in the event of spillage.

211. Provisions encouraging such private litigation
are contained in § 304 of S.3546, 91st Cong., 2d Sess.
(1970) the proposed National Air Quality Standards Act
of 1970, in the form in which it has recently passed
the Senate. On a state level, see, e.g., MICH. COMP.
LAWS ANN. § 691, 1202 (1970).

212. Another device for this purpose is the provision in Section 16 of the Rivers and Harbors Appropriation Act of 1899, 30 Stat. 1153, 33 U.S.C. § 411
(1964), which authorizes payment of half of the fines
collected for wrongful pollution of navigable waters
and other offenses to the person or persons who give
information leading to conviction.

213. Actions of this kind might be authorized by the Hart-McGovern Bill, S. 3575, 91st Cong., 2d Sess. (1970).

214. <u>See</u> p. 217 <u>supra</u>.